CULTURE, CHANGE, AND CONTINUOUS IMPROVEMENT

From Bankruptcy to Industry Leadership
A True Aerospace Story

Colin E. Cramp and
Martin R. Lodge

ISBN: 978-1-4834-9657-3 (sc)
ISBN: 978-1-4834-9659-7 (hc)
ISBN: 978-1-4834-9658-0 (e)

Library of Congress Control Number: 2019900549

Lulu Publishing Services rev. date: 04/11/2019

Dedicated to our wives, Gaye and Janet, who supported us throughout the compilation of this book, and of course, through the many ups and downs of our working lives in Aerospace.

Contents

Acknowledgments ix

Preface...xi

Introduction xiii

Chapter 1   The Beginning, Growth at any Cost and a
            Burning Platform...1

Chapter 2   Organization, how the Business was being
            Managed and Moving Forward..............................25

Chapter 3   Learning 51

Chapter 4   Aligning the Business 89

Chapter 5   Integrating Engineering, Research and
            Development 158

Chapter 6   A Maturing Business Firing on all Cylinders...........198

Chapter 7   Growing Pains 225

Chapter 8   Culture and Leadership...257

Chapter 9   Lessons learned, what we underestimated,
            missed or got wrong..274

Summary...285

Appendix 299

The Authors 323

Acknowledgments

- Rohr and Goodrich Aerostructures employees who, over the years, dedicated time and effort, beyond expectations, and drove changes that resulted in the business improvement outlined in this book, and provided many anecdotes, some of which are included in the following pages.
- United Technologies Aerospace Systems employees past and present who also provided much input and insight.
- Adrianna Hernandez, Constituent Services Representative, Office of the Mayor and City Council, City of Chula Vista, who provided some details of the continuous improvement efforts at the City.
- Tanya Carr, Librarian, City of Chula Vista who provided access to archived Rohr documents that enabled many historical details to be confirmed.
- Book cover sourced from www.istockphoto.com
- Some graphics sourced from creativecommons.org

Preface

This book is the chronological story of how Aerostructures, a Chula Vista California based supplier to all major aircraft manufacturers, made a business transformation from being "two days away from filing bankruptcy papers to unparalleled leadership, performance and business returns in the Aerospace industry."

The Company, initially Rohr Aircraft Corporation founded in 1940, had finally achieved their goal of annual sales of $1 billion in the early 1990s and undoubtedly some sense of achievement was experienced. However while the company store made a profit each year in the same period, company profits were minimal to none.

In 1993 Rohr Industries, as it was then known, was in trouble and headed for bankruptcy.

The organizational structure was cumbersome. Functional fiefdoms were in place across the company; management techniques were lacking. Morale was low; attrition was high. Acquisition "vultures" were waiting in the wings; the business was under serious threat. Customers were concerned, and several were preparing to exit.

Many employees were working hard, but only the status quo was being maintained.

Offers of help, from some customers, over several months, to "improve the business" were being rejected.

Bankruptcy was avoided at the last minute by the infusion of cash from two major customers who did not want, nor could not afford the chaos in their supply lines that would ensue, following a bankruptcy filing by one of their major suppliers.

The chronical of the remarkable industry leading cultural transformation at Rohr from this near insolvency, to years of increasing income and margin over the next decades is our story.

It is one of a commitment to change, a broad Positive Employee Philosophy and a culture that created a highly productive and successful business. This was all underpinned by Leadership, Constancy of Purpose and managed deployment of the Toyota Production System in an aerospace environment combined with the development of an effective operating system.

We hope you find this story interesting and of some use if you are desperate enough and are looking for a way to change and improve your business for the better, or fortunate enough and see opportunity in your business for greater results.

Rohr Industries, as it was known at the time, was bought by Goodrich in 1997 and became known as Goodrich Aerostructures. United Technologies Corporation (UTC) then bought Goodrich, in 2012 and Goodrich Aerostructures became part of UTC Aerospace Systems (UTAS), retaining the name Aerostructures.

We have used the names Rohr or Aerostructures aligned with the years and issues being discussed.

Colin E. Cramp   **Martin R. Lodge**

Introduction

We believe that a positive, enabling and inclusive business culture supported by leadership and constancy of purpose is always the foundation for sustained high-level business performance.

Our purpose in writing this book is threefold:

1. To record a valuable "learning history" of a 20 plus year's journey that continues to this day. And to hopefully help ensure future possibilities and opportunities are recognized, seized and leveraged by both the current and next generations of Aerostructures employees.
2. To outline for readers of any business what was done to change a culture and move a struggling business from bankruptcy to outstanding business results.
3. To possibly inspire readers to consider their respective businesses, identify improvement opportunities within and to act upon them leading to increased business success.

While this book is not another "how to" change a culture and improve business results, the reader has the opportunity to gain insights into managing effective Culture Change, implementing Continuous Improvement processes and tools and how developing a viable Operating System brought together Culture, Values, Continuous Improvement and Leadership resulting in the success noted.

The authors include details of the 20 plus year journey including things we got right, lessons learned, and the reflection, learning and adjustments made during the journey towards Enterprise Excellence. It is a story of "what we did" to change and improve a business, based on what we understood, believed to be appropriate and applied as effectively as we knew how to, to change a culture, drive continuous improvement and improve business results.

Over time and with learning, the changes made resulted in sustained world-class business performance driven by engaged teams operating in an environment that enabled their potential, and the potential within the business, to be exposed and leveraged.

However, these results did not happen without structure and process. The layout of the book is first to set the stage for change, responding to the crisis we experienced, and then to record the leadership actions and behaviors, the processes and systems deployed that drove positive change, including what worked and what did not.

The financial situation and severe customer dissatisfaction resulted in a first crisis, a "Crisis of Survival" or as we called it at the time a "burning platform."

Two other crises were encountered over the years; both are outlined and discussed in the narrative. While neither were as distinct nor as urgent per se as the burning platform, both needed focused understanding and attention.

Our experience has led us to believe that any form of broad, meaningful business "change" must first be built on the solid "foundational requirements", of Values and Leadership, then integrated with three other "Principles of Change" - Culture, Lean and Operating System, to successfully drive industry-leading business results expanded upon in this book.

In more detail the various foundational and change elements are:

Values and Leadership (Foundational)

Values, ethical guidelines and service commitments we regard as binary.

It is well documented that Leading and Managing are two different things. Successful organizations are invariably led. "Where we are going, how we are going to get there, the processes and tools we are going to use and the required and acceptable behaviors on the journey," have to be clearly articulated and demonstrated by leadership. This requires active and visible leadership engagement from the "front" every day.

Management then is the art of getting things done within solid principles established and supported by the use of selected processes and tools, led and sustained by leadership.

Culture

Significantly, the development of a positive culture where employees work together towards common goals. Where employees have mutual trust and respect for each other, and adult to adult discussions can take place without fear, retribution or "hidden agendas." A culture that puts the customer first has a resolute focus on the identification of issues, problems and opportunities, and how they are going to be addressed or leveraged in real time, driving performance improvement. Where responsibility and accountability are clearly communicated, understood and accepted. A culture that "everyone" understands, is committed to, engages in and consistently supports and maintains.

Lean (Continuous Improvement)

We do not profess to be anything beyond two people who contributed to the deployment of the Principles of the Toyota

Production System as we understood them in an aerospace environment. We believe we implemented the processes and used the tools of the Toyota Production System to effectively remove waste from, and improve the performance of, the business.

Operating System

The development and deployment of a strategically anchored, and actionable operating system based upon Toyota Production System principles. One that provides meaningful information "real time," rather than one that invariably produces old data that, at best, requires further analysis to begin to possibly understand. At worst, causes bad decisions to be made.

We also realized that we were going to have to change, do many things differently and be prepared to learn as we moved forward. Educating ourselves primarily as leaders and then everyone else to stand any chance of changing the business and achieving any measure of success. It was apparent that changes both large and small, many of both, were going to be necessary and that broad engagement of the entire team in the change process was going to be crucial.

The Change Process

A recognized four step change process has been used by many, for some time. The steps take different names depending on who is suggesting them. We are accustomed to these four:

- **Awareness**
  - o Providing information as to what the change is, the intent, the timing and who it will impact.
- **Understanding**
  - o Ensuring employees have adequate time to gain an appreciation and understanding of the change.

- **Commitment**
  - Gaining buy-in from those affected by the change and securing their inclusion in the transition.
- **Habit**
  - Achieving and sustaining the new process, the new way of doing things is indeed what employees do.

Our challenge was to take a "broken organization" on a journey, create a new environment, and a new organization with new "habits."

While firm financial business goals were in place, we did not start with a grand master plan to achieve the overall performance levels those goals would require. We did not have the experience, knowledge or time to attempt to put one together given the complexity and urgency of the situation - the burning platform. Following initial actions to stabilize the business we had to continually identify the next step or two, take action, review, reflect, and course correct as necessary as we traversed the years.

Guided by foundational principles, we knew where we were going and what we needed to achieve, but did not have the route, obstacles, and opportunities, identified, understood or mapped out.

One thing we learned over time, was to consider Leadership, Lean, Culture and an Operating System and the multiple subcomponents of those elements, as strands in fabric. This helped us as we struggled to make sense of the plight we were in, and all the things we felt we needed to understand and do.

We thought it highly likely that at some frequency we would have to deal with broken fabric strands. And on many occasions, we found ourselves dealing with multiple broken strands. However, as we developed and "repaired" the strands, and wove them together, the breaks became fewer, and the fabric became more cohesive and stronger.

Looking back, we believe we got "most things" right, the generated business results certainly support that position. What was created was a positive, enabling and inclusive business culture with a constancy of purpose, leadership leading and aggressive, effective, continuous improvement deployment. All supported via timely and appropriate metrics enabling course corrections and achievement of outstanding business performance.

We have attempted to record key events and processes rather than people. Although a number of highly engaged participants, who made vital contributions during the journey, are named in the book. Many other contributors to the business transformation are included in the Appendix, and we apologize in advance to any that we may have missed.

Where the Information Comes From:

All referenced activities, process information, and data are from the two author's direct knowledge, participation, and experience.

Interviews with Aerostructures employees past and present, published company data, local newspapers, public records, and web-based public domain sites were also additional sources of information for this manuscript.

General data included in charts developed for this book is generated from public records indicated above. Where data records were not current, the authors have estimated input and trends based upon their experience of the processes.

Industry standard strategy and assessment tools such as Policy Deployment and Assessment Matrices have been modified to include the principles of construction and use.

At the end of Chapters 1 through 8 we have included:

"What we learned on the way – a summary" – things that were new to us, things that we did not fully appreciate, issues, problems, and opportunities we encountered.

"Things you may want to consider – a summary" – things that may be important to your situation and may require deliberate pre-thought and planning if you are considering embarking on positive change and improvement.

Chapter 9 is one where we reflect on:

Lessons learned, what we underestimated, missed or got wrong.

Summary:

- The crises experienced and outlined.
- A detailed Change Pyramid.
- The salient points of the cultural transformation and changes that took the company from the brink of bankruptcy to a position where market share is now well over 50%, business results are predictable, achieved and have been invariably excellent.
- An evolving fourth crisis. Perhaps a second burning platform.

Appendix:

- Key contributors to the cultural and business transformation.
- Acronyms, words, and phrases explained.
- A Positive Employee Philosophy overview.
- Leadership and Continuous Improvement books that were significant and influential on our journey.

The Authors:

- Brief biographies.

Chapter 1

A *brief history of Rohr, its post-World War II activities and the positive growth of its business over the two decades that followed. Diversification in the 1960s that proved to be less than successful. A refocus on its core business, nacelles and pylons, in the mid-1970s. A deployed "Centers of Excellence" strategy and work transferred to perceived low-cost locations. An outline of elements focused upon to rectify and resolve the predicament that Rohr found itself in and the fundamental Values and Principles that were identified to overhaul the business and make it successful.*

The Beginning: Growth at Any Cost and a Burning Platform

In 1927 Fred Rohr was employed by the Ryan Aircraft Corporation in San Diego. Among other responsibilities, he oversaw the fabrication of the cowling, fairing and fuel tanks for the Spirit of St Louis Aircraft in which Lindbergh made his historic trans-Atlantic flight.

With four associates, Fred founded Rohr Aircraft Corporation in August 1940. Their first production building was at the intersection of Eighth Avenue and J Street in downtown San Diego California. Subsequently, land was purchased in Chula Vista, a San Diego

1

suburb, where a new 37,000 square feet facility was built. Fred served as president and general manager and with World War II already being fought in Europe and beyond, he saw that there was a role in the rapidly expanding aircraft industry for a manufacturing subcontractor that could provide the prime aircraft builders with structural components and assemblies.

As the war spread across the globe through the 1940s, Rohr manufactured engine cowlings and then assembled the cowlings with the engines to produce over 38,000 power plants for the B24 Liberator in the now expanded Chula Vista plant.

At the conclusion of World War II, the facility had grown to over 600,000 square feet of manufacturing space, and of course, military business declined significantly. Seeking stability, Rohr Aircraft became a subsidiary of a larger company whose primary business was domestic appliances.

As business conditions changed, Fred repurchased the business in 1950 and pursued the soon to be booming commercial aerospace market and also benefitted as military business ramped back up as a result of the Korean War.

In 1952 Rohr purchased land in Riverside California and built a second large facility to accommodate its increasing workload. The subsequent facilitation of that site included the installation of chemical process lines for metal bonded components and subsequently, equipment and processes for complex composite bonded components. Both of these capabilities were increasingly required by airframers in the manufacture of aircraft with high-performance requirements.

Through the 1950s business increased, various components for multiple customers were being manufactured, including fuel tanks for the B52 and by the late 1950s fuselage sections for the Boeing 707. To support these activities, total employment had reached more than 10,000 by 1958.

In the 1960s Rohr sought to increase its business through several diversification efforts and acquisitions, expanding its product portfolio into a number of additional markets.

This included securing contracts for the design and manufacture of rail cars for the San Francisco Bay Area Rapid Transport system (BART), the Washington DC Metro, Amtrak, and large metro buses and people moving systems for shopping malls. Additional business ventures that also consumed resources were the design and manufacture of marine landing craft and other marine-based technologies, large radar antennas and prefabricated, modular housing.

This mixed portfolio quickly caused significant stress on the business, and the less than satisfactory business returns saw a subsequent refocus on the core business of nacelles and pylons. The aforementioned other businesses being wound down or sold. The last divestiture, The Flxible Company, a bus manufacturer, was made in the late 1970s.

Despite these diversification activities throughout the 1970s, the company had continued to develop core technical aerospace expertise and production capabilities, producing multiple aerospace parts and assemblies for the major commercial and military airframers. This included nacelle and pylon components for McDonnell Douglas, the inlet and nacelle components for the Grumman F-14 Tomcat fighter and booster rocket motor components for the Titan III Expendable Launch System program used for both military and NASA applications.

The following illustration outlines Rohr's primary and core competency and product expertise - the design and manufacture of inlets, fan cowls, thrust reversers, exhaust cones, exhausts, and pylons:

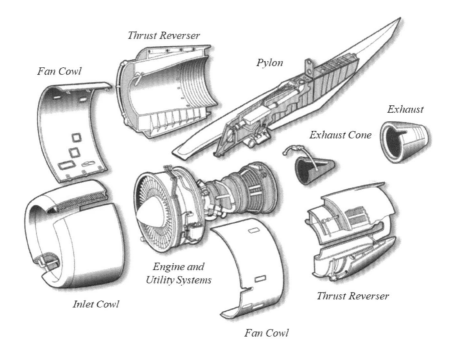

One substantial development in the 1970s was the relationship, and ultimately a commercial agreement with, the then three-year-old Airbus Industrie which resulted in a facility being established in St Martin, a suburb of Toulouse France. From this site, Rohr initially assembled and delivered to Airbus components for the A300 and A310 aircraft.

Rohr built a second French facility in Gramont, Toulouse, opening in 1990. This site now serves as Rohr's primary Airbus supporting facility with St Martin currently an aftermarket distribution center for spares and a Maintenance Repair and Overhaul location.

In the early 1980s, Rohr was awarded contracts for significant nacelle components for the V2500 engine. This engine powers the Airbus A319, A320 and A321 aircraft and as of this writing, variants of this plane and its engines have been in production for 32 years.

In this same period, and despite the focus on core business, overall business results degraded. Contributing to this situation were some onerous commercial contract conditions accepted on new nacelle, pylon and other work, combined with poor operational performance. While these commercial contracts provided multiyear platforms for continued employment, business results consistently fell well short of expectations and needs.

A factor that would contribute to the financial plight of the coming years.

The business that the company did win in the 1980s required extensive modernization and expansion. Capital was invested, providing unique aircraft component processing, production, and testing facilities, all adding to the financial strain being experienced in that period.

The Chula Vista facility was now over two million square feet under roof accommodating manufacturing, engineering, aftermarket, multiple support functions and corporate offices. Further expansion was underway to collocate engineering, support functions, and the corporate offices.

Chula Vista Facility Footprint circa 1989

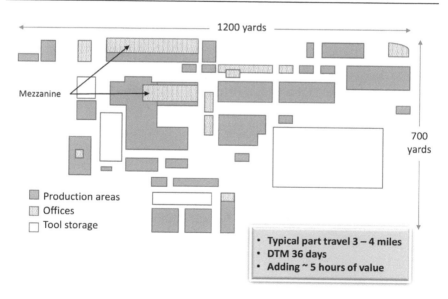

1200 yards

Mezzanine

700 yards

Production areas
Offices
Tool storage

- **Typical part travel 3 – 4 miles**
- **DTM 36 days**
- **Adding ~ 5 hours of value**

Not to scale.

In addition, the Riverside facility had been expanded to over one million square feet under roof accommodating manufacturing and some engineering activity.

In these expanded facilities Rohr was the primary provider of nacelles and pylons to McDonnell Douglas and was also providing hardware to Boeing, Airbus, Lockheed and Northrop Grumman.

Organization structures were traditional and top-heavy, with many having significant sub-departments and extensive, supporting staffs. Management techniques were dated and ineffective.

Engineering functions were physically distant from manufacturing. Supply chain activities were focused on the lowest lot cost alone, and production was driven by homegrown production control systems that were overloaded and under-supported.

Functional silos were apparent, as were the entourages that can accompany them, and adversarial managerial and union relationships added to the confusion and tensions.

The company culture was in need of attention.

Growth at Any Cost

By this time, the company had earned a reputation for niche product expertise - nacelles and pylons, manufacturing and design capabilities, unique processes, multiple patents and a highly skilled, if underperforming, workforce.

Financial results through the 1980s however, continued to be disappointing, and well under peer companies results, with some years negative.

Erratic delivery performance, occasional significant quality escapes combined with consistently under par financial performance were beginning to stress the business, shareholders, and customers. Typical development costs were out of control, with some programs unable to generate positive cash flows over the 20 plus year's production life of the program and many more years of in-service support.

A key goal of company leadership was to achieve annual sales of $1 billion. This goal became a distraction from running the business effectively and drove a culture of accepting contracts where the company was unlikely to ever make a profit. This lack of profitability continued despite the advantages of contract accounting rules being used at the time.

Actions taken in support of the $1 billion annual sales goal combined with a bureaucratic management organization structure and hierarchy, led by an almost military style of management, contributed to the financial malaise Rohr was about to face.

In the 1980s the issue of culture had raised its head. Relations with the Union at the two California locations left a lot to be desired. The contract negotiations of 1987 resulted in a strike that on occasion turned violent. The company - union relationship was at an all-time low. It was clear that this type of relationship needed to be improved and earlier initial steps had been taken to make such a transition.

In 1983, as Rohr was expanding, a Positive Employee Philosophy was introduced to help develop an inclusive work environment at a new Rohr assembly location in Foley Alabama. The Positive Employee Philosophy was subsequently deployed across the business but, beyond the Foley facility, gained little traction.

Principles for Excellence, the forerunner of what was to become the "Values," were introduced in the late 1980s, and rolled out company-wide. However, much like the Positive Employee Philosophy, little was done to promote or leverage them in any way.

As a result, with the exception of the Foley business, both the Positive Employee Philosophy and the Principles for Excellence drifted into the distant background.

Both the Positive Employee Philosophy and the Principles for Excellence are discussed in greater detail in this and other chapters.

Against this background, a "Centers of Excellence" strategy was being developed and implemented that would:

- Reposition work to states with more business-friendly environments.
- Secure lower labor rates.
- Enable the development of a culture that embraced the Principles for Excellence and the Positive Employee Philosophy.
- Establish facilities where it was believed that technical and manufacturing excellence could be achieved through focus, familiarity, and repetition in the manufacture of specific nacelle components.

By the early 1990s, Rohr had expanded to three locations in Riverside and had built and opened three new out of state facilities. These new facilities were at Heber Springs and Sheridan, both in Arkansas, producing nacelle component assemblies, this work moved from Chula Vista and Riverside, and a facility at San Marcos Texas, where a high-temperature diffusion bonding processes had been placed. The San Marcos process and product line had formerly been in Chula Vista and was relocated in the late 1980s to leverage local incentives and perceived lower utility rates.

A large composite bonding facility in Hagerstown Maryland had also been purchased from Fairchild Industries. A third facility in Arkansas was being considered. The company was clearly and energetically moving work out of California.

As a result of this Center of Excellence strategy, two of the three Riverside facilities were closed as the business moved to the new locations.

The manufacturing "Centers of Excellence" footprint was now:

- Machining and fabrication of metal parts in Chula Vista California.
- Metal bonding in Riverside California.
- Composite bonding in Hagerstown Maryland.
- High-temperature diffusion bonding in San Marcos Texas.
- Assembly of Inlets in Sheridan Arkansas.

- Assembly of Fan Cowls in Heber Springs Arkansas.
- Assembly of Thrust Reversers in Foley Alabama.
- Auburn Washington the delivery site supporting Boeing.
- Gramont Toulouse, the delivery site supporting Airbus.

Planned alignment of intended operations across those locations proved elusive driven by various factors including the complex linkage and flow requirements of product and information across a larger "manufacturing footprint." Adding to these issues was an apparent imbalance of space requirements and woefully cumbersome product linkage and flow, within and between facilities, combined with a lack of available employees with the required level of "aerospace-type" assembly experience.

One upside was that the Positive Employee Philosophy and Principles for Excellence were deployed with some success at the new Sheridan, Heber Springs, and San Marcos locations.

However, various functions across the company worked to compete, almost negatively, with other functions in managing this complex manufacturing process footprint and product flow.

Operations, Production Control and Supply Chain, were constantly uncoordinated and at odds with each other. Engineering was figuratively and literally distant from manufacturing which proved to be counterproductive to the Centers of Excellence strategy. Manufacturing Engineers, many of them with limited aerospace experience, were located in all facilities and were invariably in offices and on mezzanines away from the product they supported. Large Finance and Industrial Engineering Departments produced extensive data and charts of little to no consequence, SPC departments produced yet more data that few understood.

Continuous improvement activities, as they were, yielded little. Communications were infrequent and ineffective in explaining company progress or aligning employees with shared beliefs and goals. Delivered quality and performance to schedule continued to be below customer expectations.

Rohr US manufacturing locations at the outset of the Centers of Excellence strategy:

The Auburn, Washington State facility, opened in 1957 had grown to over 100,000 square feet on 20 plus acres, and as noted, was the delivery center for Boeing products.

The $1 billion in sales goal was achieved in the early 1990s, and at the time Rohr had 13,300 employees in 16 worldwide locations. However, financial problems were many, and in 1992 sales per employee were only $75K and income per employee nominal, not enough to cover costs.

The new corporate headquarters building in Chula Vista had been completed, equipped and furnished, contributing to the extensive financial problems. Cash flow was in crisis mode.

As a result, the Auburn facility was closed and sold. Multiple company assets were subsequently sold to finance companies and leased back. Required equipment maintenance was deferred or not done at all. Accounts payable held payments until the last day of contractual terms, and beyond.

These and other draconian moves were made to access or hold cash to ensure key suppliers and employees could be paid.

Additional problems were looming, and due to ongoing performance issues, Rohr was disqualified from bidding on the Boeing 777 nacelle.

The Riverside facility was of particular concern to several, if not all, customers. A number of them had on-site representatives in Riverside, and they were well aware of performance issues in the facility that were not being addressed.

Both General Electric Aviation and Pratt & Whitney were offering continuous improvement help, but those offers were being rejected.

In the early 1990s, the company flirted with bankruptcy and in 1993 reached this point and prepared bankruptcy papers. As noted earlier, two days before filing, an influx of cash from two primary customers, combined with asset sales and additional financing staved of the bankruptcy filing and the production line chaos that would have ensued.

Finances for this period:

	1991	1992	1993	1994
Sales (B)	$1.300	$1.000	$1.100	$1.100
Net Income (M)	Nominal	Nominal	Nominal	$77
Employees	12,775	13,300	11,750	8,150
Sales per employee (K)	$101	$75	$94	$135
Income per employee (K)	$0	$0	$0	$10

However, this infusion of cash was only a reprieve from the "Burning Platform," a crisis was at hand:

> ## A Crisis of Survival
>
> Poor customer schedule support and quality issues
>
> Customer dissatisfaction
>
> Investment community dissatisfaction
>
> Employee unrest
>
> Leadership unable to resolve performance or financial issues
>
> One step away from bankruptcy
>
> Adrift without a plan

It was from this "Burning Platform" that a remarkable business transformation was made.

In late 1993, early 1994 the Board of Directors and a newly installed president recognized that significant changes within the business were required. The first move made by the new president was to reduce the "indirect to direct" employee ratios which resulted in lower overhead costs and of course decreased indirect support staffing levels.

The second was to change the general manager at the Riverside location. This new general manager was given the mandate of either making the plant a vibrant, viable business or to close this one remaining Riverside facility and move production to the other "Centers of Excellence" sites.

The new general manager was Greg Peters, who was to become the indefatigable leader of cultural change and performance improvement at Aerostructures.

Some at Rohr Corporate and the new general manager in Riverside recognized some critical issues:

- Customer expectations, both commercial and military customers, were getting increasingly more demanding regarding cost, quality and schedule. And Rohr was already well off the pace.
- The old school organizational structure, command and control, had passed its sell-by date.
- Continuous improvement within Rohr was virtually nonexistent.
- The industry was monitoring Rohr, looking for the first signs of collapse with potential "vultures" ready to access high-value assets at low cost.

And more importantly:

- Rohr employed some highly skilled people who wanted to be successful.
- Long-term orders were in place for unique products with production and aftermarket life cycles of over 20 years.
- The potential for business success was exciting with potentially, very profitable product lines.
- The Aftermarket was where Rohr had strong prospects, and this part of the business was about to see significant growth across all programs as the global fleet of commercial airline aircraft increased and aged.
- Radical change was needed.

As previously mentioned the Positive Employee Philosophy and Principles for Excellence were in place and active in some facilities.

What was missing was a cadre of leadership, across the company, prepared to comprehensively address the issues and the potential in the business using a combination of what we later recognized as the development of a culture that embraces change and one that utilizes an efficient and effective operating system.

Riverside

The Riverside team, given its mandate, initially struggled to identify a meaningful improvement strategy. However, they did identify elements of a plan that in time became the foundation for change, continuous improvement and a significant turnaround of the entire business.

The new general manager, and what became a new leadership team, embarked upon the task of changing how the business was led and managed.

Turning managers into leaders, developing a culture that created an open work environment where inclusion and engagement were encouraged. This, in turn, led to and enabled meaningful continuous improvement and a means of managing and measuring progress – an operating system.

It was clear that we needed to "change the business" and that continuous improvement needed to be a significant feature of that change.

What we didn't know was what continuous improvement process to launch, or how to deploy and sustain one successfully.

In the spring of 1994, we contacted Ingersoll Consulting and met several times with one of their senior staff to discuss and better understand this conundrum.

His input was insightful and centered on a "Cellular Manufacturing" strategy and tactical deployment. We were later to understand that "Cellular Manufacturing" as discussed, utilized many processes and tools from the Toyota Production System toolbox, that at the time we had not yet discovered.

As previously noted, an early issue was one of stabilizing Riverside, and an initial macro plan was developed that identified the significant issues that needed to be addressed quickly.

This macro plan included:

- Organization changes
  - Removal of management layers
  - Removal of blockers (invariably employees in leadership positions)
  - Filling critical roles via new hires
- Stabilizing the business
  - Enhanced controls to eliminate quality escapes
    - Checks and balances established
  - An overhaul and reset of the data and information being produced to manage the business
  - Leadership responsibilities and expectations, defined and documented
  - Accountability clarified
- Meaningful and frequent communications with customers and the workforce established.
  - Both still rated us poorly but were encouraged by the focus

The new general manager worked closely with corporate to ensure high-level support for significant personnel and business changes. This was essential.

Riverside as noted earlier, was over one million square feet under roof, multiple buildings housing a myriad of metal and composite bonding processes with various and numerous material handling and transportation issues.

Significant linkage and flow opportunities, at this stage production operations focused, were in clear view but had not been recognized by the previous leadership. Some hardware was literally "traveling miles over months" for completion of operations with minimal value-added activity.

The plan developed included the identification of where key production processes were performed within the facility, the linkage and flow of those processes and where their support staffs were located.

Subsequently, a partial but significant, re-layout of the facility and the relocation of some production operations and support staff was completed.

Several buildings were vacated and utilities disconnected, including the affectionately named "mahogany row" that formally housed the Riverside senior staff.

Riverside Facility Footprint circa 1989

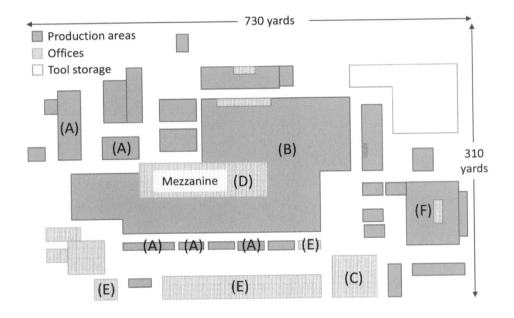

Not to scale.

The first attempts at leveraging linkage and flow were to move a number of production processes from smaller outer buildings (A), to the central production area (B).

Engineering was in its own building (C) distant from manufacturing and was relocated onto a large mezzanine (D) in the middle of the production area. Several support functions were also moved from outer buildings (E) to the mezzanine (D).

The area (F) was where the Titan III rocket system operations were based.

In addition, some significant and distracting leadership performance issues, remaining from the command and control days, were addressed and closed out appropriately.

As these primary business and continuous improvement activities were taking place in late 1994 and early 1995, we were able to gain some measure of clarity on the areas of focus required for success with leadership and management activities.

Building on comments made in the Introduction, what we believe to be necessary business requirements were identified as Foundational Requirements with three others labeled as Principles of Change. All of these requirements being enablers, that we believed would when deployed successfully, drive a successful business transformation.

The Foundational Requirements identified were:

Values and Leadership

An organization must have documented and communicated Values. It is imperative that leadership emulate these values in their daily activities. This emulation must include a constant display of the necessary leadership and management behaviors. How they act and react to issues and challenges, how they communicate, what they communicate, their actions and their areas of focus. Their listening and motivation skills must fully align with the organizational values.

There are many coined phrases that we all have heard, "People are led, things are managed" and "Culture reflects Leadership and Leadership reflects Culture" are two of them. Both are true, and both needed to be addressed if we were to drive change and improve performance.

If leadership does not embrace and emulate the values and behaviors reflective of a Culture driving positive Change then:

- Culture and change will meander and evolve on its own - and we will undoubtedly not like the result.
- Someone else might influence the culture and change - and we will, quite probably, not like the result.
- Our competitors may develop a culture, drive change and improve their business performance – and we will ultimately, lose business.

The environment, the culture, must be managed and developed into one that enables, encourages and supports positive change. It is a fundamental leadership responsibility.

"People are a key asset," how many times have we all heard that agreed with this, and then moved on to the next subject? People, employees, are one of the few business assets that can appreciate in value over time, as knowledge, skills, and experience are developed and increased. Developed effectively they can become a competitive advantage by "enabling you to do, what you do, better than the competition."

It is leadership's responsibility to provide leadership and guidance to all employees so they can achieve their potential and thereby contribute to the potential of the business.

The Principles for Change identified were:

Culture

All the enablers are important, non-more so than this one. A primary component of the cultural change at Rohr was the previously mentioned Positive Employee Philosophy. The Positive Employee Philosophy Principles are:

- Mutual Trust and Respect
- Effective Two Way Communication
- Identify and Eliminate Negatives
- Training and Development
- Employee Engagement
- Competitive Wages and Benefits

It is worth pointing out that the Positive Employee Philosophy is principle based, not rule-based. This can be a hard transition for anyone who is accustomed to operating to rules, which require compliance only, versus working to principles which require thought regarding circumstances, decisions, and consequences.

An overview of the Positive Employee Philosophy is included in the Appendix.

As noted earlier, Principles for Excellence, also essential when molding a culture, were generated and launched in the late 1980s.

They were:

- Service
- Commitment
- Ownership
- Teamwork
- Ethics

Foley, Heber Springs, Sheridan and San Marcos progressed with the deployment and integration of the Positive Employee Philosophy and the Principles for Excellence into their business culture.

These were new facilities and had employees who were much more open to change versus some of the leadership and operator veterans at Chula Vista and Riverside, previously conditioned by the business environment and company - union relationships of previous years.

As noted, at Chula Vista and Riverside, little to nothing had been done to actively deploy the Positive Employee Philosophy and the Principles for Excellence.

Lean (Continuous Improvement)

In the early 1990s, we were not using the word "lean," it had not made its way into our understanding or lexicon. However, we did understand that we had quality and rework issues, many ineffective processes, mounds of inventory, and an abundance of non-value added production area activities in place.

These non-value added activities included significant material handling, storage, and transportation processes, within facilities and between facilities, all contributing to poor performance and cost overruns.

It became quite clear that continuous improvement was an essential and much-needed component of any change process.

Operating System

Over the years, the growth and complexity of the business had not been matched by the required maintenance, or introduction and support of, business systems and processes required to run a complex, multi-facility high tech business.

Fundamental manual processes such as Strategic Planning, the foundation of any businesses focus, and its flow down into coordinated and deployed actions to achieve that strategy, were ineffective in their support of this now billion dollar plus business.

The limited Strategic Planning process in place consisted of an outline of business opportunities and goals, summarized by selected senior staff members. These opportunities, goals and supporting metrics were generally not well developed, communication flows were minimal, and the plan was not aligned or linked to any meaningful mechanism to achieve the plan goals.

Computer and electronic systems such as master scheduling, production control, shop floor management and a myriad of financial systems were woefully inadequate and ineffective. Legally required employee record keeping was a significantly manual process. Many environmental, health and safety records were also kept manually.

Production schedule meetings invariably focused on inaccurate reports and handwritten "hot sheets," themselves, more often than not, incorrect.

What was in place to manage the business on a daily basis, was a poorly aligned and inadequately linked network of over 75 outdated "software systems," some large, some small, many of which were no longer supported by the software developers. On top of this, many processes were managed, and metrics were developed, via a labyrinth of Excel spreadsheets and Access databases.

Systems and processes to effectively operate and manage the business were in dire need of attention.

Engineering systems were in better condition as they had been maintained to ensure alignment and interface with customers systems and compliance with FAA requirements and standards.

Change Pyramid

On reflection, the journey we embarked upon can be described as following a "Change Pyramid," and the next visual illustrates the three "Principles of Change" set upon the foundation of "Values and Leadership."

Where we were headed was towards "Enterprise Excellence," not a destination per se, but rather a continuing journey towards the sustained achievement of high-level performance in full support of customer and business requirements.

This diagram was put together following reflection on the actions and activities of 20 plus years, with the goal of illustrating them as they were deployed on our journey.

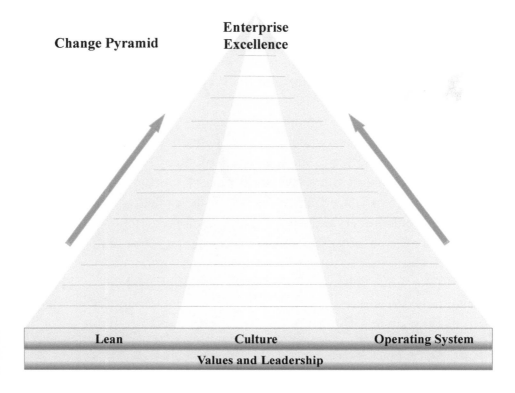

Change Pyramid

Enterprise Excellence

Lean	Culture	Operating System
	Values and Leadership	

At this stage, suffice to say that each of the steps, the sub-elements of the Principles of Change - Lean, Culture and Operating System, had to be understood and deployed effectively.

Each of the Principles, of each of the steps, had to be implemented in close sequence as we progressed towards Enterprise Excellence. Not necessarily in "lockstep" with each other, but with enough deployment and understanding by "everyone" to gain traction of each step to support progress of the whole.

We have used this visual at various points in the book in an attempt to show steps taken, and progress made, towards Enterprise Excellence.

What we learned on the way – a Summary

- We had a flawed and inadequate strategy and "old school" style of management.
- We did not fully realize how significant defining, developing, nurturing and sustaining the appropriate culture would be in the business transformation.
- We quickly realized that we did not have the time to develop a comprehensive plan to save the business. We first needed to stabilize the business, then identify incremental but significant steps in the "direction of improving business performance," take those steps and determine the next ones as we went.
- We had gained the first line of sight on linkage and flow, albeit product-centric, in selected areas within a facility.
  - o Recognition and understanding of the value of linkage and flow across _all business processes and all sites_ was yet to be realized.
- Some hard decisions had to be made.
  - o Not pleasant ones, but necessary to move the business forward.
- Running with 80% of a plan and getting it half right _now_, is much better than waiting for a more complete plan sometime in the future.
- We needed to identify some basic business fundamentals and build from those.

Things you may want to consider – a Summary

- What are our customer's perceptions of us?
- How would a knowledgeable visitor describe our environment and culture?
- Do we have a burning platform we can leverage to change the business?

- o If so, are we prepared to go with less than a comprehensive plan?
- Are our business principles and fundamentals documented, communicated and understood?
- Do we have an overall path or plan defined and developed to enable at least a start to change?

Chapter 2

*O*ffers of help from customers initially rejected. The identification of significant issues at Riverside and the launch of Cellular Manufacturing. Securing the support of a Sensei with erudite continuous improvement insight and experience. Our initial Toyota Production System education and deployment. Engaging the State, County, and City of Riverside in the identification and leveraging of "opportunities to reduce the cost of doing business."

The Organization, how the Business was being Managed and Moving Forward

Jet engine manufacturers General Electric Aviation and Pratt & Whitney both expressed concerns regarding Rohr's poor performance. They had on-site representation to protect their interests and, as previously mentioned, offered continuous improvement assistance throughout 1992. While the Riverside facility did not directly deliver any product to either General Electric or Pratt & Whitney, the Riverside site did ship bond panel components to Rohr's assembly locations which then delivered products to all customers. However through their onsite representatives, both General Electric and Pratt & Whitney identified Riverside to be at the root of Rohr's poor performance issues on a wide front - cost, quality, schedule and – most frustrating – responsiveness.

Their angst was compounded by the fact that they had adopted many of the Toyota Production System based principles in their own facilities and were beginning to see benefits. Both companies offered specific help to the Riverside facility in the form of continuous improvement training and "kaizen event facilitation."

Within Riverside leadership, there was a nominal understanding of what the suggested continuous improvement training may entail, but little to no knowledge of what or how the "kaizen events" or "facilitation of events" would be of any benefit. This ignorance contributed to the almost belligerent stance of leadership that led to the barely concealed brusque rejection of both engine maker's offers of help.

The message from Riverside leadership was clear – "Thank you for the offer of help... but please go away; we will fix any issue we may have ourselves." Undoubtedly not the best response to endear oneself to primary customers.

While one could not describe the Riverside leadership team as having a strong Theory X style, they did reflect an old school "top-down" aerospace management approach. They were parochial, viewed problems as belonging to someone else and considered offers of help as interference in their areas of responsibility, pushing back accordingly. The working environment in Riverside reflected this style of leadership and left a lot to be desired.

As noted, the general manager of the Riverside facility was replaced in early 1994. The new general manager, Greg Peters, inherited both the former general manager's staff and the burning platform. It's important to note that Greg came from the Rohr Heber Springs, Arkansas facility where the Positive Employee Philosophy and Principles for Excellence had been deployed. Consequently, he had an understanding and appreciation for both. But not of the wholesale cultural change and continuous improvement journey we were about to embark upon.

Although it was not publicly stated, corporate had placed Riverside on a two-year "performance improvement plan." This was well understood and not seen as a hollow threat, as 80% of composite bonding work had already been relocated from Riverside to the facility Rohr had acquired in Hagerstown, Maryland. In addition, all of the component assembly work previously at Riverside had been transferred to the facilities, identified in Chapter 1.

Expanding on the Center of Excellence Strategy described earlier, the transfer of this work resulted in the two satellite facilities of the larger Riverside facility – the Arlington and Moreno Valley locations – being closed. These two locations formerly housed assembly and some tooling operations. What was left at Riverside was core fabrication, metal bonding activities, the remaining 20% of composite bonding and scaled back tooling operations. As a result, employment at the Riverside facility was more than halved between 1988 and 1994, plummeting from 3,300 to 1,600.

During this same period and in support of an aftermarket "out of production" component spare part venture, Rohr was building a metal bonding capable facility in Arkadelphia Arkansas. This business opportunity did not materialize. However, the construction and subsequent availability of this facility and its capabilities did open up the prospect and possibility of relocating the remaining metal bonding operations from Riverside to Arkadelphia. While this option would have been somewhat challenging to complete it was undoubtedly viable, should that decision be made.

Pressure from the customer was appropriately unrelenting, and the requirements for continuation of their business with Rohr were explicitly stated in a communique, from a supply chain executive of a major customer to the president of Rohr in 1994.

Those requirements were:

- 100% on-time delivery
- 100% delivered quality
- 75% reduction in cycle time

- 75% reduction in "flow time"
- 25% cost reduction

The burning platform flames grew bigger and hotter.

The Positive Employee Philosophy and Principles for Excellence

We at Riverside did not realize it at the time, but the two nascent behavioral initiatives – the Positive Employee Philosophy and the Principles for Excellence would become a significant part of the cultural change that was to take place.

In the early 1980s, there was growing recognition that the culture in the Rohr facilities left something to be desired. The Positive Employee Philosophy – or PEP – that had been introduced at Foley, Alabama was being deployed in various forms in other industries and businesses at the time. The primary deployment and communication of the "Positive Employee Philosophy" and its Principles, at Rohr, was via week-long, off-site clinics.

By 1989, most Rohr locations were participating in the Positive Employee Philosophy clinics. However general follow-up and support at the California home locations of clinic attendees was inadequate and did not support or enable them to weave the behaviors of the Positive Employee Philosophy into everyday activities.

The Principles for Excellence were scarcely mentioned in any form of communications. Beyond initial "team meeting communications" indicating that they had been developed, and posters put on walls listing those Principles, little to nothing was done with them or regarding them. They drifted into "communication obscurity."

However, and to the credit of the Human Resources leadership, the Positive Employee Philosophy and the Principles for Excellence continued to be supported and deployed despite the aforementioned issues. As a result of this constancy of purpose, the week-long Positive

Employee Philosophy clinics prevailed with attendance from all locations.

However, clinic graduates still lacked the leadership support to enable integration of the Positive Employee Philosophy and the Principles for Excellence behaviors into everyday business activities.

The link between Principle for Excellence that outlined values and beliefs with the Positive Employee Philosophy, which detailed how we treat and work with others, had yet to be made and leveraged. They stood as two separate company initiatives.

With the new Riverside general manager in place, discussions were held with his inherited staff and with smaller groups that were interested in "change." It was readily agreed that the issues needing attention in the business fell into two categories.

The organization

Virtually every aspect of the organization demanded attention. This was evident in the multi-layered organizational structure itself, the inherent bureaucracy, the inefficiency and the rules-based approach to managing employees and running the business.

All of these issues affected everyone in the organization, how expectations were established, how employees were motivated, and how everyone interacted.

As noted previously, Rohr was not a strong Theory X environment. However, decision making was solely and undeniably in the hands of leadership.

Riverside and Chula Vista were, and still are unionized facilities, which raised the issue of union job classifications. Across the two facilities, there were more than 150 of them that were populated. Leadership was generally culpable for this proliferation of classifications and over the years and had created classifications to protect "valued," selected employees, from seniority-based layoffs. This protection from layoffs did on occasion extend to family and friends.

Many mid-level leaders had a generally cozy relationship with local union officials and creating those new classifications was done with little negotiation or trouble.

The out-of-control bureaucracy was also rampant. For instance, in the late 1980s, a Purchase Request for safety equipment was several months past the equipment's need date and was not progressing through the procurement system. The request was found languishing with a still "active" status in the system. It had seventeen signatures on it, three of which were the previous general manager's, with five months between his signatures alone.

Another example, in the early 1990s, there were up to nine layers of leadership between the employees on the floor and the facility general manager, making communication, decision making and problem-solving difficult, confusing and ultimately ineffective endeavors.

How the business was managed

The new general manager and the facility staff he inherited held multiple discussions in 1994 to identify options to enable change and drive business performance improvement.

Initially, as may have been predicted, traditional firefighting tactics were suggested:

- Adding inventory buffers
- Increasing production lead times
- Increasing production lot sizes
- Adding employees
- Increasing the work week
- Creating "Tiger Teams"
- Installing "catalog automation"

All of those ideas were dismissed as alarming "business-as-usual quick-fix actions" doomed to failure. In addition to not addressing root cause resolution of problems, it was agreed that they would all add a mixture of inventory, complexity and increased management combined with increased risks and cost. There was a firm belief that none of them, or any combination of them, would result in any meaningful change in how the business was being run.

We had stock rooms full of parts, the lot sizes were already too large and the lead times were too long. We already had too many employees, the leadership team was already operating as a Tiger Team, and we believed that catalog automation – equipment or software that promised the world – offered little in return.

In addition to the chaos being caused by the organization itself, multiple metrics, charts and data were already in place providing nominal information as to the status, performance or issues in both manufacturing and support areas.

This proliferation of data did not enable sound business decisions of any sort to be made.

At one point in the early 1990s and prior to the general manager change, leadership almost reluctantly accepted that the in-place data and metrics were not providing actionable information. In an attempt to remedy this situation, additional data and charts were identified and developed.

In one memorable and thankfully short-lived period, the Executive Conference Room at Riverside had in excess of three hundred charts posted on the walls in an attempt to understand cost, quality, schedule and a myriad of other issues deemed important.

Few if any of these charts captured critical driver measures. Generating this vast array of data required time and significant resources. Leadership however, were none the wiser, but indeed more confused.

This lack of meaningful metrics fueled the uncoordinated and ineffective management approach. By way of example, a common occurrence for production control was to release production work orders to the shop floor on schedule, a seemingly required and admirable thing to do.

These work orders invariably had multiple parts on their pick lists. Unfortunately, many of the work orders that were released did not have all the required parts and therefore could not be started. These jobs were consequently pushed off to the side, somewhere out on the shop floor, requiring material handling aids and space, creating additional management issues beyond the schedule problems driven by the part shortage itself.

Production control leadership's typical response to this action was, "We released on time. The shortage, or shortages, are from one or more suppliers. Talk to them."

Production control leadership believed this absolved them from any form of follow-up with regard to shortage problem resolution and any further culpability. Particularly if the missing part was from an external supplier, the issue was then deemed a supply chain problem. This philosophy naturally caused havoc with the production schedule, an aspect of the business that production control should have zealously guarded.

Another example of this chaotic management approach was a weekly metric that provided the "variance" between the labor hours booked to a job, and the applied labor standard - the time on the planning considered to be the time it should take to do that job.

Not only was the data of no use but it was taking time and effort to generate – and causing problems and driving poor decisions.

The underlying cause was the fact that the applied labor standard times were not derived from actual observations. They were entered on the shop planning as an estimate, by a project engineer who developed the original shop planning.

Many, if not all of these standards, were inaccurate, significantly over or under the actual time it took to do a job, with much of the planning being years, and on occasion, decades old. These issues were then compounded by local team leaders who were measured by their *variance to standard*, and who subsequently chose to work the jobs that they knew would provide a favorable variance.

Of course, all these activities negatively affected production schedules and customer deliveries.

On the continuous improvement front, things were equally bleak. One unintentionally depressing and comical celebration in Riverside was when the number of improvement projects being worked by the in-place "Project Improvement Teams" reached one hundred. Achieving this number was seen as a milestone in continuous improvement.

It took little research to find that only minimal if any, improvements were made by any of the teams.

Action was taken in 1994 to address the organization and how the business was being run.

Changing the Organization

It was made clear to the existing site senior leadership that all areas of the organization were under review and needed to change. This review process included organizational structure, its method of operation and who was in the organization.

The new general manager knew he had to address current issues with the current somewhat intransigent senior leadership team. He made it clear that leadership changes would be made and a leadership team established that understood and emulated the attributes of the Positive Employee Philosophy and Principles for Excellence.

During late 1994 and early 1995 one-third of the senior staff chose to leave, one third were helped in finding opportunities beyond Rohr, and the balance were retained in their roles or redeployed while remaining on the general manager's staff. Their replacements were some of the "next-level leadership folks" who were eager to change how the business was being managed.

The general manager discussed and clarified with his new leadership team how he intended to change the organizational culture, seeking the support and advocacy of his staff to fully implement the Positive Employee Philosophy and the Principles for Excellence.

At the Corporate level, the Principles for Excellence had been updated, renamed and relaunched as "Values," they being:

- Ethical Behavior
- Customer-focused Improvements
- Accountability and Teamwork
- Openness and Trust

Much was done to increase the communications and understanding of the Values and the Positive Employee Philosophy.

The alignment and linkage of the new Values and the Positive Employee Philosophy at Riverside became apparent and key. They gained traction as leaders became primary communicators and stewards of their deployment.

The general manager was a role model for the behaviors of the Values and the Positive Employee Philosophy and made those behaviors non-negotiable for all employees, first and foremost by his staff. Participation in the week-long Positive Employee Philosophy clinics increased.

A constant focus on broad facility level communications, both formal and informal, was maintained, weaving aspects of the

Values and Positive Employee Philosophy behaviors into every communication opportunity possible.

Layers of the organization were reduced, some leadership positions were eliminated, and quite quickly the management layers between employees in the workplace to the facility general manager shrank, in some instances, to only two.

Commercial aerospace was in one of its down cycles and in 1994 employment at Riverside was, as previously mentioned, at 1,600. With the dramatic ongoing organizational and behavioral changes a number of employees chose to leave the company.

This along with the industry-driven employment reductions made the organizational transition a more challenging task to manage and accomplish than had been anticipated.

Some new leaders emerged and developed well in the new environment while some leaders had difficulty leading by Principles, a cornerstone of the Positive Employee Philosophy. Active coaching was done to reinforce the Values and Positive Employee Philosophy principles. On occasion, counseling of a struggling leader was necessary.

Fortunately, this was not a frequent occurrence, and a leader was not counseled multiple times. Mutual trust and respect were to the fore and leaders who could not support were either internally reassigned or helped to find other opportunities outside the company.

It was clear who was on board for "change," who was undecided and who was not on board. After discussions and coaching, we were able to be selective with salaried staff, as to who was to stay employed and who was to be helped finding alternative employment. During downsizing, Union employees were, as mentioned, reduced by seniority.

Changing how the business was being managed

The organization restructuring in 1994 took much more time and effort than anticipated. As a result, we were unable to identify a coherent "strategic way forward" regarding specific changes, required to enable the business to run more effectively.

Time and energy was however spent looking for answers to that question. We had finally let GE run continuous improvement activities in one core fabrication cell but with little understanding of the improvement processes and tools that they used or their origin, the Toyota Production System.

We reflected on the copious amount of data that we generated which, as mentioned, was of little to no use. We recognized the egregious error of viewing some of the metrics in this sea of data as meaningful performance indicators.

The work that GE had done in the core fabrication cell had produced some interesting, albeit high level, information. We able to see that a production work order, once released, was closed out on average, 36 days later.

This seemed alarmingly odd. Taking a closer look, we found that it took 25 minutes of "hands-on activity" to produce the "average part" in this cell, with a subsequent 300-minute oven stabilization of the core detail parts.

In total, 325 minutes of potentially value-added tasks versus a 36 day cycle time to perform them.

No matter how one may look at these numbers, 325 minutes to possibly add value, compared to the total time elapsed - 15,120 minutes (36 days, one shift, 420 minutes per shift), they indicated alarming performance.

This difference between the two numbers initially exposed a now obvious opportunity of "how do we effectively reduce the days to manufacture?" Realizing that if we did, we would need less inventory and part tracking, fewer material handling aids, and reduced manufacturing space. All of this would undoubtedly result in less cost and improved performance to schedule.

A "Days To Manufacture" metric was quickly put in place for each of Riverside's production operations. This also enabled us to subsequently track progress to the 75% reduction in "flow time," a previously stated requirement from one of the large aircraft manufacturers.

We also knew that production work orders, the paperwork itself, were issued in large batches. These work orders would sit on someone's desk until released to the shop floor, contributing to the excessive days to manufacture. This action and inaction alone resulted in work orders being misplaced and getting out of sequence.

Another factor was the number of job classifications. At that time there were more than ten core fabrication cell job classifications, each with its defined boundaries of tasks for that classification. Consequently, work would often sit waiting for the union member with the "right" classification to come along and complete the required steps in the process as defined by the classification they held. A routine occurrence, multiple times a day.

In the core fabrication activity GE had run for us, we observed that they had used continuous improvement processes and tools that were different to those we were familiar with. However, we did begin to gain a broad overview of the, still yet to be identified, Toyota Production System processes and tools.

As a result, and from the initial macro plan and facility layout review mentioned earlier, we knew we had to address opportunities in many areas including:

- Housekeeping - 5S
- Inventory – Right-Sizing
- Product "hand-offs" and excessive part travel – Linkage and Flow
- Remotely located support staff - Collocation
- Mounds of data with minimal meaningful information - Driver measures or leading indicators

We further realized that organizing into work cells would facilitate implementation of the processes and tools noted above. As a result, a consensus was gained to implement a Cellular Manufacturing structure and approach as outlined by the Ingersoll consultant and also utilized by GE Aircraft Engines

Consequently in early 1995 "Cellular Manufacturing" was launched.

We started aggressive 1S and 2S (3S through 5S came later), began to reduce batch sizes and began to understand how to link and flow work through workstation placement. Cell support personnel such as team leaders, manufacturing engineers, industrial engineers, quality engineers, and production planners were all collocated within the products and areas they supported. Data that provided no information was jettisoned, and we began to identify and develop data and driver measures, that were both meaningful and actionable.

We also called upon Pratt & Whitney and asked them to provide the "Continuous Improvement Training" that they had offered earlier. They graciously did so, providing a high-level overview of the continuous improvement processes and tools used at their facilities in the early summer of 1995.

Also in the early summer of 1995, the president of Rohr had received a personal invitation from James Womack, at the time Chairman and CEO of the Lean Enterprise Institute, to a Lean Summit in Cambridge, Massachusetts. The president was not able to attend but realizing that this looked like something the Riverside leadership may well be interested in, he passed it along to the Riverside general manager, who did attend the summit.

Over the course of a few weeks in the early summer of 1995 three things happened:

1. We learned that the Pratt & Whitney continuous improvement training was Toyota Production System based. A direct result and product of them working with Shingijutsu, the consulting company.
2. The general manager's attendance at the James Womack Lean Summit put the Toyota Production System definitively into view.
3. Contact was made with the Toyota facility nearest to Riverside. This was Toyota Auto Body California (TABC), a manufacturing facility in Long Beach, about 70 miles from

Riverside. Site leadership there graciously allowed several members of Riverside's leadership team to visit their facility and were hosted by their Sensei.

To this day, we wonder how it could have taken us so long to realize that what we were looking for was in front of us - The Toyota Production System. This was undoubtedly a reflection of our own shortcomings, as much was being published regarding the Toyota Production System at the time.

What we observed at TABC was the application of continuous improvement tools at a level none of us had seen before. The efficiency was "eye-opening."

One area in particular, was a sight to behold. A U-shaped *chaku chaku* production line fabricating and assembling catalytic converters. One operator, five machines, and process steps all linked and operating in unison. The applied and clearly visible Toyota Production System processes and tools – 5S, linkage and flow, visual controls, right-sizing and point of use – were impressive. Raw materials and parts went in at one end and product, ready for the next step in its manufacture, came out of the other end.

The TABC Sensei, sensing that we were serious regarding deployment of the Toyota Production System in an aerospace environment, went out of his way to share his knowledge and experience with us. Over the course of several weeks, we had many long and late-into-the-evening discussions when he visited the Riverside facility on his own time.

A fourth significant step was also made that summer. James Womack was asked if he could recommend a Sensei and he suggested Bob Pentland. Bob had worked at Jacobs Vehicle Systems, the company known widely as "Jake Brake" who had previously used Shingijutsu, the business consulting firm founded in the US in 1987 by Chihiro Nakao, an ex-Toyota executive.

Fortuitously, Bob at the time was consulting at a company in Riverside. At a meeting at the Mission Inn, Riverside in the summer of 1995, we explained our plight, challenges, and needs, Bob listened intently throughout the session. His services were secured shortly after that.

Bob engaged as our consultant, our Sensei, in the late summer of 1995 and had an immediate impact. His knowledge, experience and teaching abilities were readily shared with, and consumed by, an eager-to-learn Riverside team.

Under Bob's guidance, the deployment of continuous improvement, now commonly called lean, followed a disciplined and structured path. Early lean implementation efforts focused on basics.

However, we were able to clarify and accelerate implementation of the previously launched "Cellular Manufacturing plans" and to build on the facility-wide 1S and 2S efforts. In addition, some secondary linkage and flow moves were made while collocation of shop floor support employees was solidified.

The consultant also provided formal and informal continuous improvement training and coaching on every visit. The initial formal training provided was excellent in content, limited in detail and rudimentary in format – it was on overhead "view foils."

That training covered 5S, linkage and flow, point of use, right-sizing, the "Seven Kinds of Waste" and several associated Toyota Production System Tools.

The Seven Kinds of Waste being – defects/rework, overproduction, waiting, transportation, inventory, movement, over processing.

One point repeatedly emphasized at the start of our lean journey by Bob was "If you can't master 5S, you will never master the balance of the Toyota Production System." He wanted us to thoroughly understand a basic continuous improvement tool, and to appreciate the time and effort to do so. Another was "Don't even think about countermeasures to a problem until you have documented reality." Documenting reality as we learned, was another fundamental continuous improvement process step to be taken and understood before applying countermeasures.

Bob wanted us to develop a deep understanding of the basics and have a structured, measured deployment of continuous improvement, emphasizing that this was not going to be a quick journey.

We worked diligently developing an understanding of the Toyota Production System processes and tools. This included the somewhat obvious, but not to us at the time, difference between value-added and non-value added activities and the nuances and differences between driver measures and result measures. All of this was combined with education, guidance, and direction on how to run well-structured, successful kaizen events.

The issue of "driver measures and result measures" was not only important at the time, but was, as we came to find out, a vital element of a process we were to shortly develop.

The first actual "visual" of the continuous improvement path we were embarking on was drawn on an easel during many of the late-night discussions of the mid-1990s as we "unfolded the lean journey map" and made progress.

The initial Continuous Improvement model:

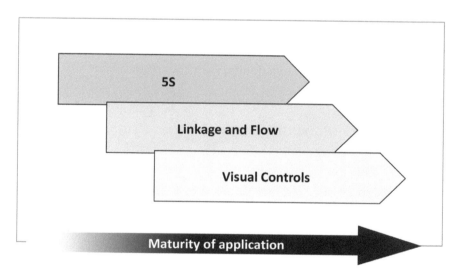

As we began to run multiple kaizen events under the guidance of our consultant, we encountered opportunities and used tools that were not previously understood or readily evident in our business:

- Creativity Before Capital
  - o Developing "made in-house" tools, fixtures and supporting equipment.
  - o Avoiding "catalog type" solutions that invariably came at a cost, with high hopes, and were not available in real time.
- A Bias for Action
  - o Taking action now rather than adding an issue to a list.
  - o Implementing Countermeasures during an event, to significantly improve the processes rather than waiting for perfect solutions.
- Heijunka
  - o Developing a visual shop floor schedule management process.
  - o A process that one facility found to be invaluable to manage closely interlinked manufacturing processes and one they have perfected over the years.

It is worth noting that although we were aggressively driving change and performance improvement, we were learning as we made headway, identifying tactical steps along the way and often making course corrections.

As we embarked on changing – and saving – the business, we realized that this would require the focus and attention of everyone in the company, in addition to all the other issues requiring support.

Two obligations that could not be compromised were deliveries and responsiveness to the customer. Discussions around these subjects highlighted that while senior leadership were spending much if not all their time "leading change," we still needed to focus on and ensure that we were delivering on schedule to the customer and responding effectively to their inputs.

To this end, one of the senior leadership team stepped to the fore. This was an individual with much production control and manufacturing experience. It was agreed that his primary responsibility would be to ensure customer requirements – deliveries, were made on schedule. A complex and full-time job given the chaotic state of the business at the time. This included working with, and providing direction to, production control, supply chain, and operations.

This assignment enabled the bulk of leadership to focus primarily on change and the deployment of the Toyota Production System.

On occasion, to make a delivery, we would knowingly violate a Toyota Production System principle or two, to ensure customer requirements were achieved. To keep a production line moving this included applying quick fixes to problems rather than "formal line stopping and root cause resolution." Or on occasion, taking a product out of the production flow and completing it with experienced employees, in a triage manner, to quickly get the job done to ensure a delivery.

We were extremely cautious when doing this and communicated real time with employees in the affected areas, as to what we were doing and why. Employees invariably understood these decisions. Stabilizing the business, doing some non-lean things to ensure that customer deliveries were made on schedule. These decisions needed close attention and communication while the business was being "changed."

In addition, recognizing that general business operating costs for the Riverside plant were high, a cross-functional "Red Team" was established, made up of City, County and State representatives along with Rohr employees, both salaried and union, with the goal of identifying and implementing means and methods to reduce plant operating costs. Over a relatively short period of intense, focused efforts, overall business costs were significantly reduced enabling a more competitive operating cost basis.

The city, county, and state understood and appreciated that to retain a business that had been in Riverside since 1952, and was capable of providing employment for hundreds of people, was a good thing to do for all concerned.

By the fall of 1995, barely 18 months into the "improve performance or close the business" threat, performance was improving significantly.

- Overall days to manufacture had reduced 30%
- Direct labor costs had reduced 15%
- Scrap rework and repair had reduced 45%
- Late deliveries to the internal customer, and subsequently the paying customer, had reduced 60%
- The overhead costs of doing business in Riverside was down significantly.

Why was this the case?

The Red Team had had a positive effect on cost. More importantly, employees were beginning to appreciate that they were being listened to, being treated as adults, and thus became increasingly engaged in the business – and actively engaged in change. They were buying into and becoming advocates of the Values and the Positive Employee Philosophy resulting in the Continuous Improvement processes and tools being deployed with increasing effectiveness and impact. Real performance improvement could be seen and was being sustained.

As noted previously, the down cycle in commercial aerospace was upon us, with inevitable and ongoing layoffs occurring as we drove change. This issue tempered the positive emotions of employees but did not in itself disrupt the ongoing changes.

Both salaried and hourly employees were being trained in the Positive Employee Philosophy and the Toyota Production System. Kaizen events became a significant and frequent process to focus upon and eliminate waste/non-value added activities.

Kaizen events have a structured process, each starting with a "kick-off" attended by the event team participants, senior and local leadership, continuous improvement facilitators and employees from the areas of event focus.

On two separate occasions, two different union employees who were participating in events, stood in front of their respective "event kick-off" audience and said, almost verbatim, "I know we have a layoff of 30 people scheduled in four weeks' time. I also know I am in that layoff group given my seniority, but I am participating in this event because I want to make positive change and contribute to improvement in the business so that it is still around for me to get recalled back to."

Momentous occasions given the state of relations between the company and union well into the late 1980s and early 1990s. We were gaining the hearts and minds of employees. The culture was changing.

What Riverside was doing and the impact on the facility metrics was easily seen, and the threat to the facility began to ease to the great relief of the Riverside employees in the fall of 1995.

Senior company leadership understood that Lean Manufacturing, the Principles for Excellence, the processes and tools being deployed and the results they were producing at Riverside were real and sustainable. Further, they believed that they could also be successful if deployed with discipline across all operations facilities. In late 1995, the Vice President of Operations set the expectations for all facilities to deploy lean as it had been deployed at Riverside.

How this deployment was enacted at each of the locations beyond Riverside is discussed in later chapters.

In early 1996, we received a copy of the *"Executive Summary of Lean Thinking,"* the book by Womack & Jones. This 25-page document became our "go-to" source for continuous improvement guidance and information until the book *Lean Thinking* itself was published later that year.

Defining Value and an organizational Value Stream structure were discussed in this executive summary. This was the first time our leadership team had seen anything regarding that type of structure, which many of us found to be intriguing. It was to be a significant feature in the organizational changes we made in future years.

Most importantly in 1996, this summary outlined the steps taken by companies that were successfully removing waste/non-value added activities and improving their performance significantly. We translated those steps as being:

- How to get the lean journey started, being clear as to what the goal was, that being perfection.
- Dealing with people problems up front and removing those not on board.
- Finding and engaging a proficient Sensei to help guide the journey.
- Starting out small, establishing linkage and flow, right-sizing processes and tools and demanding results in one particular area of the business.
- As progress is made, mistakes will be made and are acceptable as long as you learn from them.
- Being transparent on progress and setbacks, recognizing progress through some form of profit sharing for all employees.
- Fix something and fix it again, this is continuous improvement.
- Once progress is made, expand the scope and begin to link improvements together and develop a "pull system" to start to optimize the whole.
- Ensure every employee shares in performance improvement through a compensation link.
- Include suppliers, as difficult as that may be.
- Make a plan for growth, for as waste is identified and removed, then capacity will be created.

A comment on union job classifications, in the late 1980s, as noted earlier, there were more than 150 job classifications at Riverside and Chula Vista. It was clear that this was an impediment to both shop floor and support efficiency. Through the course of two union contract negotiations in the 1990s, these job classifications were reduced to a total of ten.

Production employees were predominantly in one of three classifications. The other seven were for skilled trades such as electrician, electronics technician, plumber, and other facilities engineering trades. This significantly reduced, and in many instances eliminated, the issue of waiting for an employee with the "right union classification" to complete a task and move the job to the next operation. This alone contributed to positive, meaningful change in how production was able to run its business, improve efficiency and effectiveness and reduce cost.

Through 1996, we were making headway as reflected on the "Change Pyramid."

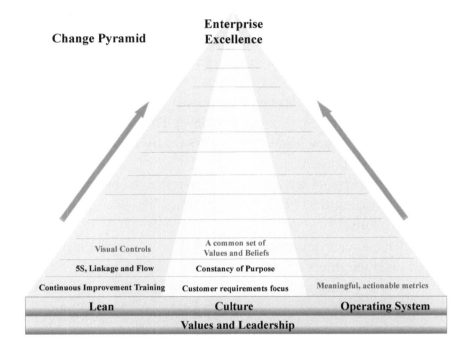

Steps taken and proficiency achieved through the years discussed to this point are shown in **BOLD** black font advancing from the bottom of this visual to Enterprise Excellence at the top. Progress but with less than required proficiency is shown in a light grey font.

What we learned on the way – a Summary

- We were not listening to customers.
  - o We should have been doing this habitually and responding positively.
- Leadership responsibility and accountability was not a strong point with a number of in-place leaders. As accountability increased, many leaders were unable or unwilling to function appropriately in the new environment.
  - o Some became part of what was called "The Government in Exile" and became critics and subversives until removed.
- Traditional organization structures had become unwieldy
  - o When we de-layered and flattened organizations, information flow improved and ownership increased significantly.
- Traditional style leaders were not always suited to Principles-based leadership (Positive Employee Philosophy)
  - o Many new leaders emerged who flourished in the new environment.
  - o Some long-service leaders who remained became divisive hoping that "This too shall pass." They had to be dealt with.
- Face-to-face discussions were held between senior leadership and their direct reports. The critical question posed was: "Are you on board with where we are about to take this business and with how we are going to operate, and are you prepared to fully support and engage?"
- Our organizational structure needed attention, but we were unsure of how to address this issue.
- More data does not mean more knowledge
  - o More charts mean nothing if there is no information to drive the right decisions and actions.
- As change was implemented, there were some levels of confusion.

- o Some were genuinely confused, and we helped with extra attention and training.
- o Some chose to be confused, a somewhat obvious tactic to "not engage" and were counseled as necessary.
- Some organizations wanted to leap to what they perceived as being the latest technologies rather than focus on the unglamorous basics.
- The Positive Employee Philosophy had an unexpectedly supportive influence upon the business as employees began to be led rather than managed.
  - o "Identify and Eliminate the Negatives." Removed significant obstacles to progress including the elimination of Probationary Periods for new employees.
  - o Focusing on doing "the right thing" for the 95% positive employees rather than rules for the marginal 5%.
- Continuous improvement as we knew it was ineffective
- Simple visual controls were needed to understand the basic health of the business and performance to customer requirements. Meaningful driver measures and metrics did not exist:
  - o Shop floor metrics
  - o Support function metrics
  - o Financial metrics
- Focusing on "days to manufacture" was quite possibly the most significant single meaningful metric that led to a wealth of opportunity.
- We needed external, knowledgeable help, and stimulus.

Things you may want to consider – a Summary

- What is our process for customer feedback?
  - o Is it effective?
- How would we rate our responsibility and accountability?

- How would a knowledgeable visitor rate our responsibility and accountability?
- Is our organizational structure effective?
  o How do we know?
- Do we have comprehensive, integrated, communicated and sustained Values and a People Philosophy culture?
  o Can our culture be defined?
  o Can it be seen?
  o What would people "knowledgeable" about employee relations, work environments, and culture say about our work environment?
- Are all employees "on the same page?"
  o How do we know this?
- Where do we find a competent Sensei?
- Are we prepared to listen to and take Sensei input?
- Are our metrics timely, meaningful and actionable, do they measure something we can change to impact the customer and or our bottom line positively?
  o Are these metrics understandable and meaningful to employees and do they act upon them in real time?
- Do we understand our days to manufacture? The number of days a "work order/shop order" is open?
- Do we have a coherent picture of basic, applied continuous improvement?
  o How are we communicating this and is that communication effective?
  o How do we know?
- Do we have union representation in any of our facilities and how is our relationship with the union?

Chapter 3

*D*riving to a Goal we could define, but lacking a defined roadmap to achieve that Goal. Identifying and developing an understanding of the steps required, to reach the Goal as we made progress. Increasing our continuous improvement knowledge and capabilities. Actively learning as we made progress. Standardizing continuous improvement processes and tools. The development of the culture we believed we needed, through the linkage of Values and a Positive Employee Philosophy. Ensuring comprehensive and effective communications. The introduction of Policy Deployment and an initial Operating System.

Learning

We knew that we were on a path where our knowledge and experience base was limited. It was imperative for us to progressively learn as we made progress and we were committed as a team, to that process. We believed that whatever progress we made would undoubtedly be an improvement over past results.

At this stage, we still had not fully recognized the potential impact of the linkage and integration of the Values, the Positive Employee Philosophy, and the Continuous Improvement processes. These elements as a combined system, would in time produce outstanding and sustained results. This system recognition was to be understood and leveraged later.

With constancy of purpose and alignment with our strategy to save the business, many incremental but substantial changes were deployed in the 1994 and 1995 period. It became clear that these actions were indeed changing the Riverside organization and how the business there was being run.

Basic but timely, meaningful metrics were developed and displayed on Driver Measure Boards accessible and visible to all team members. Many of the prior resource intensive but ineffective business metrics were discontinued.

We had learned from the study of the Toyota Production System about seven different types of waste, and the development and display of these driver measure metrics exposed vast amounts of waste in, what appeared to be, all our processes. This represented a tremendous visible opportunity to improve the business by applying fundamental continuous improvement tools and techniques.

Riverside resources were appropriately seen as a growing knowledge base for continuous improvement and change. This resulted in the additional challenge of supporting the operations-wide deployment of new methods and processes that we were only beginning to understand.

To this end, we started down several paths of learning:

Increasing our knowledge of and proficiency with continuous improvement

Recognizing the failure of prior ineffective leadership techniques combined with the need to fully understand required continuous improvement tools and techniques, a simple "Learning Together" process was developed and implemented. This helped ensure that essential knowledge, process methods, and calibrations were in place on the journey forward.

This was initially led by the general manager who with his staff read and studied books and articles on two subjects – Leadership and Continuous Improvement.

We were very selective about what passed our filters as "viable sources of subject information," often guided by our consultant. A vast selection of books and articles on Leadership were available and multiple books on Lean Manufacturing, and the Toyota Production System were already available, with many more being published at the time.

The Learning Together process became one of – identify an article or book, read a chapter or article per week and record a summary, on a preprinted one-page form, the following:

- What does it say, what are the facts?
  o What did I learn?
- How may it apply to us?
  o What should I, or we as a team do, as a result of this learning?

At senior staff meetings, brief book/article reviews and a discussion of the notes taken were permanent agenda items. As a result of this process, continual learning and alignment of the staff, regarding leadership and continuous improvement, was apparent. Subsequently and over time, a number of course adjustments were made to the broader "leadership, continuous improvement and change" strategies and tactics being deployed.

The next level of leadership quickly adopted this Learning Together process with much success.

Leadership, recognizing the need to learn and taking the time to study in their own time, evenings and weekends over the initial years of "change," was in itself a humbling step, taken willingly and with fervor.

A Bibliography of books and articles, which we read and found to be helpful, is in the Appendix.

A second significant step taken, with the support and guidance of our consultant, was the update and expansion of the continuous improvement training materials.

They were significantly updated, including the identification and addition of next level Toyota Production System tools and techniques such as Standard Work.

The modules on Standard Work were utilized later on our journey following development and application of fundamental 5S, linkage and flow and other continuous improvement tools.

The graphics and visuals in the training modules were significantly improved, and the complete training package was formalized, structured and captured electronically as we entered 1996. The initial continuous improvement training agenda and schedule was developed for the year. Each session was four and a half days with a class size of thirty people.

To supplement the training course, a "virtual kaizen event game" was subsequently developed and added to the schedule. This challenging game, based upon real company data, took an additional four and a half days to complete. Participants were divided into teams and were required to use continuous improvement processes, tools and countermeasures covered in the training curriculum to remove waste and improve selected driver measures, all within strict budgetary constraints. This valuable learning addition increased the continuous improvement training course duration to a second week.

The training became known as "Continuous Improvement boot camp." Leadership were the first required participants through this training. Subsequently, and to this day, senior leadership team members, including the president, knowledgeably present multiple training modules in each Aerostructures "Continuous Improvement boot camp."

This type of visible Leadership engagement contributed significantly to the positive change taking place.

These training materials were routinely updated over many years of deployment and learning, and are currently in place and used at many, if not all, United Technologies Aerospace Systems locations. They have been incorporated into UTC's continuous improvement process known as ACE (Achieving Competitive Excellence).

Over the years, numerous suppliers have taken advantage of this training, participating in many of the scheduled "Continuous Improvement boot camps."

However, meaningful implementation of continuous improvement in the supply base has been disappointing, driven by their leaderships lack of support for the deployment of continuous improvement, at their facilities.

Towards the end of the 1990s, the "Continuous Improvement boot camp" had become a powerful tool in the education of employees and the business of change. A long waiting list of now Aerostructures, and supplier employees eager to attend was maintained.

Once Rohr became part of Goodrich the waiting list quickly grew longer and the "virtual kaizen event game" was dropped to add more "module only" classes per year. This change was implemented with the goal of attendees participating in scheduled kaizen events at their home locations as soon after the classroom training as possible to drive home the overall learning impact in real business situations.

To replace the "virtual kaizen event game," half day assembly line exercises were developed and introduced into the now one-week training that simulated assembly lines to help attendees understand the continuous improvement tools and how they worked together.

We also realized that continuous improvement in itself, was helping drive the cultural change taking place and that the Positive Employee Philosophy was a robust supportive element of continuous improvement.

To this end, existing modules on "Group Dynamics," that Human resources had available, were modified and subsequently presented by Human Resources personnel in all the "Continuous Improvement boot camps."

The Group Dynamics module contained many of the "traditional" behavioral issues:

- Team development.
- The emotional aspects of change.
- The highs and lows of change and how to manage change.
- Dealing with resistance to change and leveraging the support of change.
- Communications to ease and enable change.

The following diagram shows the somewhat typical emotional cycle of change:

Change, the Transition and Emotions

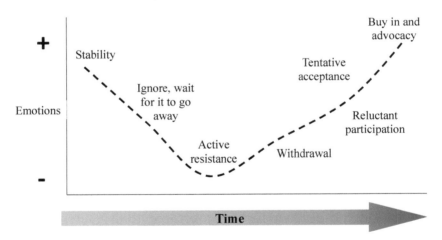

Although becoming more evident, we had still to fully recognize and understand the potentially powerful connectivity and the relationship of continuous improvement to the Values and in particular the Positive Employee Philosophy.

The continuous improvement training and its deployment evolved over the years as the modules were systematically updated and supplemented.

A visual was developed – the House of Lean. The following one is circa 2000:

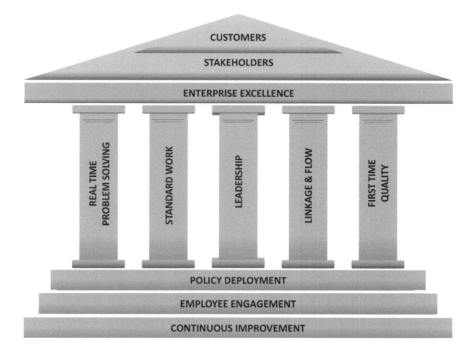

This "House of Lean" and variants of it are in the educational materials of many companies who have deployed "lean," and it has become a standard visual in continuous improvement training materials.

Reviewing this "House of Lean," from bottom to top:

- Continuous improvement is the foundation in everything we do. All underpinned by Values and a robust People Philosophy.
- Employee Engagement in continuous improvement activities is required, nurtured and sustained.
- A Policy Deployment process is in place that aligns, focusses and links employees to the right priorities. (Policy Deployment is explained in detail later)

- Leadership is the center column as it is fundamental and central to the culture, the environment, change, continuous improvement, and business success.
- Linkage and Flow and Standard Work are on each side of leadership as they are the two aspects of continuous improvement that are the platforms for the identification of waste identification and its reduction.
- Real Time Problem Resolution and First Time Quality are the outer columns as a focus on these will eliminate or reduce waste, improve performance, and reduce costs.
- On the lintel of the House, achieving and sustaining Enterprise Excellence is the goal.
- All of these aspects are in support of Stakeholders - employees and shareholders.
- At the peak of the House is the Customer, the only reason for the business to exist. Customer needs must be satisfied at all times, and the House is constructed with that in mind.

Standardizing the Continuous Improvement process

Continuous improvement in Riverside, as noted, had been previously and erroneously graded on the number of "improvement projects in work," not the measurable success of any one of them.

Kaizen events there were now facilitated effectively by our consultant when available and supported at other times by our increasingly proficient lean leaders to ensure continuity. It was clear that locations beyond Riverside needed more help and guidance regarding how to plan and run efficient and effective kaizen events.

A "Standard Work for an Event" document was developed that identified how to do this and achieve the objectives of an event.

This document also helped event participants understand how event objectives, indeed all continuous improvement activities, should be linked to and support, the Policy Deployment process and its business objectives.

"Standard Work for an Event" also aided the development of everyone's continuous improvement understanding and proficiency, and was a resource for self-sufficiency in event facilitation.

The "Standard Work for an Event" document covers in detail:

- How to identify opportunities and ensure they tie to company goals.
  - Development of a well-scripted Scope Sheet
  - A continuous improvement Management Team or Council approval filter and process.
  - Ensuring events are prioritized appropriately and tied to Policy Deployment.
- Pre Work for an event
  - Preparation of the event documents
    - Scope Sheet
    - Objectives to Goals matrix
    - Objectives to continuous improvement tool matrix
    - Starting and finishing metrics matrix
    - Completing a "Pre Event checklist"
  - Securing the participation of the identified Team Leader, Co-Leader, and team members.
  - Ensuring a proficient facilitator is available or that the team was experienced and capable of running a successful event without one.
- How to Kick Off an event
  - With senior management engagement and participation.
- How to identify the appropriate continuous improvement tools to use and when
- The steps of an event:
  - Documenting Reality
  - Identifying issues, problems, and opportunities (waste/ non-value added activities)
  - Planning countermeasures
  - Making changes
  - Verifying and quantifying changes

- o Changing any relevant specifications, processes, and documents
- o Celebrating event achievements
- o Post-event follow up
- o Doing it again
- To Do lists and their use
  - o Using two sets of To-Do lists. One to manage the team's activities during the week and one to manage the "output" of the event.
- Meeting areas
  - o Where event teams should be located, preferably in, or as close as possible, to the area of the event focus. Recognizing that this may not always be possible.
- Daily debrief meetings
  - o Attended by Team Leaders and or Co-Leaders.
  - o Events weeks usually have multiple events running at the same time, often with connected objectives. Outlined is what each team should cover, "what they have done, what they are doing, what they are going to do next and the big "Ah Ah" of the day."
  - o These meetings are for coordination, learning and training purposes.
- Standard Work and Documentation Changes
  - o Keeping Standard Work documentation, shop floor planning and other documents up to date and in line with Quality and audit requirements.
- Event Report Out process
  - o Holding a concise and successful Report Out where progress can be shared with a broad audience.
  - o How to get the event results to "speak for themselves"
- Post-event evaluation and accountability
  - o Closing out open To Do countermeasures post-event week. (A constant challenge)
  - o Completing a "post-event checklist."

While this could be seen as a little overwhelming, once understood and in practice, discipline to the process became second nature and enabled the kaizen event process to be planned, managed and executed efficiently and effectively.

To support the Standard Work for an Event process additional training manuals were also developed outlining steps for the critical kaizen event process of "Documenting Reality."

This includes in detail methods for:

- Documenting reality using standard methods
  o Time Observations
  o Process Mapping
  o Standard Work Sheets
  o 5S evaluations
  o EH&S and Ergonomic evaluations
- Documenting reality using non-standard methods
  o Voice of the Customer
  o "Supplier, Input, Process, Output, Customer" process mapping (SIPOC)
  o Statistical Process Controls
  o Lean Product Development tools such as Document reviews, FAIR reviews, and component Assembly Flow processes. (discussed in Chapter 5)

Standard Work for an Event and the Documenting Reality manuals proved to be excellent learning and reference tools for all employees, particularly those new to the kaizen event process and in need of guidance. Both documents were updated many times over the years with clarifications and additions as issues and opportunities were encountered along the way.

One practice we saw and outlawed early in our journey was when some leaders, fortunately only a few, would identify themselves as the "sponsor" of an event. While this practice in principle was appropriate, some leaders saw this as the way to "check the continuous improvement engagement box" essentially without any engagement in the actual event. We required leaders to actively and regularly, engage in kaizen events, full time when appropriate.

Developing a Continuous Improvement Guide and Assessment tool

Building on Quality Improvement Matrices utilized by many suppliers and customers, an Enterprise Excellence Assessment tool and process was developed in 1996. This assessment tool was put in place to act as a continuous improvement guide and metric, by which to set objectives and track the progress of each function and facility to those "objectives." Within the matrix, we identified and defined a number of specific annual requirements and accomplishments to ensure continued and sustained continuous improvement and positive cultural change progress.

Initial matrix categories were:

1. Organizational Deployment and Development
2. EH&S
3. Communication
4. 5S
5. Visual Management and Controls
6. Layout, Linkage, Flow, and Right-Sizing
7. Multi-Skilling
8. Quality
9. Continuous Improvement Training and Education
10. Metrics and Results

The Enterprise Excellence Assessment document contained a matrix with "tracks" for each of the ten categories. Within each of the tracks, there were five levels of achievement and progress was measured from left to right, levels 1 through to 5, as outlined on the following visual.

Awareness Understanding Commitment Habit

1	2	3	4	5	
An assessment of the functions learning opportunities is complete	A plan is in place to further the development of the organizations' employees	A Learning Together process is in place	Employees participate in events outside of the function	The organizations learning and development plan is the organization standard	Organization Deployment and Development
Employees have an awareness of EH&S	Employees are aware of EH&S requirements	Metrics are in place to monitor EH&S requirements	Activities are scheduled to address EH&S issues	Consistently meets all EH&S goals	EH&S
Leadership communicates regularly	Leadership has a posted comm's plan	Leadership is on track to its posted plan	Comm's plans are statused and on track	Comm's plans are consistently met	Communication
Awareness of 5S	All employees trained in 5S. Some 5S activity obvious	A 5S assessment schedule is developed and posted	5S assessments are being completed on schedule	Follow up items from 5S assessments are closed out real time	5S
Basic labeling and identification in place	Visual controls in place to manage throughput	Visual controls indicating throughput status and issues	Visual controls are in place the length of the functions processes	Visual controls are identifying issues in real time	Visual Management and Controls
A layout of the functions processes exists. As does a map of the functions processes	A plan has been developed to remove waste from the functions processes	An example of effective process linkage and flow can be seen	Multiple examples of effective process linkage and flow can be seen	The function is right sized. All processes are linked and flow. Next opportunities are defined	Layout, Linkage, Flow, and Right-Sizing
A skills assessment has been completed and a matrix developed	The skills development matrix has a posted plan to develop the areas skill base	The skills development matrix and plan is on track	The skills development matrix and plan 75% complete	The area has full coverage of identified skills and a plan to maintain	Multi-Skilling
A process is in place to not pass on defective product from the area	Metrics are posted that show quality level requirements	Posted quality metrics show three-month improvement trends	Posted quality metrics show six-month improvement trends	Posted quality metrics show nine-month improvement trends with zero escapes	Quality
A plan exists to increase the CI understanding of all the functions employees	15% of the functions employees have participated in the CI boot camp and 30% in at least two kaizen events	30% of the functions employees have participated in the CI boot camp and 30% in at least four kaizen events	60% of the functions employees have participated in the CI boot camp and 30% in at least eight kaizen events	75% of the functions employees have participated in the CI boot camp and 30% in at least eight kaizen events	Continuous Improvement Training and Education
Awareness of functional goals	Some goals and metrics posted	All goals and metrics posted and statused	All posted goals and metrics have plans and up to date actuals	All posted goals and metrics are up to date and are on track	Metrics & Results

For each of the five levels, there were detailed criteria/requirements that had to be achieved. An example of the criteria/requirements for the 5S track is shown below.

Awareness	Understanding	Commitment	Habit	
1	2	3	4	5
Organizations employees have an awareness of 5S	The organization has completed 5S training for all employees.	Follow up items from last 5S assessment posted on To-Do's with date/time due.	Follow up items from last 5S assessment posted on To Do's & closed out.	No follow up items open from last 5S assessment.
Focus is upon the first 3S's	Obvious 1S, 2S and 3S activity ongoing.	Obvious 1, 2 and 3S activities are ongoing.	Point of use storage for all equipment used daily is practiced.	The 5S's themselves are an indicator of normal vs abnormal.
Some recent 1S activity can be shared and is obvious.	Areas of 5S responsibility defined and posted.	A 5S assessment schedule is developed and posted.	The first three S's are linked to and are supporting, the Least Waste Way linkage, flow and rightsizing.	The fourth and fifth S's have been internalized such that the members do not consciously think about them.
Some 5S evaluations have been done.	Employees assigned to the area do the evaluations .			
A 5S evaluation schedule is being developed.	Recognition that 5S enables Visual Controls to highlight abnormal conditions.	Area employees do evaluations.		
		5S scores posted with 6-month improvement trend, current score of 3+ - all areas .	The three S's are precursors to problem-solving.	All levels of 5S are implemented and a system to maintain rating is established and practiced daily.
	5S scores posted with 3-month improvement trend, current score of 2+ - all areas .		5S scores posted with 12-month improvement trend, current score of 4+ - all areas.	Posted 5S score of 4+ maintained all areas.

Entering each year, an assessment baseline was established to indicate the current state of each function or facility relative to the required criteria. Following this baseline identification, annual objectives were set for each track.

The Enterprise Excellence Assessment was explicitly designed to ensure that several requirements were repeated every year to drive both culture change and continuous improvement.

These requirements were built into the appropriate tracks and included:

- The organizations Vice President/Senior Staff member, participated in four kaizen events, in the current year.
- The organizations Vice President/Senior Staff member presented modules in the Continuous Improvement boot camp four times in the current year.
- The function or facility leader participated in four kaizen events, in the current year.
- EH&S targets established for the current year.
- Annual communication plans and schedules developed and followed.
- Process yield, quality targets, are established for the current year.
- Achievement of training and event participation goals required for the current year.
- Leadership of the organization can share two examples of a "Learning Together" activity they did as a group that focused on leadership or continuous improvement during the current year. These were primarily book or article reviews.

Compliance with these requirements required a deliberate, annual rollback of all Enterprise Excellence baselines. This, in turn, required the continual engagement of leaders and their employees in continuous improvement activities and training, demonstrating real measurable progress to organizational results. This was a significant driver in the cultural change taking place.

The Enterprise Excellence Assessment is discussed further in Chapter 4.

Developing a closed loop Operating System

Observing opportunities to improve the way we established annual Goals and Objectives, our consultant encouraged us to develop and implement a Policy Deployment process. Explaining that an effective Policy Deployment process aligns business goals and initiatives with time bounded improvement targets. Moreover, when the process is used as intended, it can contribute significantly to the achievement of goals and improvement targets.

Policy Deployment was to become a key component of our operating system.

Given our appetite for learning, we sought out reading material on Policy Deployment processes. After reviewing some voluminous publications that we considered somewhat obtuse, we came across a soft cover book entitled "The Management Compass" by Michele L. Bechtell, published by the American Management Association.

We found this book to be a potpourri of ideas, simple to understand and full of examples to consider within a Policy Deployment process. The "Management Compass" became the basis for the Policy Deployment as deployed at Rohr.

Our first session to create and deploy Policy Deployment was in mid-1996 preparing for the upcoming 1997 fiscal year. (At the time, fiscal years were not aligned with calendar years). Rohr senior leadership and several other leaders and influential employees convened for three days offsite and went through a process specifically developed to produce a robust Policy Deployment matrix.

The starting point to the development of this Policy Deployment matrix required the identification and review of a number of external and internal factors and issues. These were primarily the expectations of the Board of Directors, customer input, strategic issues, financial considerations and perceived strengths, weaknesses, opportunities, risks and threats.

Each of these inputs was discussed, and the pertinent thoughts generated by the participants, in the discussion, documented on 8.5 X 11's and posted on walls. Brief thoughts, several words to capture the salient point, not dissertations. There were dozens of 8.5 X 11's!

Once all the inputs were reviewed, discussed and observations posted, the 8.5 X 11's were clarified and combined, by the team, into a list of "important things" to cover/address via Policy Deployment.

Each of these "important things to cover/address" were added to the X-axis of a Master Matrix and were given a color, via team consensus, which identified their importance as noted below:

"Important Things" Color Bar	
Red	Mission critical, must address comprehensively
Yellow	Very important, must address effectively
Green	Important, must address well

Against that background, the Goals, Initiatives, and Improvement Targets, in that sequence, for the first Policy Deployment matrix for Aerostructures, were developed.

Goals were typically three to five years out and reflected "What" we wanted to achieve and sustain.

Initiatives described "How" those goals were going to be achieved. They described how the business was to be managed and run and what you would see if the business was viewed "from above."

Improvement Targets were the "How much" and had to be SMART - Specific, Measurable, Achievable, Results-oriented and Time-bound.

They also had to be broad enough in collective aggregate to have an appropriate impact on the "important things" on the master matrix.

To understand this impact, the Improvement Targets, once developed, were added to the Y-axis of the Master Matrix, and at every intersection with the important things on the X-axis, the following question was asked: "to what degree does this Improvement Target support this important thing?" The team had to think about the direct and indirect impacts, of the Improvement Targets, to come to an answer.

The symbols used to identify the impact of the Improvement Targets on the important things:

Intersections could be left empty if there was no impact seen.

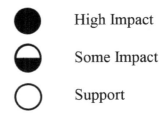

High Impact

Some Impact

Support

If any "important thing" on the Master Matrix was not adequately supported, an adjustment to an Improvement Target could be made, or one added. While sometimes challenging, we became quite proficient at wordsmithing Improvement Targets to ensure the impact of the Improvement Target itself and its impact on other "important things."

We then had to ensure that the entire Policy Deployment matrix was robust in the linkage and support of the whole.

The Policy Deployment matrix developed, followed the structure shown here:

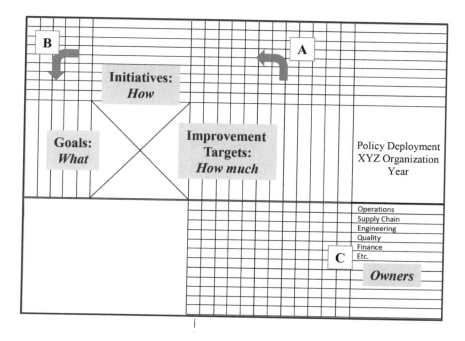

How the Improvement Targets supported the Initiatives was identified at the intersections at identified as "A," where the following question was asked, "To what degree does the Improvement Target drive and measure the effectiveness of the Initiative?"

How the Initiatives supported the Goals was identified at the intersections identified as "B," where the following question was asked, "To what degree does the Initiative support achieving the Goal?"

In answering these questions, significant value was gained through the discussions that ensued. Adjustments were made, if appropriate, as a result of those discussions.

In both instances, the answer to the question was indicated by the following symbols at the respective intersection:

● High Impact

◒ Some Impact

Intersections were left empty if there was no connection seen.

○ Support

The owners of Improvement Targets, those who would need to develop plans and metrics to make and show progress, were identified at the intersections identified as "C." Improvement Targets in support of broad business initiatives such as Safety and Compliance or Enterprise Excellence Assessment were assigned to all organizations.

Other Improvement Targets related to specific issues such as Product Quality, Cost, and Delivery, were assigned to production programs and Aftermarket spares. The introduction of say a new performance management system would be assigned to Human Resources.

If an organization may be required to support only from time to time when requested, that was also identified.

The symbols used to identify ownership of the Improvement Targets:
Intersections could be left empty if there was no "plan to support or support as requested" required.

● Owner of a plan to meet

◐ Plan to support

○ Support as requested

Should anything change over the course of the year, organizations readily stepped up and incorporated the appropriate requirements into their plans.

A typical Policy Deployment matrix is as shown next where the linkage of Goals, Initiatives and Improvement Targets to each other and ownership of those Improvement Targets is noted.

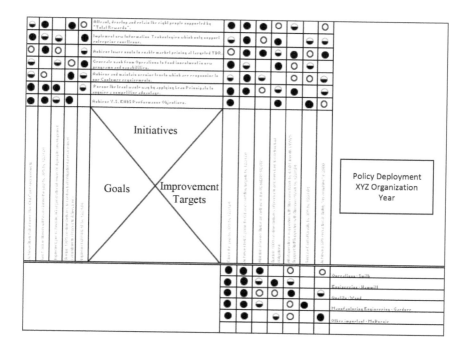

A significant intended product of the Policy Deployment development process, as it was developed, was the engagement, understanding, calibration, alignment, buy-in and advocacy of all participants.

This was achieved through discussions around the Goals, Initiatives, Improvement Targets and important things that the intersections on the Master and the Policy Deployment Matrices were designed to stimulate. These discussions were equally as important as the Policy Deployment matrix itself.

In this first session, we learned a lot about how to establish meaningful Goals, Initiatives, and Improvement Targets, how to wordsmith them so they would resonate with employees and how to flow down and use a Policy Deployment process.

One realization with the process was how team members could interpret words quite differently when discussing issues and opportunities.

An example of this occurred in the first Policy Deployment session. A discussion around the issue of "adjacent markets and potential opportunities" was seen by one person as "get the existing sales and marketing team to evaluate the adjacent market opportunities and provide feedback on this issue." Almost an add-on, part-time task by a potentially existing function.

By another team member, it was seen as "appoint an Adjacent Market Leader, establish an Adjacent Market core team to pursue and secure opportunities in these markets, set up metrics and include in the policy deployment reviews." A new, staffed and structured organization.

Two entirely different interpretations of spoken words and there were multiple examples of this interpretation issue throughout many sessions. Discussions that secure the aforementioned engagement, understanding, calibration, alignment, buy-in and advocacy of participants illustrate the advantages of a Policy Deployment process.

Along with a process to develop the Aerostructures Policy Deployment matrix, we had developed a flow down process for the next level of deployment and development. In the latter part of 1996, facilities and functions began the task of developing Policy Deployment Matrices and did so producing respectable Goals, Initiatives, and Improvement Targets.

Taking a cue from "The Management Compass" book, each organization was required to establish and maintain a Plan, Do, Check, Act document for each of their Improvement Targets.

At the time there were 28 "organizations" in the business and these Plan, Do, Check, Act documents were reviewed by senior leadership on a weekly rotational basis:

- Week 1 - Organizations 1 – 7
- Week 2 - Organizations 8 – 14
- Week 3 - Organizations 15 – 21
- Week 4- Organizations 22 – 28

Then repeat.

This review process proved to be both insightful and cumbersome. After no more than three cycles, we reflected on a couple of topics that had generated much discussion since embarking on the lean journey. They were the issues of "visual controls, driver measures and result measures." This resulted in the transition to a visual, driver measure centric, Policy Deployment review package.

The Plan Do, Check, Act documents for each Improvement Target were retained and maintained by each organization to plan, manage and drive activity at the local level. In the senior leadership Policy Deployment reviews, they were replaced by visual controls, charts, and graphics that had the goal of being easily understood by the casual observer and had a Driver Measure focus. Each Improvement Target had to have a visual control chart, that had to have a plan line, and an actual status to date line so that progress to plan, throughout the year, was readily visible.

The challenge was to develop and align driver measures with the required results to ensure that progress to business goals was visible at all times. This with the firm belief that the proficient management of selected driver measures would significantly increase the probability of achieving the required results.

The established Policy Deployment reviews ran to a rotation and schedule, each organization having 15 – 20 minutes to report out depending on the organization.

The first page of the Policy Deployment package had now developed into a "scorecard" that listed all the organization's annual Improvement Targets with actual monthly results shown against plans as the year progressed. This was a "one-stop" page with a, full line of sight of the organizations Policy Deployment, Improvement Target status.

The same "red, yellow, green color indicators" were used on each Improvement Target metric to denote:

- Green – On plan
- Yellow – Off plan but will recover
- Red – Off plan with no recovery in place

Improvement Targets indicating green did not need to be discussed, Improvement Targets indicating yellow or red had to be briefly discussed. Leadership's input was primarily to understand any issues and establish if the organization needed any additional help to get back on plan.

Somewhat ironically, "Red" items became viewed as goodness. All of these items were seen as things that we could address and improve performance.

In these weekly Policy Deployment reviews, there was clear visibility with regard to progress towards the Improvement Targets. The discussions in the weekly Policy Deployment reviews reinforced the previous calibration and alignment dialogue regarding what the actual Goals, Initiatives, and Improvement Targets were, and what the words on the Policy Deployment matrix meant.

The Policy Deployment process and its use is relatively straightforward. From a "top down" perspective:

1. Review and understand all internal and external inputs and forces.
   o Develop the company/business level, Policy Deployment matrix.
2. Review, develop Goals, Initiatives, and Improvement Targets.
   o Goals should be stable for a number of years.
   o Initiatives should be too, with some occasional adjustments to accommodate changes in circumstances.
   o Some Improvement Targets stay quite stable, such as those relating to EH&S, compliance and Enterprise Excellence, Some may change, be dropped or added, but they should always be SMART.
3. Identify which Improvement Targets are "assigned to" which Organization.
   o Improvement Targets such as adherence to and compliance with EH&S requirements and continuous improvement progress should go to all organizations.

- o Other Improvement Targets are invariably organization specific.
4. Organizations then follow a similar process to develop their own Policy Deployment matrix.
    - o The company Policy Deployment matrix is baseline input, as are other organization influencers and forces, both internal and external.
    - o Additional Improvement Targets, for issues and opportunities visible to the organization, may be appropriate. Making every attempt to keep the total number of Improvement Targets in the single digit range.
5. Develop the annual "plan metrics" for each Improvement Target.
6. Develop or update PDCA's.
7. Use the PDCA's weekly to plan and schedule activities and deploy resources effectively.
8. Capture driver measures and track progress.
9. Report Out in Senior Staff debriefs, course adjust as appropriate.

Each year steps 1 through 6 are repeated. Steps 7 through 9 are institutionalized as the Policy Deployment management and review process.

The Operating System

In the mid to late 1990s, the operating system was in its infancy. We knew that we were using a process that had much potential and that focus, care and attention was needed to ensure its development and use.

Communications and education through company bulletins and formal and informal discussions continued to bring everyone up to speed with the Policy Deployment process and the other processes being deployed.

In retrospect, the mechanics of the then relatively undefined operating system began to gain understanding, commitment, and traction.

Policy Deployment is undoubtedly a highly effective process if constructed and used appropriately. For Rohr, it quickly became, meaningful and actionable. It brought a level of timely metric transparency and clarity along with a degree of accountability that pays dividends to this day. All of which contributed to the cultural change taking place.

The discussions in the annual Policy Deployment process and the weekly Policy Deployment reviews as they developed, were open and enlightening. They enabled broad calibration, alignment and understanding of company and local area Goals, Initiatives and Improvement Targets. And in these weekly Policy Deployment reviews, there was clear visibility with regard to progress towards the Improvement Targets.

We began to see the outline of our Operating System:

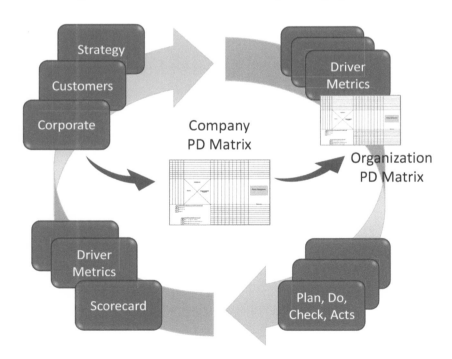

It was during this period we made progress in the development of a process for developing a Strategic Plan.

As noted in Chapter 1, Strategic Plans to date had been outlined annually by a few Senior Leaders, giving their views to a small working group who then developed a document that became the "Strategic Plan," that invariably took a "back seat," to issues of the moment, during the following year.

As we reviewed changes to the Strategic Plan development process, and its linkage to the operating system, it was determined that after senior leadership had developed an outline of the structure and content of a Strategic Plan, a broad, inclusive team, with in-depth functional knowledge, would develop the detail and body of the plan. Interspersed with frequent reviews with senior leadership throughout the development process.

Communication of the plan to a broader employee audience was also required.

The discussion around this approach prompted one team member to ask the question "if we include a broader team in the development of the Strategic Plan and communicate its contents to a broader employee audience, what are we risking?" To which the president at the time somewhat comically responded: "If we develop a plan in a vacuum and tell no one about it how the heck are we going to achieve it?"

An appropriate and effective communication flow down process was developed.

We went on to develop a "Strategic Plan development process" to advance the overall operating system as we moved forward. More on the "Strategic Plan development process" in Chapter 4.

Communications

Significant efforts were made with communication - content, distribution, and frequency to ensure everyone:

- Knew where we were going
- How we were going to get there
- The processes and tools we were going to use on the way
- The behaviors expected to create the culture required to make progress

The Policy Deployment process in itself had become a very effective communications tool. As appropriate driver measures were identified and introduced, they brought new light onto issues and opportunities, now visible to the entire team responsible for them. Who then used the Plan, Do, Check, Act process to identify, and continue activities to address problems and leverage opportunities.

A requirement in the Enterprise Excellence Assessment tool was "Effective Communications." This required each organization to have its own structured Communications plan. Daily, weekly, monthly and quarterly communications with the organizations' staff, shop floor and support employees, were hard requirements.

What needed to be in their communications plan was outlined, for example:

- Daily: Expectations and customer requirements, any overnight issues and any safety items.
- Weekly: Driver Measure progress.
- Monthly: Overall organizational progress, including the Policy Deployment review packages.
- Quarterly: Company news and financial updates.

Weekly reviews and updates of the Plan, Do, Check, Acts and driver measures by the organizational leadership team were also required.

The communications plan had to be posted with status to the plan noted.

Continuous improvement progress was shared across the company in a monthly "broadsheet" that included reports of business-wide kaizen events and their results and kaizen events and their results in specific facilities. Pictures taken before, during and after events. Articles and pictures of senior leadership, participating in events in the workplace, working "hands-on" alongside salaried and hourly operators. (Reporting on senior leadership working alongside hourly and salaried employees, in their workplaces, always had a positive impact) Continuous improvement training progress communicated and upcoming "boot camp" dates and locations identified.

As overall business performance information was routinely shared with all employees, it became obvious to everyone that collectively we were all contributing to the significant progress being made.

We were effectively utilizing new processes and tools. Our understanding and deployment of lean and the Toyota Production System tools was progressing well.

The kaizen event process had a firm foundation, and we had become disciplined with the event process. We had a good understanding of value added and non-value added activities and were becoming quite proficient and accustomed to eliminating waste and driving performance improvement.

Tempering this was our increased understanding regarding the magnitude of the task at hand, and the extent of the continued learning, focus, and rigor required to ensure we sustained the required pace of performance and metric improvements. We had a long way to go.

Although the commercial aerospace market was depressed and employment had, unfortunately, been reduced significantly, business metrics were beginning to show good progress. With the exception of "program wins."

Aerostructures was now approaching around 15 years without winning new business of any consequence, and had been retaining engineering and technical resources by accepting small subcomponent work, affectionately known as "bottom feeding."

It may be worth mentioning that we had input from a number of sources that the deployment of continuous improvement could not be successfully implemented in a "downsizing" environment.

Clearly, that was not the case as we were making good progress. We did through careful and constant communications, get employee recognition and buy-in of the business difficulties that remained, the choices we had made and the things we were doing to change the business.

Employee engagement in continuous improvement activities and change remained high.

James Womack had visited two Rohr facilities by late 1996 and the book "LEAN THINKING, BANISH WASTE AND CREATE WEALTH IN YOUR CORPORATION" by James Womack and Daniel Jones was published.

"Lean Thinking" was read with relish and became the guide for continued changes in the organization, both continuous improvement and organizational changes that continued to drive the culture.

Three Tracks

During one of the frequent informal discussions by the small group of leaders driving changes to the business and routinely identifying the next steps, we reflected on the perceived primary drivers of those changes and their alignment. The following visual was created as a result of one of those discussions. "Three Tracks" were identified that we saw as the tracks to Enterprise Excellence.

We believed that progress from left to right needed to be relatively synchronized across the Three Tracks. It is interesting to note that Standard Work although being discussed, was not yet fully understood or introduced, beyond its recent inclusion in the continuous improvement training. As a result, it was not included on this first "Three Track" visual.

This visual became part of our "communications toolbox," and was shared with employees at every opportunity. This helped the continued collective understanding and alignment across the organization, once again through constant and consistent communications that contributed to the cultural change taking place.

Metrics at the end of 1996:

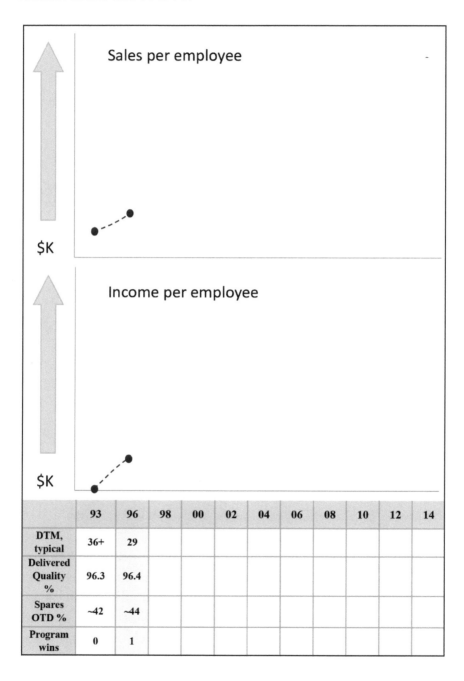

	93	96	98	00	02	04	06	08	10	12	14
DTM, typical	36+	29									
Delivered Quality %	96.3	96.4									
Spares OTD %	~42	~44									
Program wins	0	1									

Our understanding and use of the lean tools helped drive significant waste out of our processes. Our consistent focus and demonstration of the behaviors of the People Philosophy were gaining understanding and buy-in from all employees, and the culture was changing.

An initial overhaul of the Strategic Planning process had been completed, and Policy Deployment was gaining momentum as the process matured and metrics became increasingly timely, transparent and actionable. Progress was being made along the Change Pyramid steps which contributed to the very respectable income and margins in the late 1990s.

In 1997 Rohr was purchased by Goodrich, a move that brought increased financial stability. It also brought the influence of Goodrich processes on Rohr. However, over the next three years, it became clear that Rohr was running very efficiently and effectively. It was delivering solid income and margins, positioning itself to win new business and gaining much industry publicity for the changes being made in the business to achieve these results.

Continuous Improvement and the Positive Employee Philosophy were central to this performance and recognition. As a result, Goodrich began to integrate the "entire suite" of Values, Positive Employee Philosophy and Policy Deployment across all Goodrich businesses.

By 1998 both Riverside and Chula Vista had established an Office of Continuous Improvement. Both were staffed by employees who had gained experience with the continuous improvement processes and tools and had become "lean zealots."

At each location, there were around five individuals in this role at any one time. Over the years it became a full-time role for one or two employees and a development assignment for other employees who wanted to increase their breadth and depth of understanding of the continuous improvement processes and tools. Following an 18-24 month special assignment, they then went back into functional roles in various organizations with increased continuous improvement knowledge and proficiency.

With the Offices of Continuous Improvement in place, we consistently emphasized that continuous improvement was the responsibility of all employees. The resources of the Offices of Continuous Improvement were there to help, plan and facilitate continuous improvement activities and to train employees in their understanding and use of the improvement processes and tools.

Continuous improvement activities were in high gear in some locations. In others, there was less understanding, enthusiasm, and deployment.

A question that was asked of Riverside leadership by some visitors and sometimes by leaders from other Aerostructures facilities was "how much time do you spend on continuous improvement?" Greg Peters, the general manager at Riverside invariably answered, "All of it."

Although this may not have been an entirely accurate answer, it was indeed accurate in the sense that continuous improvement was a constant focus and a consideration in virtually all decisions.

By 1998 OI and OM had been increasing annually. Rohr had been a very positive aerospace acquisition to the Goodrich business portfolio which was transforming from a large industrial company to an aerospace centric business.

As noted previously, a compendium of Standard Work tools had been fully developed and added to the continuous improvement training catalog. This consisted of Time Observation, Standard Work Combination Sheet, Standard Work Sheet and Percent Load chart modules.

Over the next few years, we would develop a deep understanding and level of deployment of Standard Work that drove next level waste/ non-value added activity elimination and associated business results.

Much had been achieved through 1998 and progress along the "Change Pyramid" looked like this:

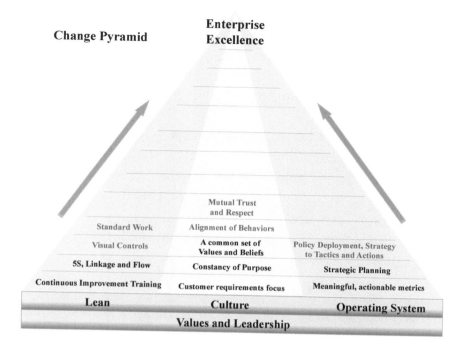

The book Lean Thinking, mentioned earlier, was a source of inspiration for us. One theme that we had initially seen in the Executive Summary of Lean Thinking and now in the book itself, kept entering into our discussions, that theme was "Value Streams."

As we approached the end of the 1990s, we were increasingly interested in this concept as we were continually mulling over our existing organizational structure which, although changed as noted, remained traditional and functional with visible issues, problems, and opportunities throughout.

One other significant development was the introduction of an all employee incentive plan. The president of Aerostructures had a long-standing belief that all employees should share in the wealth created by a successful company. That "share" was beyond the normal salary and benefits received by all employees and was commensurate with the "gain" the business made when beating financial goals.

In the late 1990s, an incentive plan for all employees, other than the senior staff, was introduced known as "Gainsharing." In the simplest sense it was made up as follows:

- The annual organizational budget developed and agreed upon.
- Stretch targets were added to those budgets that required financial results beyond the budgeted numbers.
- Thresholds of stretch target achievement were established for Gainsharing payouts, which amounted to a maximum of 10% of gross earnings for all employees.
- Annual payouts were funded by achieving the stretch target financial results.

Once launched this further increased employee's appetites for change and their understanding of the business and its workings. Engagement in change and business improvements commensurately increased and this ultimately added traction to the broad cultural shift taking place.

What we learned on the way – a Summary

- We had a lot to learn about change, continuous improvement and culture.
- Our understanding and use of metrics increased.
  - o We had recognized that we were focused on the wrong metrics. What we learned was that as well as identifying and using different metrics they also needed to be timely, meaningful to those in the workplace, customer focused and actionable. In addition, they must be regularly reviewed by senior leadership, and where possible, be linked and integrated with each other. Understanding this was a stepping stone to an operating system.

- Training was invaluable in focusing everyone on continuous improvement and the objectives of its deployment.
    - We did intend to get every employee into the full one-week Continuous Improvement boot camp.
- A knowledgeable and experienced Sensei can be, and was to us, invaluable.
- Involvement and engagement are two entirely different things.
- The development and maturity of an Enterprise Excellence Assessment tool and process proved to be a masterstroke in measuring continuous improvement deployment and progress.
- Policy Deployment enabled the business strategy to be integrated, deployed, expectations set, progress measured, and course corrections to be made all with an exceptional level of accountability.
- How to identify and understand opportunity - "waste/ non-value added."
- The opportunity was enormous. Finding improvement opportunities of 50% - 95% was typical. The scale of opportunity was challenging for some to believe. We adopted the phrase "if we get it half right, we will be streets ahead of the competition."
- The change process will trigger emotional responses of many kinds.

Things you may want to consider – a Summary

- Do we have a Strategic Planning process that results in its deployment in a measurable, actionable operating system?
- Do we have management techniques in various states of acceptance, understanding, and deployment or do we have them "woven together" to form an integrated operating system?
    - Are all our leadership on board with it?

- o Are all our leadership assertively using and driving the operating system?
- o Can it be visualized and explained easily and understandably?
- o Does it work to our satisfaction?
- Do we have a good understanding of driver measures and result measures?
- Do we even believe we have up to ~95% opportunity/waste in our business?
- How proficient are we at identifying and eliminating waste?
- Is our continuous improvement process documented and followed?
- How do we measure continuous improvement progress?
- Should business returns, beyond the committed and approved plan, when achieved, be shared with those helping generate them?

Chapter 4

*L*inkage and Flow, work transfers, right-sizing, and facility closures. Starting the focus on Standard Work, and an epiphany. The Values, Positive Employee Philosophy, and the Operating System become recognized as catalysts for each other and subsequent business performance improvement. Successes and struggles in support organizations. The development of a process and the documentation of reality that resulted in a Value Stream structure. Understanding the power of Standard Work and the introduction of Real Time Problem Resolution.

Aligning the Business

Needing to understand and define opportunities across the business in the mid-1990s we documented the cost drivers of major mature production programs. The ranges are noted below with direct labor at 16% of program cost:

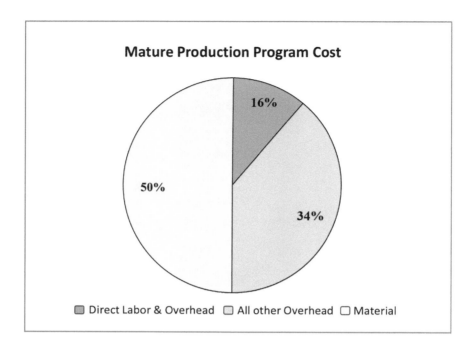

In the mid to late 1990s significant continuous improvement efforts were made to drive improved linkage and flow on all production programs. Through this period, work was again moved/relocated and concurrent supportive actions taken including implementing workstation 5S, ensuring point of use tools and equipment, establishing visual controls to communicate performance to plan and to identify problem areas where help was required. All of which had the effect of reducing costs and improving performance to schedule.

Also, required support personnel including manufacturing and quality engineers were increasingly co-located within the manufacturing cells. This greatly enhanced real time communications across the teams and increased responsiveness to required process issues and system changes.

While the momentum for change was driven from the Riverside team, engagement at other sites and functions of the business, with some notable exceptions, was mixed. Consequently, subsequent business results were in the main disappointing.

It is interesting to note that in the sites that were driving positive results, support functions such as Maintenance, Human Resources, Supply Chain, and Quality, increasingly engaged in the continuous improvement activities and changes.

Notable exceptions were the Chula Vista based Research and Development and Engineering functions which remained somewhat isolated from the continuous improvement activity that was gaining traction elsewhere. Integrating these functions into the transformation of the business is addressed in Chapter 5.

As waste was removed from the manufacturing areas of the business engaging in cultural change and continuous improvement, it was imperative to sustain their momentum and fill the capacity created through waste elimination.

This was achieved by transferring additional work into these improving areas which had the effect of reassuring team members that they were not "improving themselves out of a job," while also allowing the business to further leverage and drive the benefits of linkage and flow.

Generally, work was only transferred out of sites where business performance was static, and leadership engagement in the development of the new culture and deployment of continuous improvement was limited.

During the late 1990s through early 2000s, progress within Riverside accelerated and following the relocation of some key Riverside personnel into leadership positions in Chula Vista, engagement in change and continuous improvement subsequently accelerated there.

To ensure continued progress at Riverside while improving linkage and flow, an earlier decision was made to close the Hagerstown facility and move the composite bond work back to California. Although California had nominally higher labor and overhead costs, the gains in productivity being achieved there more than offset these higher baseline costs.

The Riverside facility was able to absorb the work without adding employees via the capacity that was being created through the elimination of waste. Leadership at Riverside were apt to say "we can absorb that work for free, given the labor required is already here."

During this same period, the Foley assembly site continued to lead with the deployment of the Positive Employee Philosophy and use of the Toyota Production System processes and tools. All of which drove productivity gains solidifying the long-term future of that site.

San Marcos Texas was a different case. Linkage and flow within the facility was virtually non-existent and anticipating workload increases, the leadership there was planning to increase employment and extend the facility several thousand square feet to accommodate the higher production volume.

A quick review of the shop floor revealed that several months' worth of inventory, in boxes, was stacked up to ten feet high in prime manufacturing locations. There were no visible activities or plans to stop the flow of this inventory. Customer dissatisfaction was high, and some were looking to remove their products from this site.

The leadership of the facility in San Marcos Texas were ineffective in driving both continuous improvement and change. The general manager and technical manager of the site were replaced in 1998 with the direction to their replacements to implement change or to close the site and transfer the business elsewhere.

The need for significant and rapid change was obvious. With strong support from leadership in Riverside, Chula Vista, and our consultant, the first Aerostructures kaikaku was held at San Marcos in 1998.

A kaikaku is an activity where fundamental and radical changes are made, usually on a large scale. Unlike a kaizen, which is focused on smaller incremental changes.

Following detailed preparation, this week-long site level event re-aligned 80% of the production activities which required moving many pieces of equipment, several of which were quite large, to link product flows. During the event, basic visual controls were introduced to understand customer demand and to support fundamental Toyota System tools and techniques to identify and remove waste. Over the next two years, productivity accelerated to that of the Riverside facility.

Over the years limited kaikaku events became a feature of our continuous improvement efforts. On the one hand, they did require pre-planning with larger teams than for a kaizen event and could be a little disruptive.

On the other hand, we got quite proficient at planning, resourcing and executing them effectively. In reality, we did not have time on our side and needed to be as expeditious as possible in driving change into, and waste out of, the business.

At Riverside and Chula Vista, much waste/non-value added activity continued to be removed from production processes. An increasing ability to document reality effectively revealed a never-ending stream of waste rich opportunities - "waiting for, looking for, going for, reworking, and other non-value added activities" that had, over time, become recognized as legitimate, required "process steps."

Through the late 1990s, we were fortunate that commercial aerospace was beginning to ramp-up. This enabled Riverside and Chula Vista to fill the capacity created, hiring only a fraction of the employees who would have been required in previous years.

At the same time, the marketplace became more competitive as customers required improved performance and lower costs to be awarded their work. Productivity gains on many programs enabled a positive response to these customer pressures for performance improvements and reduced costs.

The leadership of locations that were not driving continuous improvement with the same vigor, or at all, saw the ramp-up quite differently.

The response from these locations was "we have rates increasing, I have to get some recruiting done, and employees have to be on-boarded, trained up and ready to go." Despite urging to identify and remove waste from their processes, create capacity, absorb work and as a result reduce cost, they chose a different path and hired additional employees.

An interesting phenomenon occurred as a result. The next chart shows a significant reduction in labor hours at Riverside, by late 1998 labor hours had reduced by almost 40%. See (A) on the following chart.

At the locations where they did hire additional employees to accommodate the increased sales, traditional, outdated onboarding and training processes were followed. This entailed new employees working with experienced employees to gain some understanding of the work being done, consequently, doubling up the hours being charged to the product.

When the new employee was considered to have an adequate understanding of the task, approval to work alone was given. Rework issues often arose which again added to the hours being charged to the job.

At the sites where continuous improvement was not being deployed, or capacity created, hiring was done resulting in the labor hours being charged to the product actually increasing. See (B)

When direct labor hours for all locations were totaled the effect of the those not driving continuous improvement, but hiring more employees, reduced the overall labor hour reduction. See (C).

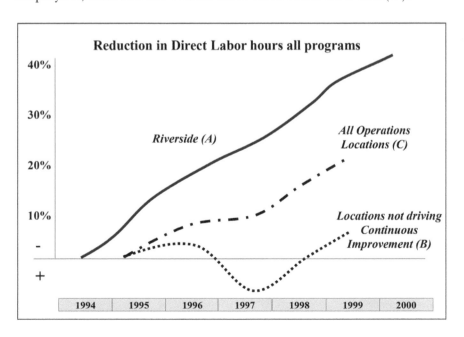

Shortly after this predictable phenomenon, leadership changes were made at the underperforming locations with the recognition from their leader that "I should have acted sooner."

With the firm belief in the benefits of linkage and flow and the need to reduce the overall footprint of the business, the Heber Springs and Sheridan facilities were closed. The assembly work at Heber Springs and Sheridan was moved predominantly to Foley, with small amounts going to Chula Vista and San Marcos.

The proficiency being achieved relative to removing waste and creating capacity at these remaining sites enabled them to absorb the incoming work with little or no additional staff.

By 2000 the mature production programs direct labor cost had been reduced by 3% to now 13%:

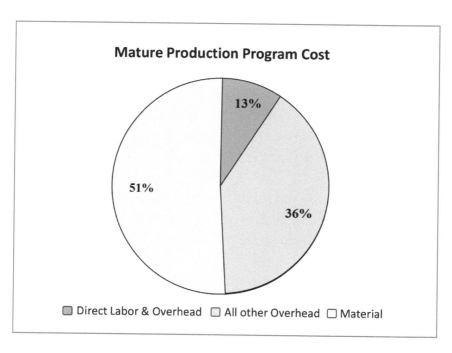

This was done without any offload or onload of any manufacturing, it was an "apples to apples" comparison, albeit as just noted, some work had moved to different Aerostructures locations during this period.

The reduction in direct labor content was achieved through the eye-opening removal of waste from production processes utilizing fundamental improvement tools and techniques deployed by an engaged workforce.

By 2000, Policy Deployment Improvement Targets required every production program to "Achieve, a 1% per month productivity improvement level entering 2000, and 1.5% per month exiting 2000." This was achieved not only through direct labor hour reductions but also via a focus on all overhead and material costs.

It is worth mentioning that this requirement translated to an overall "product cost reduction" and that most Value Stream programs in production met this Improvement Target for many years. During one of the visits from a large customer, one individual tellingly remarked - "we'd be thrilled with a 1.5% improvement a year."

As we drove continuous improvement on the shop floor, it became obvious that significant additional improvement opportunities, including cost reduction opportunities, were in other areas of the business.

By this time, the Enterprise Excellence Assessment had been revised a number of times to improve its effectiveness and care had been taken to ensure requirements were applicable to all organizations, not just manufacturing.

The Policy Deployment process required hard plans to achieve Improvement Targets, and as noted earlier, one target for all organizations was the achievement of a specific Enterprise Excellence Assessment level.

These target levels were aggressive but achievable and what we wanted to see were earnest plans, efforts, and progress to achieve the targeted level. While the achievement of the Improvement Targets was always the goal, we also recognized that earnest and consistent efforts could on occasion, be negatively impacted by circumstances beyond a team's control.

This was invariably a consideration by leadership when reviewing a team's performance and their annual Gainsharing.

In reviewing the footprint of the Chula Vista facility, it was clear that the previous forty plus years of traditional layout philosophies and planning, had resulted in the linkage of the manufacturing steps and the subsequent product flows being severely impeded.

Parts and product could be found in all corners of the facility, much of it waiting to be taken to the next step in the manufacturing process. Most manufacturing processes had their own locations that required material handling devices and transportation between each process step.

Quality had their own shop floor areas where the product was taken to for inspection. Support functions had their own locations, many of them on mezzanines away from the area they supported. Tools were stored in multiple locations and an extensive "production control, transportation and expediting department" was required to try and understand where everything was, move hardware from location to location and chase the "hot jobs." Which in reality, were all jobs. All of this activity contributing to costs that were well over business needs.

Ironically in the mid-1990s, it was recognized that producing hardware through the Chula Vista manufacturing facility took so long that an "Express line" was established to do the "hottest of the hot jobs."

The "Express Line" was equipped with machinery and equipment for most manufacturing processes and had the Quality inspection personnel and process collocated in the area. However major manufacturing steps such as chemical processing and welding still required completion in other locations. These became known as "Curtain Operations."

It was quite a surprise to many when it became evident that it took longer to manufacture parts through the "Express Line" than it did to let parts meander through the normal channels.

There were also some long-tenured, entrenched leaders in the facility who, when continuous improvement or change was discussed "provided the right input or gave the right answers" but through their actions demonstrated that their commitment to continuous improvement and change, was far below requirements.

As happened in Riverside some of these leaders chose to move on, some were helped to move on, and some were reassigned.

We had to be clear that the cultural change was going to be made and continuous improvement was going to be driven with leaders willing and able to lead that change and work within the Values and the Positive Employee Philosophy.

By 1998 the footprint of the Chula Vista campus had been reduced, with many buildings closed and demolished, primarily to reduce the costs of maintaining such a large facility. Resultant linkage and flow opportunities had been leveraged as work was absorbed into the remaining buildings.

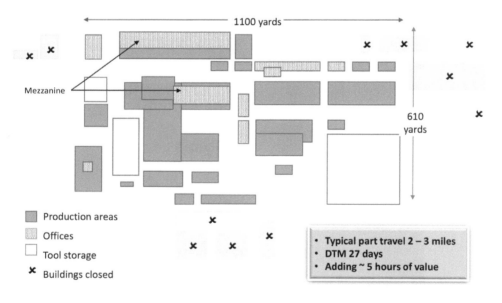

Not to scale.

The Corporate offices are not shown and are to the left of this illustration.

The gains from these efforts contributed to the 1998 metrics:

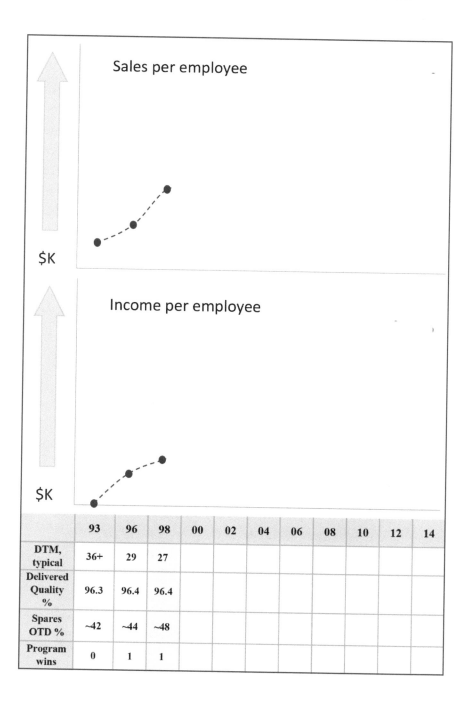

	93	96	98	00	02	04	06	08	10	12	14
DTM, typical	36+	29	27								
Delivered Quality %	96.3	96.4	96.4								
Spares OTD %	~42	~44	~48								
Program wins	0	1	1								

As a result of the focus on "linkage and flow," the days to manufacture metrics were now dramatically reduced from the levels of 1993. As noted earlier, following the closure of some sites and the transfer of their work to the remaining facilities, progress continued to accelerate.

By 1998, the slump in the commercial aerospace market was rebounding. Through the downturn, we had been careful in the management of overall staffing levels. In prior decades reducing staffing levels had primarily been managed and achieved through layoffs and attrition. We were cautious regarding layoffs and had communicated that no one would lose their jobs through continuous improvement. However, we did communicate that business conditions could result in that unfortunate necessity.

Within the new culture, actual attrition rates were falling as employees began to see real improvement and regained their confidence in the business. Continuous improvement activities were resulting in much capacity being created, including staffing capacity. The ramp-up in sales enabled us to fortuitously fill this capacity as it was being created.

Standard Work

The focus on Standard Work did not begin until early in 1998 in the assembly operations at Foley.

The continuous improvement training materials, as previously noted, had been upgraded and further developed to include Standard Work elements such as Time Observations, Standard Work Combination Sheets, Percent Load charts and Standard Work Sheets. The Enterprise Excellence Assessment tool had the requirement for frequent leadership engagement in continuous improvement activities. This now included "Leadership Event Weeks" where participation by the Aerostructures president and his staff was a requirement.

Event focus in manufacturing was moving quickly to Standard Work, and leadership's engagement in the development of Standard Work became conspicuous and had a positive impact in the workplace.

This had a noticeable influence on continuous improvement engagement and the "cultural change" taking place.

Our consultant educated us regarding what made the Toyota Production System different from other continuous improvement efforts and "programs" that abounded in the manufacturing and business world.

The primary differentiator being the constant pursuit of waste, where the goal of "Cycle Time equaling Takt Time" is pursued but never achieved. (Takt Time is an expression of customer demand, detailed in the Appendix)

For example, as waste is eliminated from individual processes, and actual cycle times are improved (reduced) the staffing, as shown in a percent load chart, changes to support the new process.

Achieving a complete balance of "Cycle Time equaling Takt Time" across an entire process/percent load chart, with multiple employees, invariably never happens. However, pursuing this goal ensures that the next level of opportunities are consistently exposed.

The consultant made it abundantly clear why Standard Work was so important and valuable while stressing the difference between value added and non-value added tasks. He talked at length of the importance of identifying and recording short elements (process steps) when doing time observations and always reminded us that Standard Work represented the Least Waste Way as we knew it, at that point in time.

And that tomorrow, after further waste identification and elimination, the Standard Work should change to support the revised process.

With our growing understanding of Standard Work, we had now updated our Continuous Improvement model:

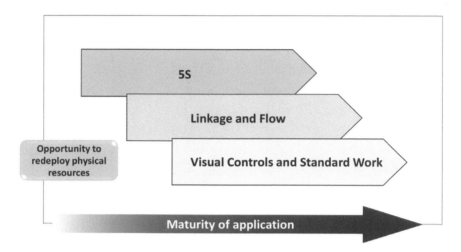

One anecdotal episode occurred in Foley, in 1999 during an event where time observations were being made on a 717 component assembly. The person leading the time observation activity was the 717 program leader. Our consultant asked to review the time observation sheets, and upon doing so directed the 717 leader to "do them again, the observed elements need to be smaller." Early the next day our consultant reviewed the new time observation sheets and again directed that "the observed elements needed be smaller." Later that afternoon the scene repeated. The 717 leader, exasperated, asked, "how small do you want these elements?" To which the consultant replied, "how good do you want to be?"

Is this an anecdote about Standard Work? Alternatively, is it an anecdote about leading, the understanding of value-added, non-value added and how attention to detail can lead to the elimination of waste and meaningful business performance improvement? Possibly a little of the former and much of the latter.

To this day the 717 program leader in this engagement, who subsequently became a successful Goodrich Executive, will say that this was a "continuous improvement epiphany" for him. He quickly became a knowledgeable, engaged driver and advocate of continuous improvement and of maintaining an environment that enabled it.

As our understanding and proficiency with Standard Work improved, our identification and elimination of waste became quite effective. Hours per unit across multiple programs, in multiple locations, were continually being reduced and with them the actual costs of the programs also reduced.

As this was happening finance reported that overhead rates were, of course, increasing as a result of the lower direct labor hour base, driven by the ongoing productivity improvements. Some amusement was generated when two options were suggested. One "tongue in cheek" option was to stop reducing direct labor hours; the other was to increase the focus on productivity improvements and drive continuous improvement into the overhead costs themselves. The latter was thought to be the much better option!

There were some monumental hours per unit reductions. One memorable one occurred during a focus on the layup of an Inlet Inner Barrel, part of a metal bonded assembly used in the nacelle of a single aisle plane in high production. Layup is the task of placing contoured, metal parts and other metal details onto a bond jig (a mold) with layers of adhesive in between the parts and then curing this assembly under pressure and vacuum.

This layup task was taking 36 hours and had been doing so for several years. The two employees who did this work had also been on this task a number of years.

Leadership of the area determined that the next step of continuous improvement for the layup process was to develop and implement Standard Work. Following completion of time observations, involving the two employees doing the task, waste was identified and, countermeasures were implemented to remove this waste and improve the process. Standard Work to support the new method was developed showing a cycle time of around 18 hours per unit. A good, and not unusual reduction for first generation Standard Work. The Standard Work did, of course, have well defined and detailed process steps.

Expectations were set, but unfortunately, the two experienced layup operators did not believe in or follow the revised process detailed in the new Standard Work. In fact, they continued to follow a sequence and process they had become accustomed to and continued to take around 36 hours. While expectations were repeatedly set to work to the new Standard Work, their process did not change or the hours per unit improve.

The Team Leader at the time removed them from the task and reassigned them to other roles. They were replaced by two employees who had no experience with the layup of the inner barrel. They did, however, have explicit directions to follow the Standard Work.

Within a month, and around 48 inner barrels later, they were sustaining this task at 18 hours per unit.

Over the next six months, the Standard Work was updated as more waste was identified and removed with the layup process time reducing to around 7 hours. As of 2016, the Standard Work had been reduced to 4.75 hours and operators were routinely completing the task at close to 5 hours.

By 2003, prior to the introduction of Standard Work, around 2,000 of these units had been built, at an average of something greater than 36 hours.

Looking back and given the 31 hours difference (36 hours vs 5 hours) one begins to understand the opportunity presented by the identification and elimination of waste/non-value added activities with the implementation of Standard Work. A total of 2,000 units, at a difference of 31 hours and an hourly burdened rate of $110, this amounts to a "loss" of $6.8M. (2,000 units X 31 hours X $110)

Looking forward, 10 years at say 400 units per year, 31 hours savings at $110 per hour, a minimum cost savings of $13.6M, in 2003 dollars, can be achieved. (10 years X 400 units X 31 hours X $110)

In this instance, it pays to look forward.

Throughout the 2000s there were many similar such examples across Aerostructures. With the high number of new programs going into production in the late 2000s into the 2010s plus, this phenomenon and opportunity repeatedly presented itself on all these programs and products in multiple locations.

Our consultant insisted that all time observations and workplace Standard Work be handwritten. This caused some unrest particularly with the employees who were computer savvy and looked upon anything that could be done electronically as an upgrade to manual operations of any kind.

The reason for this insistence was, to some, quite apparent. As we manually, and painstakingly, record time observations and build the standard work, we began to develop a visceral understanding of what is potentially value added and non-value added and what is required to complete the various tasks and activities. We gain an appreciation for how work can be planned, distributed and scheduled across multiple operators working on the same assembly. As the Standard Work is developed from the time observations, each and every element from the time observations can be reviewed and challenged as the Standard Work Combination Sheet is constructed.

This furthers a deep understanding of value added and non-value added and what is required to construct a viable set of work instructions, with the entire task potentially distributed and balanced across multiple operators, seen visually on the percent load. All with the goal of supporting the Takt Time in the Least Waste Way.

Conversely, we may well fall into the trap of believing the computer is doing some of, or all of this analysis, thought and decision making.

Time observations and Standard Work were handwritten for three years until the green light was given for "computer generated Standard Work Combination Sheets." This was restricted to programs with seventh and eighth generation Standard Work. Time observations are still done manually.

As we progressed and gained proficiency with the removal of waste/non-value added activities, Standard Work became second nature, and the next "learning opportunity" for us came in the form of Standard Work In Progress – SWIP. In the simplest sense, SWIP is the required inventory that must be in place to support customer demand. To determine SWIP for a process requires knowledge of the particular Takt Time and the time required to complete operations.

For example, if an oven cure requires two hours and the customer demand equates to a "unit" every 20 minutes, there should be a minimum of six pieces of SWIP in cure at all times in support of that step in the process. There should also be as many as six pieces ready to be loaded into the cure once the previous "batch" is unloaded to maintain process cadence. In some cases, additional temporary safety or buffer stock may be considered to protect against process yield and machine reliability issues with the clear expectation of near-term problem resolution of the process yield and machine reliability issues themselves.

It was quite a task to determine SWIP levels across multiple process steps and locations, especially when including transportation times between those locations. It was and is, however, "just math" and SWIP can be calculated with due care and attention to detail. Managing SWIP levels can free up vast amounts of cash and does require constant attention given the number of issues that may arise in a production environment.

Many continuous improvement books give detailed explanations of SWIP and SWIP calculations.

The Three Circles

In 1999 we stepped back and summarized that on the one hand our binary Values, integrated with the Positive Employee Philosophy, were enabling culture and work environment change.

On the other hand, continuous improvement was the basis and driver of our Operating Approach. We somewhat belatedly realized that collectively, they were catalysts and drivers for each other!

This was quite a revelation for us as we immediately saw how we could communicate and leverage this in communications and training as we moved forward.

Realizing that as leadership's behaviors followed the intent of the Positive Employee Philosophy and employees were treated in an "adult to adult" fashion, in an environment of mutual trust and respect, the more they engaged in the business.

The more employees engaged in the business, through continuous improvement activities, the better we became at identifying and removing waste. This, in turn, drove performance and employment stability and created a level of employee buy-in and advocacy to the entire "change process" that was well underway.

The Two Circles became the Three Circles, and extensive business-wide communications were in place to ensure all employees understood what the interrelationship of the Three Circles represented and enabled:

Also in 1999, a supportive process of the Positive People Philosophy was introduced. It was a Positive Climate Index (PCI) process that required leadership, organizational leaders and above, accompanied by a Human Resources representative, to meet with groups of around

20 employees to solicit input as to "what was working, or being done well" and what was "not working, being done well."

These sessions were held with employees from outside of the leader's area of responsibility. This process was done company-wide and was invariably an "agenda item" when leaders were making offsite plant visits.

The process was:

- Brief introductions of everyone and an overview of the Positive Climate Index process.
- Attendees take a survey and are asked to identify what they perceive as:
  o Working, or being done well
  o Not working, or not being done well
- Presentation of company business metrics and items of interest, by the leader and questions and answers with attendees.
  o Concurrently, the Human Resources representative tabulates the survey input
- Presentation of the tabulated input to the attendees by the Human Resources representative
  o Top three - what is working, or being done well
  o Top three - what is not working, or not being done well
- Discussion with the attendees to focus on and understand the top three "not working or not being done well" items, why they thought that and what they believed could be done to improve them.

Follow up was done and actions were put in place for issues raised. Human resources kept trend data, and if trends or themes were seen, in local areas or across the business, broader countermeasures were pursued.

The top two issues encountered over the years, with little variation, were "communications and supervisor feedback."

These are the two "not working or not being done well" issues that seem to be timeless and universal. Regardless, actions were taken to address these issues each time.

Annually in the region of eighty to one hundred PCI's were completed. This process helped identify real concerns and issues, enabled countermeasures to be developed and put in place, was an avenue for communications, and helped the overall cultural development and sustainment.

Continuous Improvement beyond Operations

By 2000 we had run around 1000 employees through 35 "Continuous Improvement boot camps." In addition to Aerostructures personnel, other Goodrich business unit employees and supplier employees had also attended that training.

The Aerostructures president and the senior leadership were now a fixture when it came to the presentation of the continuous improvement training materials and modules in the "boot camps." Leadership's engagement in this training was a visible contributor to the cultural change taking place.

The opportunity and need to move continuous improvement activities into the office environment became apparent to most. Many employees in the office environment had attended the "Continuous Improvement boot camp" and participated in several shop floor kaizen events. They routinely identified and discussed opportunities to improve performance in their own areas of responsibility, and although some areas made good progress, overall continuous improvement activities were not being deployed with the same enthusiasm or speed as in operations.

However, over time and with the active support of site continuous improvement resources, kaizen events, and other performance improvement activities in the office environment, became the norm.

Some early successes:

Finance:

Compiling month ending and quarter ending reports was problematic and invariably took excessive overtime hours to complete to required deadlines. After a brief discussion, site continuous improvement resources and some finance employees realized that this was being driven by a number of quality issues. Some in finance had difficulty understanding this being the case, as they were after all, in finance and had nothing to do with hardware where quality issues were generally seen. After some coaching, it became obvious to all that many of the multiple inputs coming in from various locations for the month and quarter ending reports could not be used as they were incomplete, in error, or required further interrogation. These process inputs did indeed have quality issues.

Through a series of kaizen events, the teams documented reality to understand and categorize issues, problems, and opportunities, then identified their root causes and applied countermeasures. This was accomplished with great success. The finance team concurrently developed a visual control, which was used monthly and quarterly to show the required sequence of inputs, when they were due, if they were completed on time, and were error-free. As late deliveries or errors were observed, reality was again documented, issues, problems, and opportunities identified, root cause determined and countermeasures applied. Over several months major quality problems were significantly reduced, excessive overtime and stress greatly reduced. This was one of many successes in Finance.

Supply chain:

Continuous improvement in the supply chain presented both a huge challenge and opportunity. The supply chain had its own extensive internal operations to manage while also charged with the oversight and development of dozens of external suppliers. Initial continuous improvement activities were focused first on supply chain internal operations.

The supply chain was organized into small groups that focused on Long Term Agreements, Contracts, suppliers by region or commodity and then others on supplier development.

Supplier on-time delivery and delivered quality were two primary issues for the supply chain, and metrics were in place for the overall status of each. However, the status of issues at or by supplier, and projected resolution dates with individuals responsible for closure, were not apparent. Individual supply chain employees had much of this information but a visual to understand the detail was not available.

The supply chain leader at the time made the creation of this visual and the management process that went with it a personal quest, ably assisted by supply chain employees eager to engage in the continuous improvement process. This visual became known as the "Watch List" and covered all key suppliers and those who fell into the "not performing to requirements spotlight." The visual was mounted in the entrance to the supply chain area covering an area five foot high by 20 feet across. It was maintained by the supply chain team, reviewed daily by the supply chain leader and his team and any "Program leaders" who needed real time information or for them to provide real time input. It was a process that needed little explanation, driver measures, additional appropriate data and visuals were developed and matured over time. One could understand the "health" of the supply chain and each of the suppliers within it quickly when viewing the "Watch List" and its visual metrics. With this in place, attention to issues became increased, and supplier delivery and quality improved measurably.

Supplier development activities focused on specific short-term issues and problems through to resolution. Continuous improvement concepts being deployed internally at Aerostructures were introduced into the supply base and were met with mixed receptions and results that continue to this day.

Aftermarket:

The Aftermarkets primary customers are airlines. Products are individual parts or structural components such as an inlet or fan cowl. As the Chula Vista site was being right-sized in the late 1990s, the aftermarket team moved their Spares warehouse into a vacated building. Using this move as an opportunity for change and performance improvement, they implemented multiple visual controls, and the identification and storage location of thousands of parts was significantly improved. Other improvement initiatives addressed improving the linkage and flow of incoming spare parts into stock, their retrieval, and global shipment. These improvements also covered all associated paperwork, packaging and shipment-processes. Visual controls were installed to track all these order fulfillment activities.

The warehouse inventory of nacelle spare parts is estimated to have been over $100M at the time, to ensure the availability of multiple parts for on-time airline support. Continuous improvement tools and techniques were extensively utilized to ensure spare parts inventory levels were managed in the Least Waste Way to maintain a balance between on-time customer support and the level of capital investment in spares inventory.

Traditionally, when an airline customer required a structural component, a nacelle sub-assembly, for a currently in production program, it would take a full manufacturing cycle to meet that demand supported by scheduling efforts to add the extra requirements to the production line. As a result of the much-improved efficiency and velocity of production parts passing through the manufacturing facilities, a different option became available.

When a spare assembly was required for an Airline customer, we were now able to pull the unit out of the Least Waste Way production process and satisfy the demand knowing full well that we were able to make up the production need quickly within a production line operating to Standard Work and being managed by visual controls on the shop floor. As the days to manufacture, the velocity through the production process were half of pre-improvement "days to manufacture," opportunities to increase on time delivery to airline customer need dates were realized. Delivery on schedule to airline customer requested need date was improving year over year.

Human Resources:

One issue that plagued organizations was the time it took between completing the required paperwork for a new hire and the time it took to for the person to be on site, in place and functional. Human Resources took the challenge, and through a thorough documentation of reality - detailed process mapping, they identified multiple issues, problems, and opportunities. The days to process were determined to be in the 60 to 90+ days range. With good countermeasures applied this process was reduced to <30 to 60+ days dependent on the skill set need and availability.

One comment that was heard in the office and the shop floor environments when uncovering monumental amounts of waste/non-value added activity was, often incredulously and occasionally defensively - "it's always been like that." A comment not unique to Aerostructures.

As we advanced the deployment of continuous improvement, the Toyota Production System, into the office support areas, other pushback comments we occasionally heard were– "we are not production, we are XYZ function" or "it's called lean manufacturing for a reason, and we are not manufacturing."

We explained to the skeptics that the Toyota Production System/Lean Manufacturing principles applied anywhere and everywhere. Helped them with continuous improvement activities, the identification and elimination of waste, improved performance, and moved on. The progress and improvements in the office support areas ensured that these comments quickly died out.

There was of course less than full support and engagement from some leadership and staff in the support organizations. There was coaching and some reassignment of leadership, but in retrospect, there should have been more of both. There were other pockets of hesitation, push back and on occasion a lack of continuous improvement understanding. We made every attempt to encourage and train employees to help them do the right thing, and they usually did, with the appropriate support.

Reflecting on leadership engagement - over the years, particularly the early years, some leaders chose to see, and do, things that they thought to be more important than their engagement in culture change or continuous improvement activities. Other leaders chose to engage in culture change or continuous improvement activities at every opportunity.

It is a recognition of how opportunities and priorities are seen and then a choice a leader makes. It is a characteristic that separates leaders from others.

Real Time Problem Resolution

On several occasions early in our lean journey, our consultant was asked: "how quickly can we drive continuous improvement?" His answer was always the same – "what is your problem-solving capacity?" We came to realize and experience, that when employees, engaged in continuous improvement activities, identified problems and opportunities, they understandably had the expectation that countermeasures would be promptly applied to resolve the problems or leverage the opportunities.

This concern did indeed come to the fore as we were beginning our understanding and deployment of Standard Work. The kaizen event teams were gaining understanding and competency, not only with the kaizen process itself but also at finding waste. Issues, problems, and opportunities were being identified at a rapid pace, and not all countermeasures were being put, in place real time.

Some perceived as being a little more challenging or requiring additional information to resolve were put onto To-Do lists to be dealt with later.

Our consultant insisted that if we addressed all issues, problems, and opportunities when identified, rather than thinking that some of them needed some further analysis, we would find that we could resolve many more of them in real time.

The team on the 717 program rose to the challenge and in a Standard Work focused kaizen event in Riverside they outlined a process to both capture and resolve problems in real time. Once back in Chula Vista, where additional 717 work was done, the team quickly matured a simple process. Which was - once a problem has been identified, usually by an operator detecting a problem, turning on a red light at their work station, and documenting the problem on a To Do sheet, the collocated support team met with the operator and made every effort to quickly document reality, identify root cause and solve the problem, real time. If not resolved there and then, twice daily status and coordination meetings, by the collocated program support team, focused upon it incessantly, through to resolution.

The 717 manufacturing support teams in Riverside, Chula Vista, and Foley were all collocated or close to Operations, and as this process gained traction, it changed their priorities from a focus on old issues and problems to one of supporting a Real Time Problem Resolution process. Invariably the lists of past issues and problems, reduced significantly as they engaged in the new process. Inactive issues and problems, languishing on lists, were minimized considerably.

Real Time Problem Resolution proved to be quite a challenge to the cultural momentum of what employees saw as priorities. It did, however, become a process we continued to pursue, across all programs and locations, and it was added to our evolving Continuous Improvement model:

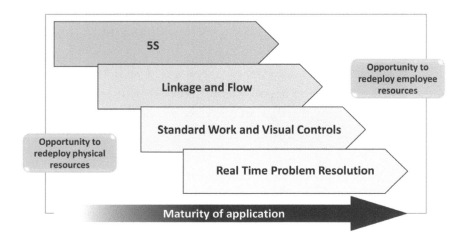

We had spent four years addressing and unraveling the knots in the production processes and leveraging linkage and flow. We had dealt with large production machines and equipment and had moved many of these "monuments" in line with their associated process steps or alternatively, moved their associated process steps in line with the monuments. Often the latter.

In one memorable kaikaku week in the Chula Vista facility, we spent high six figures with the international large equipment mover Mammoet, to move several large machines and pieces of equipment to align with the processes they supported, leveraging linkage and flow opportunities.

Although positive progress was made regarding process and monument alignment, some monuments such as clean rooms, chemical process lines, and autoclaves remained challenges to efficient product linkage and flow.

Support organization processes, tasks and activities

As we had looked at and learned about the support processes used or relied upon by the shop floor, we saw that virtually every support process had steps that passed through a labyrinth of functions, with delays experienced in most, if not all of them.

By way of example a Quality tag, a discrepancy finding with a part or product on the shop floor, has to pass through many functional steps that may include - Operations, Quality Assurance, Material Review Board, Engineering, Supply Chain, and Program Management for resolution and buy off. In this type of process, communications between functions were generally ineffective with impaired flow of data and information and functional priorities invariably misaligned.

We had started to look at "functions" as monuments. Big, slow, entrenched and not easy to move. Certainly not anywhere close to having the flexibility and nimbleness we were seeking in support of overall performance improvement.

Value Streams

As mentioned previously, we had become ardent students of the book "Lean Thinking." The concept of Value and Value Streams, discussed in some detail in Lean Thinking, had piqued our interest.

Our understanding of Value and Value Streams subsequently became as follows:

- Value – things or actions that a customer is willing to pay for.
- Value Stream – a sequence of steps whereby a product or process is manufactured and or completed, in a Least Waste Way, in support of a paying customer.

We also applied the label Value Stream to an organizational structure that is put in place to lead and manage an organization charged with satisfying customer demand.

We also recognized that:

- We were undoubtedly providing things or taking actions that the customer would not see as adding value.

The president of Aerostructures at the time, Dave Watson, a fully committed and actively engaged supporter of continuous improvement, was supportive of an effort to understand and improve support function processes and like ourselves was intrigued by the concepts of Value and Value Streams. So much so that he committed to a detailed evaluation of a potential Value Stream organizational alignment. The details of which, and how such a structure could be effectively utilized at Aerostructures, had yet to be understood.

We needed to understand value, recognizing what activities added value, to what the customer wanted, and what activities did not. Then eliminate non-value added activities, while improving those that are value added. Concurrently gain an understanding of how do we address all the activities that we may be required to do, regulatory and other, which do not add any value?

With regard to Value Streams, we did have an understanding of the revenue generating aspect of Value Streams given our program accounting methods. However defining the revenue generating Value Stream structure, understanding its activities and level of control in a cost-efficient environment was yet to be determined.

We wanted to engage the "right employees" in an activity or process that would shed light and clarity, on Value and Value Streams. And much like a Policy Deployment process, ensure their engagement, understanding, calibration, alignment, buy-in, and advocacy of the process and its eventual outcome.

Any process of this type would require a detailed documentation of reality to understand the issues, problems, and opportunities. Followed by the identification of potentially multiple countermeasure options. In this instance, the documentation of reality process used must be sufficiently robust and logical enough to engage, what was to be, the entire Aerostructures senior leadership team.

Our challenge was to come up with a process to document the reality of, what was at the time, a $1.2 billion and 4,500 employee, complex aerospace business.

Working with our consultant, late 1998 into early 1999, time was spent developing a process to document reality at this "whole business" level.

A detailed process, plan, and schedule was developed and shared with the company president in early 1999, and he bought into the process with minimal discussion. The process had six steps, and we were asked to plan and schedule them as soon as possible.

The six steps were:

1. Development/update of a Strategic Plan
2. Development of Aerostructures Policy Deployment
3. Documentation of Reality of the current organization structure and processes
   - Identification of issues problems and opportunities
   - Identification of Value Stream centric countermeasures relating to the organizational structure
4. Identification of Value Stream Leaders
5. Development of Value Stream Policy Deployment
6. Identification of Value Stream tasks and activities and assignment of employees

Communications were developed and shared with all employees in all locations that outlined:

> Via a defined and structured process, activities to understand organizational structure, and the associated issues, and opportunities, were to take place over the coming months. And that we would regularly be communicating progress as we went.

Our first challenge was to develop a meaningful Strategic Planning process.

1. Strategic Plan development

The process outlined below was developed and used:

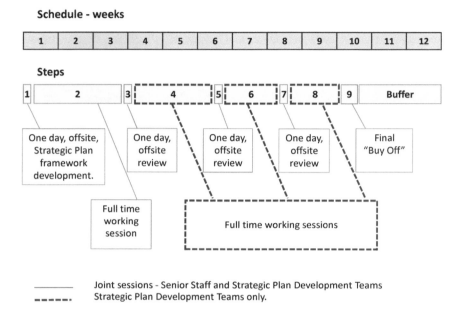

Schedule - weeks

| 1 | 2 | 3 | 4 | 5 | 6 | 7 | 8 | 9 | 10 | 11 | 12 |

Steps

Joint sessions - Senior Staff and Strategic Plan Development Teams
Strategic Plan Development Teams only.

This process ensured leaderships engagement in the beginning to frame the plan, their participation throughout the process to provide further input and guidance, and again at final buy off.

Strategic Plan sub-teams were made up of leaders and other influential members from organizations such as Business Development, Research and Development, Operations, Program Management, Finance, Procurement, Operations, and Human Resources.

Sub-teams would be focused upon different aspects of the business such as commercial markets, military markets, operations, and training and employee development.

Each sub-team had a leader and was tasked with developing their section of the Strategic Plan and coordinating with, and across, the other teams during the process.

There was also one overall leader to ensure coordination, alignment and schedule management of all the sub-teams through to completion of the plan.

One brief discussion was a reflection on the number of years that had passed since Aerostructures had had a significant business win. Options had been previously discussed with this in mind and were, basically, "grow the business _or_ harvest the business."

The business had ongoing programs, a strong Aftermarket, and new business potential. Given Goodrich's purchase of Rohr in 1997 "grow the business" was the clear choice.

There had also been previous discussions around an appropriate Strategic Plan "thrust/direction."

Three primary options had been considered, they were:

- **Innovation**, an effective and efficient new product development pipeline - 3M, Apple, Tesla, Monster Beverage
- **Customer Intimacy**, face to face care and attention, with the customer, real time – high-end stores and hotels
- **Enterprise Excellence**, operating the company in such a manner that customers and shareholders keep coming back – Amazon, Walmart, Chick Fil A

Innovation in nacelle design was quite active, all of our competitors focused on this issue and the Aerostructures Research and Development team continually focused on improvements to nacelle weight, size, sound attenuation and thrust reverser abilities which are the primary attributes and requirements of a nacelle.

Customer Intimacy in the "store/hotel" mode was thought to be inappropriate. The commercial aerospace business around the world is a small community. Business relationships are close. Most if not all commercial deals are based on product performance and price with the occasional political decision in the mix. Four customers, Boeing, Airbus, Bombardier, and Embraer, account for most of the world's commercial airplanes. Emerging airplane manufacturers may at a later date change this customer profile.

Recognizing that other attributes of the business playing field we were in were quite level, Enterprise Excellence was the obvious focus.

What we needed to do was achieve and maintain Enterprise Excellence in all we did. Since 1999 we had become accustomed to defining Enterprise Excellence as "doing what we do better than the competition." The Strategic Plan was completed by May 1999.

2. Aerostructures Policy Deployment

The Policy Deployment process had matured over the previous years and was getting to be well understood and reliable, producing a Policy Deployment matrix each year that had meaningful, focused Goals, Initiatives, and Improvement Targets.

This process was followed once again and the SMART Improvement Targets, at an Aerostructures level, were developed for 2000 and included:

- Targeting and winning new business.
- Development and implementation of a least waste cost/ pricing model.
- Defined goals for engineering cost reduction.
- Defined productivity improvement, and cost reduction goals, for both mature and new programs.
- The launch of the all employee incentive program - Gainsharing.
- External and internal customer support and delivery goals.
- Meaningful and measurable progress towards Enterprise Excellence by all organizations.
- Development and execution of a new ERP system.

Riding on the wave of meaningful continuous improvement activities and annual margin and income increases, the Improvement Targets as developed above clearly "raised the bar." This step completed in June of 1999.

3. Documentation of Reality

If ever there was a documentation of reality that took on gargantuan proportions, this is a candidate for that honor.

The Senior Staff and fifteen plus "next level" leaders and influential team members participated in this activity. Thirty people in total working in three teams of ten.

The intent of this step was to identify all the tasks and activities, done by all functions, at Aerostructures. Quite a challenge.

This meant the norming of a "flight level," the level of detail to be identified and captured by each team to make sure we had information we could ultimately compare and contrast across all three teams.

Multiple scenarios were discussed with the team in the effort to calibrate the "flight level" of their outputs, an example of how we accomplished that successfully is shown next, where a ground level activity and the flow of that activity up through the business is depicted:

	Activity	"Flight Level"
7	Design, Manufacture, Integrate and Support Aerostructures components - Company	"Upmost level activity"
6	Finance data roll up and review – Leadership	100K'
5	Issue Labor Reports – Finance Org	40K'
4	Capture labor hours – Finance Org	20K'
3	Employee secures supervisors labor approval, weekly – Employee / Supervisor	5K'
2	Enter labor into system – Employee	1K'
1	Go to PC, enter employee number, access labor screen, entry job number, enter labor hours, visually check screen, correct any errors, close and exit labor screen – Employee	"Ground level activity"

At the top #7, what the company did. At the bottom #1, a discreet activity within the company.

On reflection, this example, and some others we discussed had some shortfalls, but on the day, after discussion, they held up and worked to level set the teams.

The instructions to the teams were to identify all the tasks and activities done within the business at a 5K' level. Enter each task or activity being performed on a "stickie note," color code the tasks and activities by function, via the "stickie note" colors, and put all the "stickie notes" on wall mounted butcher paper.

We knew that asking the teams to identify all the tasks and activities was a tall order, but we could not have documented reality without this detailed level of information.

This step looked like this, with significantly more stickies, literally thousands more, than shown here:

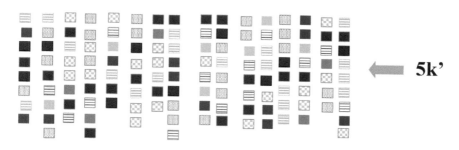

⟵ **5k'**

From this point, we asked the teams to identify natural groups of tasks and activities and identify each group with a 20K' Umbrella Statement, containing a verb, that described what that group of tasks and activities represented.

Such as:

- Identifying and requesting a staffing requirement
- Processing a quality tag
- Purchasing a non-standard item
- Making an engineering drawing change
- Designing a new material handling aid

This step required lots of stickie review and movement, to ensure team understanding and calibration, and alignment of the stickies to the correct higher level task and activity:

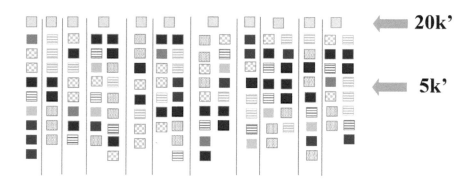

From that point, we asked that the teams to further identify natural groups of tasks and activities and identify each group with a next level 40K' Umbrella Statement, containing a verb, that described what that group of tasks and activities represented.

Such as:

- Hiring and onboarding of new employees
- Inspecting and assuring quality
- Purchasing, scheduling and releasing to production contracted production materials
- Supporting, making and deploying engineering changes
- Facilitating the movement of parts, in and in-between facilities

And more importantly, at this point, identify all the steps that were rework, corrective action, redo loops or potential non-value added steps:

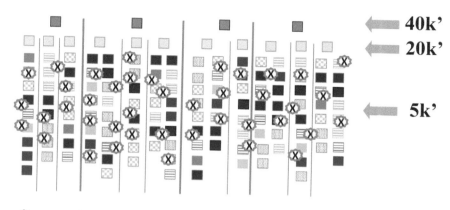

⊗ Rework, corrective action, redo loops or potential non-value added.

Checks were done throughout these activities to ensure the teams were in close "flight level formation."

All processes showed steps that were rework, corrective action, redo loops or potential non-value added steps. Further confirmation that we were replete with opportunity.

The next step was somewhat complex, at least to outline here. It involved the identification of existing functions that were active in a 20K' task or activity and information relative to each of those tasks and activities.

Each team developed a large matrix with 20K' tasks and activities on the X-axis and existing functions on the Y-axis. The functions that engaged in which tasks and activities could be then identified at the appropriate intersections.

The teams were asked to identify and interrogate these intersections with the four questions below:

- What was the frequency of occurrence of that task/activity, in that function?
- Who was the perceived task/activity owner?
- How many employees were engaged at any one time in the task/activity in that function?
- What was the opportunity with the task/activity to positively impact the business?

We kept the answers to these questions as simple, but as representative as possible and required the answers to be in estimated percentages.

An example of a typical "four quadrant" intersection:

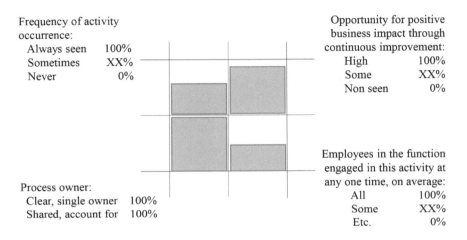

Frequency of activity occurrence:

Always seen	100%
Sometimes	XX%
Never	0%

Opportunity for positive business impact through continuous improvement:

High	100%
Some	XX%
Non seen	0%

Process owner:

Clear, single owner	100%
Shared, account for	100%

Employees in the function engaged in this activity at any one time, on average:

All	100%
Some	XX%
Etc.	0%

Exposed were: things believed to be "occasional" happening daily, tasks and activities with no clear owner, tasks and activities with multiple owners, and the number of employees engaged in the various tasks and activities were, on many occasions, different from perceptions.

Opportunity for improvement was obvious, with the waste/non-value added activities, on this visual, along with the rework identified in the previous step, leaving little to the imagination.

At this point, all three teams presented their documentation of reality to the other teams. The similarities across all three, regarding the complexity of the business and the opportunities made visible, while possibly to be expected, were still quite remarkable.

What was not so remarkable was the kaleidoscopic nature of virtually all processes. The sheer number of processes that passed through multiple functions was painfully evident. There was little doubt as to the issues, as the three teams had each posted close to ~6,500 stickie notes each to document the reality of the Aerostructures processes and had very similar outputs.

Qualitatively the teams did a thorough job. Quantitatively they hold the record for the number of stickie notes used to document reality in an event at Aerostructures, ~19,500.

Once again the desire to understand a Value Stream focus and its structure was a priority for the entire team through 1999.

James Womack, in his visits to a number of Aerostructures facilities and discussions with leadership and others, had explained his views on Value Streams and the benefits of such an organizational structure. The entire team had spent many hours in large and small groups, in formal and informal discussions on the subject of Value Streams and their potential benefits and challenges.

There was also the expected clear understanding and agreement that the only reason for the companies' existence was to continually win new business, support the customers that bought our products and to make money for all the stakeholders. Stakeholders defined as shareholders and employees. This readily translated into "we need to make those business winning, revenue generating areas of the business as efficient and cost-effective as possible and all support areas equally as efficient and cost-effective as possible."

Revenue generating Value Streams had struck a chord. Anything we were doing that we could not connect to revenue generating, consequently a high probability of being non-value added, became an obvious opportunity for attention and improvement.

Against this background, the entire team reviewed the three, very similar documentations of reality, the ~19,500 "stickie note" visuals. They reflected on their areas of responsibility, the processes that they used, the often conflicting priorities and mixed messages across the organizations and the lack of clarity as to where multiple business responsibilities resided.

They came to a common collective conclusion best summarized by comments at the time that echoed - "It's no wonder it takes so long to get things done, we have multiple handoffs, across multiple functions, often in different facilities, with at best, misalignment of priorities and often incomplete information to get the job done at many of the process steps."

The then President, Dave Watson, with that clear line of sight on the inefficiency, ineffectiveness, and opportunity, within the business he was responsible for, asked the team if they saw the "documentation of reality" the same way. They did to a person. Dave asked each of the teams to put together what they saw as Value Stream structure options.

Specifically, the teams were asked to:

- Identify what the high level, overarching Value Streams may be, and what they should be responsible for, not what they may be titled.

Not as easy as it possibly looks and there was much discussion around the flight level of a Value Stream and what, organizationally, may be a subset of a Value Stream.

However, with "revenue generating" in mind, each of the three teams completed this step, identified the higher level Value Streams, and then convened and normed on:

Acquiring Business	Defining the products and processes	Supporting the production Customer demand	Supporting the user Customer demand

All three teams recognized that some important activities did not fall clearly into these "revenue generating Value Streams" and looked much more like support functions. Such as Human Resources, Research and Development, and Information Technology. Organizational detail that was yet to be worked.

Dave Watson closed the week:

He thanked everyone for their participation in the activities to date and for leaving behind any "baggage" they may have had and spoke of the realization that everyone had experienced. That being the need to do something different if we were to build upon the Lean Enterprise that was being created. He reinforced the fact that pushing continuous improvement into a functional organization was ineffective, leaving much on the table. That the safe thing to do was to continue to optimize pieces or sections of the organization through continuous improvement, as we were doing quite successfully at this point, but to ultimately sub-optimize the whole.

He emphasized that 4,500 employees depended on the leadership team to provide direction and advocacy on a broad scale.

To ensure alignment of understanding and commitment he encouraged the team to answer the questions "what are you folks doing in these events and what should we expect as we move forward?" by responding "we are developing a process and structure so we can grow as a business, increasing sales, income, margin, and stability."

He outlined the next planned steps of the process, which were to identify and solidify the Value Stream structure, identify leaders for the new organization, identify the tasks and activities that would be placed "in and reporting to" the Value Streams and said that we would enter 2000 in a revenue generating Value Stream structure. He added "we must achieve performance levels and costs so that we can choose our customers." (A bold statement, but one that reflected the challenge, opportunity and passion we had for change)

He concluded by saying "when you are discussing the process with employees or anyone else, do so with conviction. Tell them where we are in the process, where

*we are going and how we are going to get there. If you
find that you cannot do that please come and see me."*

The entire team was encouraged by the process and progress to
date, their engagement had been outstanding, and everyone looked
forward to the next steps.

Communications with all employees, on progress to date, was
done via company-wide newsletter and flow down staff meetings.

Feedback from employees was positive as they had engaged
sufficiently in change to date, that they too, could see the inefficiencies
in the current organizational structure.

The president was undoubtedly leading "change" through his
conviction, and we were fortunate to have a leader who was focused,
engaged and utilizing a process to make changes, rather than by fiat
or directive.

He explained to the team that before the next session that he
would personally develop a draft of the next level "Value Stream"
structure to be reviewed, discussed and agreed to by the full team
before any broader communications took place.

Over the next two weeks, the president, coordinating with his
staff, discussed the higher level Value Streams and renamed them:

Acquiring Business	Defining the products and processes	Supporting The production Customer demand	Supporting the user Customer demand
⬇	⬇	⬇	⬇
Business Acquisition	Product and Process Definition	In Production Business	Aftermarket Services

... and the initial Value Structure was developed:

Customers

Business Acquisition			Product and Process Definition				In Production Business					All Other programs	US production facilities	Overseas production facilities	Aftermarket Services		
Core Business Nacelle and Pylons	Military and Space	Other Commercial Aerospace Components	Program A	Program B	Program C	Program D	Program A	Program B	Program C	Program D	Program E	All Other programs	US production facilities	Overseas production facilities	Spare Parts	Technical Services	MRO

Human Resources

Quality, Technical and all other Compliance

Enterprise Support Services - Finance, Supply Chain, IT, R&D, Test Labs

Higher level revenue generating Value Streams can be seen as "In Production Business" and "Aftermarket Services."

The new organization also retained some functional organizations seen at the time, and ultimately, as necessary.

Human Resources remained as a whole entity supporting all Value Streams.

While acknowledging that compliance is "everyone's responsibility," it was also determined that maintaining core teams to retain focus, visibility and "audit readiness" across the spectrum of compliance related activities required clear separation from revenue generating Value Streams. These core compliance elements included finance, quality, environmental, health and safety and International Trade Compliance.

Enterprise Support Services also had some "central functions" that we needed to retain at some level and format, recognizing that some employees in those functions, such as supply chain and finance, would be assigned to Value Streams.

It was already understood and agreed that the revenue generating Value Streams would be in "full control" of their destiny. This meant giving them all the resources they needed, to do all the tasks and activities required of them. And to have those resources, regardless of any existing functional alignment, report directly to the revenue generating Value Stream Leader.

This Value Stream structure was agreed upon by the Aerostructures senior staff and their roles and responsibilities, at the Primary and Support Value Stream levels, were defined before the next session.

There were no changes in overall responsibilities at this level per se. The significant leadership assignments and changes were to be made at the Parallel Value Streams, and the second level, of the Support Value Streams.

This step completed in July 1999.

4. Identification of Value Stream Leaders, and Tasks and Activities

A step needed to help identify leaders for the Parallel Value Streams was to define where responsibilities "started and stopped" for each Primary Value Stream. Options were discussed and clarified, pros and cons identified and with relative ease the "start and stop" points of each was identified.

They were:

Business Acquisition
Start - Identification of opportunity, usually within the Strategic Plan
Stop - Signed Contract

Product and Process Definition
> Start - Notification of award
> Stop - After XX units have been built to "Standard Work" cycle times.

In Production Business
> Start - After XX units have been manufactured and assembled to "Standard Work" cycle times.
> Stop - All hardware built through "end of contract," all materials dispositioned, all tools and documentation stored or supplied to the customer per contract requirements

Aftermarket Services
> Start - 90 days prior to entry into service
> Stop - Program life ends as defined by contract

It was recognized that on occasion these start and stop points would not always be as precise as defined here. Such as Product & Process Definition participation may be required during the Business Acquisition phase. Or In Production participation during a number of the Product and Process Definition phases.

It was also realized that Aftermarket should be engaged in the Product and Process Definition phase to understand and plan for opportunities once the aircraft was in service, sooner rather than later. Much of this overlap was clarified during the identification of the tasks and activities and associated resources that each Parallel Value Stream was to have responsibility for.

The identification of leaders for the Parallel Value Streams was now the challenge. Existing "Job Descriptions" did not include Value Stream Leader or the process required to select them. The team subsequently developed the "attributes" and the "roles and responsibilities" of a Value Stream Leader.

The attributes and roles and responsibilities were defined with reflection on the requirements of the Three Circles, predominantly the Environment and the Operating Approach.

The Environment was defined by the Positive Employee Philosophy and the behaviors required by everyone, leaders in particular. Reinforced by constant communications on the subject.

The Operating Approach was gaining understanding, broad acceptance and traction.

By 1999 Policy Deployment was in its third year, as was the Enterprise Excellence Assessment. Our understanding and deployment of the Toyota Production System was increasing rapidly, and aggressive business results were being achieved each year.

We were fortunate to have no issues with the Values.

Attributes were subsequently defined, and each was given a weighting to be used in the upcoming Value Stream Leader selection process. The first three below receiving the highest weighting and the last three all close seconds.

The attributes were:

- Consistently demonstrates the attributes and behaviors of the "Three Circles," with a focus on customer support.
- Is a "Continuous Improvement Leader"
- Is a "Change Agent"
- Has a "Bias for Action"
- Is "Process" oriented
- Has good "Communication skills"

Roles and Responsibilities for a Value Stream Leader were then developed reflecting these attributes.

Role	Responsibilities
Cultural Development Leader	• Demonstrate mutual trust and respect and adult to adult behaviors that ensure leadership credibility • Demonstrate and ensure ethical behavior in all areas of the Value Stream • Ensure the Values and the Positive Employee Philosophy principles are developed into the Value Stream culture through clear demonstration, education, and expectation • Communicate frequently and effectively
Business Leader	• Ensure contractual compliance with external agencies, customer requirements, and supplier contracts • Ensure sound business principles are understood and applied in the Value Stream • Be accountable and responsible for Value Stream profitability • Effectively communicate and maintain an environment that ensures two-way communication in all areas of the Value Stream • Employee Resources – recognize the value of and develop the employee resource • Effectively communicate and ensure the necessary Policy Deployment elements are in place to implement Initiatives and achieve Improvement Targets
Continuous Improvement Leader	• Know, Lead and apply the application of Lean Principles toward developing the Value Stream a "Least Waste Way organization" • Change Agent – create and maintain an environment that encourages and supports change while maintaining compliance and protects the business • Bias for Action – execute a change strategy in line with the Aerostructures Policy Deployment in a timely fashion while protecting the business. • Nurture an environment that enables real time problem identification and resolution

The senior leadership team identified a list of 43 candidates for Value Stream Leader roles, some of whom were either existing functional or department leaders and others who were on the cusp of leadership roles. All 43 were assessed against the attributes, roles and responsibilities and ranked using the weighting.

The attributes, and the weighting of them in particular, had set the bar high, and the results of the process caused a pause for concern. Only seven individuals passed what had been established as the "weighted score waterline" for a Value Stream Leader role.

To the amusement of the senior leadership team, the president had assessed himself against the attributes and weighting and failed to reach the "watermark." As noted, the bar had been set high.

The discussion that ensued was around the perceived strengths and weaknesses of the candidates, the attributes and weighting as used, and where everyone, Value Stream Leader candidates and Senior Staff themselves, were regarding their understanding and deployment of the "continuous improvement and cultural change journey" we were all on. This discussion allayed concerns and Parallel Value Stream Leaders were identified and their roles communicated to them.

To further fulfill the intent of what we understood as a Value Stream structure involved the identification of the tasks and activities required of a Value Stream, what they were responsible and accountable for, to control their destiny and operate as a fully functioning revenue generating business.

Another large visual was created to facilitate this step.

A matrix was posted the X-axis extending many feet to the right. On this axis, all the existing functions and their previously identified "20K flight level tasks and activities" were listed.

On the Y-axis, the Aerostructures Improvement Targets were listed. Also on the Y axis were the Value Streams, aligned with the designated Improvement Targets that each would have "flowed down" to them along with the associated responsibilities.

With this in place, a question was asked, for each of the Improvement Targets of each of the newly identified Value Streams, "what tasks and activities does the Value Stream need to have in their control to successfully achieve the assigned Improvement Target?"

The answer to this question was identified at the matrix intersection of the Value Stream Improvement Target and the functional tasks and activities listed on the X-axis.

For example, if an In Production Business Value Stream were to reduce costs through addressing quality issues, it would need the responsibility for those tasks and activities that identified, and resolved those quality issues in the Value Stream, enabling them to be addressed immediately with, at best no handoffs or conflicting priorities.

Using this extended matrix proved to be necessary, exhausting and productive. Possibly the most challenging step in the process for the team to align on, but the team achieved what it set out to do - identify what tasks and activities were currently residing in which functions that needed to be in the Value Streams.

Communications were developed and deployed to bring all employees up to speed with Value Stream development to date, outlining:

- A process summary.
  - Strategic Plan Summary
  - Enterprise Excellence business approach
  - Year 2000 Policy Deployment
  - Task and Activity definition
  - Thoughts, observations and results of the "documentation of reality to date"

- Value Stream high-level structure.
  - "New" Value Stream Leaders, roles, responsibilities and expectations

Concurrent communications with on-site Union officials were also completed, securing their understanding, agreement, and buy-in. These broad communication steps were completed in August of 1999.

5. Development of Value Stream Policy Deployment

The new Value Stream leaders were given the opportunity to designate a core group of two to three employees who would become part of their Leadership team. Value Stream Leaders identified employees many of which were already supporting their new organizations, albeit in the functional structure.

The environment was such that this was accomplished with the right people being placed in the right Value Streams in the right roles. A "competitive draft" was avoided, some functional angst was not, but communications allayed concerns quickly.

Most if not all of the newly identified Value Stream Leadership team had been taking part in the development, deployment, and use of the Policy Deployment process for some time, most if not all having leadership roles in their functional organization. For them developing a Policy Deployment matrix was reasonably straightforward although the focus was quite different from a Value Stream perspective. This step was completed quite quickly and effectively in September 1999.

6. Identification of Value Stream tasks and activities and assignment of employees

The newly identified Value Stream Leaders and their new small leadership teams joined the team that had been documenting reality through the year. Another challenging but necessary step was necessary.

Using the matrices with the "four quadrant" intersections, developed in step 3, linking tasks and activities to the function currently performing them, and the matrix developed in step 4 identifying particular Value Stream Improvement Targets, the teams were charged with:

- Understanding the tasks, activities and the opportunities at each of the relevant "four quadrant matrix intersections."
- Asking "is the task or activity necessary, does it add value?"

- Confirming that the task or activity is required to achieve the Value Stream 2000 Improvement Targets.
- Asking "is anything overlooked, that should be in the Value Stream?"
- Reviewing the documents in all three-team rooms for any task and activity clarification.
- Identifying the number of employees, not names, that were estimated to be needed for each task and activity.

Challenges arose. One was the size and complexity of some of the Value Streams that required a significant number of employees with specific functional skills, such as Manufacturing Engineers. Other smaller Value Streams appeared to need a fractional number of employees with specific functional skills.

The identification of what skill sets was somewhat straightforward, the number of required employees with those skill sets in each Value Stream was "best estimate." The overall availability of employees in certain functions with the specific skills required in the Value Streams was an initial issue.

The next challenge was to place employees by name in the new Value Stream organization. Some assignments were relatively easy, such as employees in operations already manufacturing or assembling product for "Program A" went into the "Program A" Value Stream. Engineers working on specific programs went into those program Value Streams.

What we wanted to assure was that the Value Streams got the skill sets and the individuals with those skill sets into the Value Stream where they would provide the "most effective support" for the business.

Aftermarket was generally already in a Value Stream structure with the subsections of Spares, Technical Services and the Maintenance Repair and Overhaul facilities, each one of which was self-sufficient and self-supporting. Little further adjustment was needed in this part of the organization.

Human Resources managed the process and leaders of the functions where employees were currently assigned provided insight and guidance on the skill sets, performance, and potential of employees in those functions.

The process completed relatively quickly and with the minimal discord as up until this point, only "functional skill set" requirements in terms of numbers had been identified. Employee names previously and purposely had not been used.

The reassignment of the employees into the appropriate Value Streams included both a direct reporting relationship and also, where possible, a physical collocation. Both of these steps were an intricate undertaking. This step completed in October 1999.

The application of continuous improvement tools on the processes they all used in their functional and soon to be Value Stream roles was to follow, and staffing was further defined and adjusted in the following months.

The process that the Aerostructures president, his staff, and the broader team had undertaken across the six long weeks, with much time in between the scheduled weeks, had a profound impact on all employees.

The documentation of reality activities, the constant communications of progress and the final output of the endeavor were instrumental in clearly demonstrating meaningful change and contributed to molding the culture in a magnitude not seen previously.

It is interesting to note that the leadership of Goodrich chose to let the Aerostructures leadership proceed with the "documentation of reality" process throughout 1999 followed by the restructuring into Value Streams entering 2000, without intervention of any kind.

1999 had been a pivotal year. Rohr had been part of Goodrich for over two years and during that time had returned operating income and operating margin in excess of that estimated by Goodrich prior to the purchase of Rohr.

Continuous improvement deployment, abilities, and successes were being noticed by many in Goodrich and beyond. Major customers and others continued to send groups of people, to Aerostructures, to get an understanding of how the business was being turned around from the "almost bankrupt" days.

Groups of 50 to 60 visitors at a time was now the norm. The number of visitors we had hosted was around 1000 by 1999.

Value Streams

During 2000 the Value Stream organization and the assignments of employees into the Value Streams stabilized. Waste elimination and process improvement stuttered at first as employees adjusted to the new structure but then noticeably accelerated.

A critical feature of the organization structure was the revenue generating Value Streams, predominantly "programs," and the relationship with the leadership and teams in the facilities through which their product passed during its manufacture.

Employees in those facilities who were working on a specific Value Streams hardware would report up to the revenue generating Value Stream leader. The facility general manager and his core team would function as landlords and providers of services shared with other revenue generating Value Streams. These services included paint booths, furnaces or autoclaves that could not be isolated and placed in each revenue generating Value Stream.

On a daily basis, the resident facility general manager would ensure the smooth running of operations in the facility, managing overall staffing assignments and overtime as required, while dealing with the issues of the moment, local politics, regulations, and requirements. Then coordinating these daily requirements and decisions as appropriate with the respective Value Stream leader.

"In Production Business" had four vice presidents at the Primary Value Stream level: one for Boeing programs, one for Airbus programs, one for the balance of customer programs and one for operations. Program Value Streams reported to the respective vice president and the facility general managers reported to the vice president of operations.

This was an interesting facet of the organization we launched and caused many furrowed brows, with visitors in particular, as to how this could work in practice. It worked and continues to work, extremely well.

A somewhat simple visual example of the program Value Stream and facility alignment:

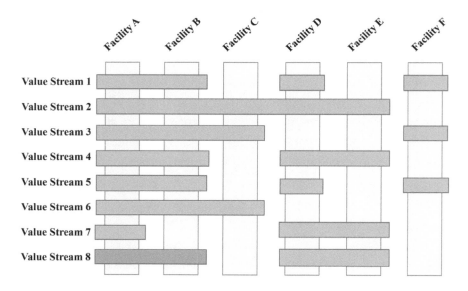

In this example:

- All program Value Streams had fabricated parts in Facility A.
- All program Value Streams had bonded panels from Facility B except program Value Stream 7.
- Program Value Steams 2, 3 and 6 had work in facility C.
- Facility D was where the assembly work was done for most of the program Value Streams.
- Facility E was the delivery center for the primary customer in the US.

- Facility F was the delivery center for the primary customer in Europe.
- Program Value Stream 6 shipped a component directly to a customer, the component did not pass through a delivery center.

The revenue generating Value Stream Leaders had full responsibility and accountability for the program, profit and loss.

The facility general managers provided services and local daily management. The two had to work together to ensure efficient and effective operations. The work environment that had been created and was being sustained went a long way to make this possible.

Metrics through this transition period of 2000:

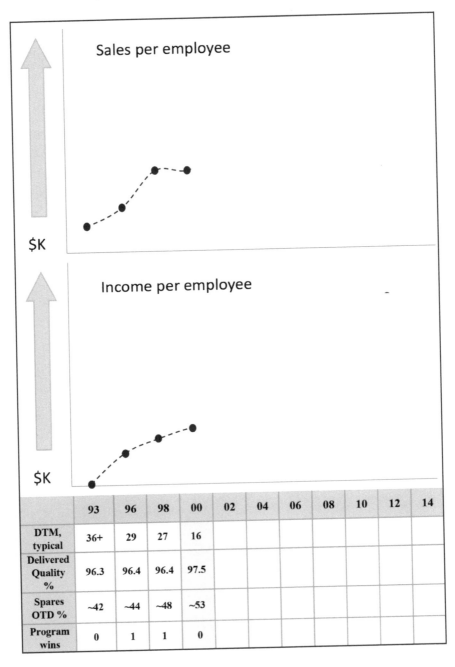

	93	96	98	00	02	04	06	08	10	12	14
DTM, typical	36+	29	27	16							
Delivered Quality %	96.3	96.4	96.4	97.5							
Spares OTD %	~42	~44	~48	~53							
Program wins	0	1	1	0							

Ongoing Continuous Improvement Activities

As outlined earlier in this chapter, continuous improvement on the shop floor had continued to identify and eliminate waste/non-value added activities through linkage and flow, 5S, point of use, right-sizing, visual controls, some total productive maintenance, and a number other Toyota System Tools. The focus of continuous improvement had moved to Standard Work, or what became known as "the triplets."

The triplets being Standard Work Combination Sheet, Standard Work Sheet and Percent Load chart.

Multiple books cover Standard Work in detail, suffice to say we were getting proficient at time observations, identifying waste/non-value added activities and developing Standard Work that reflected the Least Waste Way. We were diligent in driving to smaller and smaller work elements when doing time observations which in turn yielded more opportunity.

In every Standard Work event we identified labor hours that were being booked on a job, the time we observed when doing time observations, the time on the generated Standard Work and the time that represented Value Added only activity. It invariably revealed:

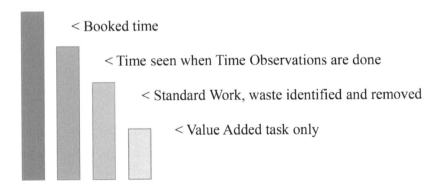

< Booked time

< Time seen when Time Observations are done

< Standard Work, waste identified and removed

< Value Added task only

The challenge, of course, was to identify all the waste/non-value added activities that we could and deploy countermeasures to get as close to "Value Added task only" as possible.

This activity became known as "closing the gap."

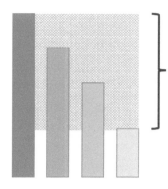

This is the gap, the difference between booked time and the Value Added only. Should a competitor choose or develop the ability to step into this gap and offer a lower price, subsequent work may be awarded to them.
Giving them the opportunity to drive OI and OM to their bottom lines.

A telling instance of this occurred in the mid-1990s. A product that Aerostructures manufactured was taking a six-figure loss on every one shipped and at the time, approximately eight a week were being shipped.

By 2000 a flurry of engineering change activity was taking place with multiple technical folks and engineers assigned to the program, to reduce cost through design changes. The team had been in place for some time contributing much in the way of cost but little in the way of return.

A competitor was interested in this work. Some discussions took place and thought was given to "selling" the product and relieving ourselves of a money-losing product. The new Value Stream leadership, all of whom were experienced with and fully bought into continuous improvement, saw the "waste within the program" and the opportunity it presented. They lobbied for the work to stay and aggressive continuous improvement be applied. The team was given the opportunity. All engineering change activity on the program, except that required from a safety or compliance aspect, was stopped and the technical folks and engineers assigned to other work that needed their skill sets.

Standard Work for production activities was developed, and multiple "close the gap" activities found a treasure trove of waste/ non-value added activity. The direct labor hours were reduced dramatically and within two years that product, which was still being shipped at approximately eight a week, was making a six-figure profit on every one shipped.

A massive swing, achieved by a hard focus on Standard Work, closing the gap. That product was still being manufactured as of 2018, and ongoing close the gap activities continue to reduce direct labor costs.

By 2003 the Enterprise Excellence Assessment was in its fourth revision. Requirements had been clarified and two added, they being:

1. **Strategy and Policy Deployment**
2. Organizational Deployment and Development
3. EH&S
4. Effective Communication
5. 5S
6. Visual Management and Controls
7. Layout, Linkage, Flow, and Right-Sizing
8. **Standard Work**
9. Multi-Skilling
10. Process Yield
11. Continuous Improvement Training and Education
12. Metrics and Results

In the again updated Enterprise Excellence Assessment, the bar continued to be raised, Strategy and its linkage to Policy Deployment as a process required much greater emphasis as did leadership engagement in the change process under the Strategy and Policy Deployment requirement. Communications requirements increased with a concise focus on continuous improvement, driver measure performance updates and "Change." Standard Work came to the fore with explicit requirements on the development and updates to Standard Work and "close the gap" activities.

Every effort was made to keep every update to the Enterprise Excellence Assessment as concise and straightforward to understand as possible while being explicit enough regarding requirements and progress to those requirements.

The Enterprise Excellence Assessment process, as previously outlined, was straightforward. Entering the year each organization, now Value Stream, would develop its baseline against the criteria for each column. A target for each column would be given that was closely aligned with the needs and opportunities of the Value Stream. The Office of Continuous Improvement established this target, supported by senior leadership, who had high confidence in that office to set meaningful targets. Over the course of the year, each organization followed the Enterprise Excellence Assessment as a guide and roadmap "doing those things" that led to the achievement of the target and to improved performance.

At the end of the year, the organization would self-assess their progress and have that validated by the Office of Continuous Improvement.

In the early years, organizations tended to be overly optimistic and rated themselves beyond actual achievement. After a couple of years of calibrations, organizations became competent at reporting factual progress and invariably aligned with the Office of Continuous Improvement in their assessments.

Enterprise Excellence Assessment requirements by design, drove the required culture and Enterprise Excellence Assessment progress was a component of "Gainsharing."

An activity of consequence

One other significant development in the early 2000s was as a result of the issues relating to the inadequacies of the multiple, often inadequately linked, software systems that had become unsupported or obsolete, as noted in Chapter 1.

A new ERP system had been identified in the late 1990s and funded entering the 2000s.

A massive, almost two-year data cleansing and system definition effort was undertaken to ensure that processes to be included in, and supported by an ERP system, were indeed structured in the Least Waste Way. This effort required significant functional and continuous improvement resource expertise to be engaged, particularly with the Support Value Streams, where many woefully inefficient processes were driven to the best Least Waste Way configuration possible given the timing and resource availability.

This was completed in late 2001. The new ERP system went live entering 2002.

Entering the 2000s, Standard Work was being applied across all programs, and all sites and the benefits were clear to see:

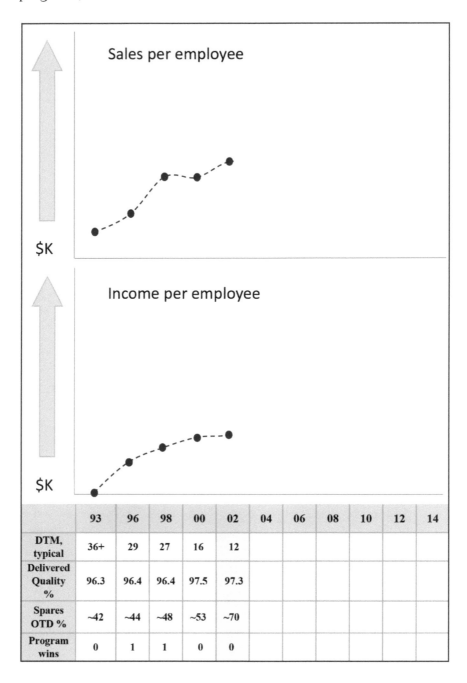

	93	96	98	00	02	04	06	08	10	12	14
DTM, typical	36+	29	27	16	12						
Delivered Quality %	96.3	96.4	96.4	97.5	97.3						
Spares OTD %	~42	~44	~48	~53	~70						
Program wins	0	1	1	0	0						

Days To Manufacture and Spares On Time Delivery were now showing outstanding progress.

The cost make up of programs by 2002 looked like the chart below. Direct labor costs continued to decrease, to now 10% and again this was done without any offload or onload of any manufacturing, it was still an "apples to apples" comparison:

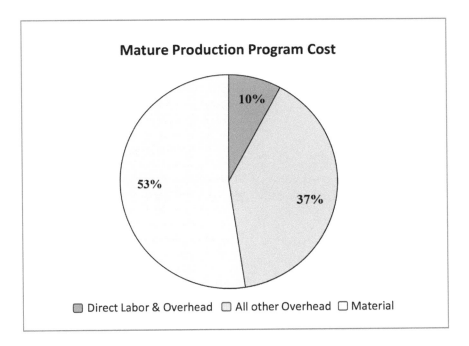

We had made significant progress in developing the culture we believed necessary, and the operating system and its processes were becoming "habit."

The Enterprise Excellence Assessment had become a tool and process that was valuable as a continuous improvement guide and metric.

Progress along the "Change Pyramid," now looked like this:

Aerostructures continued to receive recognition from a wide range of interested parties. Customers, suppliers, the Lean Enterprise Institute and the press. The number of visitors into Aerostructures to understand what was changing the business had reached around 1500 by 2002. The customer's perception of Aerostructures had changed dramatically. We were consistently delivering a quality product on schedule, we were attentive, responsive and performance improvement across the Aerostructures business could be clearly seen.

The cost reductions we had achieved enabled us to update some commercial agreements/contract extensions that benefitted and were well received by, the customers.

New product opportunities in the commercial aerospace marketplace were ramping up. Specifically at Boeing with the 787 and Airbus with the A350. Right behind them Pratt & Whitney were making progress with the Geared Turbo Fan engine destined for application across multiple aircraft platforms. Aerostructures, with the progress it was making with meaningful change, and it's now good reputation was positioned to benefit from these opportunities having garnered the favorable attention of existing and potential new customers.

What we learned on the way – a Summary

- The Linkage and Flow of data and information across the business functions were areas of great opportunity.
- The cost of linkage and flow is not just inventory or transportation. It's the inability to identify and resolve problems in real time and consequently the significant resources consumed when addressing the problem after the fact, across locations, languages and time zones.
- An effective positive people philosophy linked with an equally effective continuous improvement strategy can be catalysts for each other.
- Our organizational structure was an impediment to significant efficiency gains.
- Significant change to the organization structure was a complicated process that took time and effort to accomplish effectively.
- Realigning leadership and their priorities proved to be challenging.
- We needed to clearly and regularly communicate where we were going, how we were going to get there and progress being made.
- Toyota Production System Principles, Processes and Tools are easy to understand, it does not require specialized talent or training. It does require that understanding becomes commitment and habit through engagement.
  - The "Seven Types of Waste" are deceptively simple in theory. In practice finding waste is reasonably

straightforward. Eliminating it can be a little more challenging, but the savings are invariably huge.

- Applied, followed and maintained Standard Work can produce substantial cost reductions through waste/non-value added identification and elimination.
- Standard Work needs to be developed at a detailed level – small elements.
  - o Understanding that smaller and smaller elements in time observations yielded more and more waste
  - o Driving to Cycle Time equaling Takt Time delivers performance improvement.
- The actual hour gap presented a tremendous opportunity
- Some things within a process you may choose, for good reason, not to do. Understand all the consequences before making those decisions.
- Over 90% of all process changes were driven by utilizing basic Toyota Production System processes and tools in kaizen events and in daily activities.
- Moving continuous improvement into the office/support organizations required "a push" in some areas and was "pulled" in others.
- Continuous Improvement Principles, Processes and Tools, as reflected by our understanding of the Toyota Production System, apply to every business process. It is leadership's responsibility to thoroughly understand these Principles, Processes and Tools and engage in their deployment across a business, all functions
  - o We had to learn and understand how to apply these principles and tools across our entire business and all its functions
- As waste is removed from processes additional improvement opportunities, previously not visible, are exposed.
  - o We "didn't know what we didn't know" until we begin to peel back the layers of waste.

Things you may want to consider – a Summary

- Is our organizational structure contributing to or hindering waste removal, efficiency, increased performance, reduced cost and business return?
- How effective is our Strategic Plan process, development, and deployment?
- Are initiatives and measurable improvement targets linked to the Strategic Plan?
- Do we have a clear picture, literally a visual representation, of our support process flows?
- What is our cost makeup – direct, indirect, overhead, material?
  - Where are the opportunities for cost improvement?
- Are we satisfied with our continuous improvement process, deployment, and resultant performance improvement?
  - Do we have a tool to guide and measure continuous improvement progress?
  - Can we measure performance improvement in all areas of our business?
- Do we drive continuous improvement across all our organizations/functions?
  - Is everyone motivated, encouraged and rewarded appropriately?
- Do we understand how much labor is charged against each "work order/shop order?"
- What is our understanding of Standard Work?
- Do we have Standard Work in the Toyota sense?
  - Is it detailed with average element sizes of around 15 seconds, derived from time observations, or is it "shop floor planning" with steps described at a high level and times estimated?
- Is Standard Work in place and followed?
- Do we understand our performance opportunities – the gap?

Chapter 5

C *hange and continuous improvement in Engineering. The need to reduce non-recurring engineering and recurring production costs. The early adoption of fundamental continuous improvement processes and tools in engineering, evolving to an environment where visual controls, engineering standards, and Standard Work were deployed and became the norm. Changes in the product and process definition process that went through some distinct phases enabled by a steady influx of new programs. A transition of thought and behaviors, and of the actual product and process definition process itself.*

Integrating Engineering, Research and Development

To place the changes driven within engineering and product development in context, it is appropriate to spend some time describing and defining the somewhat complex high-value nacelle product designed and manufactured by Aerostructures.

Aircraft engine nacelles provide critical functions in support of the engine and aircraft to ensure safe, efficient operation within strict safety and performance boundaries including:

- Airflow management and drag reduction, both contributing to fuel efficiency.
- Reverse thrust aircraft stopping power
- Acoustic systems to reduce engine noise
- Protection of engine and aircraft systems
- Load sharing to reduce engine weight

In development and manufacture they utilize:

- Advanced design and analysis techniques
- Advanced lightweight complex composite and metallic material systems

Below is a photo of an installed nacelle with the inlet cowl attached in front of and around the fan blades, the fan cowls and thrust reverser sections behind the inlet, both open for inspection/ maintenance.

Aircraft and their nacelles have a useful lifespan of over 25 years and are produced under strict Federal Aviation Authority guidelines and required certifications.

Historical Perspective-Setting the Stage

As noted in the previous chapters, moving continuous improvement into the office environment had early successes in areas such as Finance - Least Waste Way processes for month and quarter end reports, Aftermarket Spares - linkage and flow of operations visuals and metrics and Supply Chain - visuals and metrics, Human Resources – the hiring and onboarding process.

Significant continuous improvement progress in product development/engineering was a different story given the lack of any significant new nacelle program opportunities and a somewhat hesitant embrace of the Toyota Production System processes and tools in the engineering environment.

Through the 1990s the engineering/technical organization and its support of operations was quite traditional, manufacturing engineering and quality personnel were assigned to the operations teams, but most were not collocated within the manufacturing cells themselves.

As most programs were in production and mature and had been so for many years, technical product engineering personnel and their activities were accomplished by small engineering teams reporting directly to the program, but again, not collocated with the program. Small central Engineering, Quality and Research and Development organizations to ensure design integrity, specialty analysis, customer protocols, certification, compliance, and configuration control, were based in Chula Vista. Riverside also maintained a relatively large Materials and Processes organization required to manage complex non-metallic material processing across multiple programs.

Drivers for Change:

With a developing culture and increased success across the business, the life cycles of mature programs became strategic concerns as these programs were advanced in years and would eventually come to the end of production and move into an aftermarket phase.

Customers were proposing new aircraft with potentially new nacelle designs, and the decision had been made to win and invest in this new business. Not a decision made lightly, as development, design, manufacture, test and certification cycles for each new nacelle generally extends over a four to five year period. The extensive non-recurring costs incurred and expended over this time frame include substantial investments in engineering personnel, tooling, capital equipment and program resources.

Product and process development "sets the stage" and determines program manufacturing methods and strongly influences resource requirements for the next 20 - 30 years. A big decision had been made as outlined in Chapter 4. Investment and business growth was the strategy.

Rohr had not won a major program since the early 1980s, the V2500 Nacelle for the A320 program. This program was typical of earlier development efforts within Rohr, and although the end-product was technically very sound and structurally robust, non-recurring and recurring cost overruns were extensive resulting in losses of around $120 million taken in the late 1980s. Significant additional losses were taken in later years.

In the late 1990s, with reflection on the continuous improvement activities in operations and office environments, we recognized some parallels. They were that new product development activities, as few as there had been, were accomplished within a "functional type organization" analogous to "operations monuments" resulting in impaired linkage and flow of data and information, unaligned processes, and conflicting priorities. Potentially there was significant opportunity to transition the existing functional engineering and product development methods and approaches to aligned product development Value Streams, learning from the successes of other areas of the business. This opportunity is captured in the next illustration showing total non-recurring and "recurring non-recurring" engineering costs and ongoing production costs:

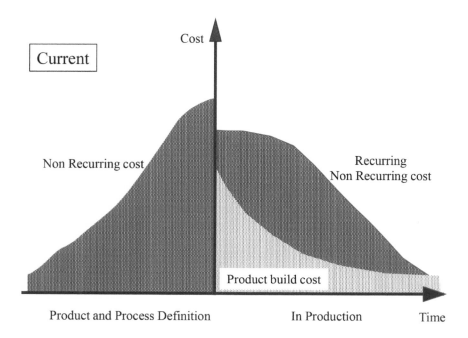

Initial, and often excessive non-recurring cost with a nacelle, is generally a consequence of "engineering development and iteration" of the plane, its systems, the pylon, the engine and the nacelle itself.

This progresses as data becomes available relative to how all systems perform, and interfaces align, to assure the performance of the whole. The challenge is to spend time and resources, expend cost, when interface data and engineering changes are known to have stabilized, be stabilizing, or to be least required or expected. Invariably a constant product development challenge across diverse companies attempting to integrate and interface complicated engineered products and systems.

Recuring non-recurring cost is a result of the ineffective management of the iterations of the initial non-recurring phase and the clean up activity required as a result of those iterations.

It can be extremely costly if every single element of input is reacted to and accommodated upon receipt. This can be minimized if incoming requests, information, and data are managed within the scope of the contract and by using an efficient and effective "Lean Product Development" process.

We recognized that:

- We had great engineers.
- We needed highly effective engineering processes to enable them to succeed and compete.
- We had an opportunity to accelerate the application of continuous improvement tools into the product and process definition processes and infrastructure.
- We also recognized that unlike operations, where continuous improvement was common practice, engineering did not have the same focus. No amount of operational improvement can overcome the inherent waste locked into a poor part design.

We undoubtedly needed to overhaul the entire product and process definition process itself.

It was critical to have a competitive edge for the current and the future. This would require a significant cultural adjustment in the Engineering and Research and Development departments. An adjustment that would result in new hardware development costs being reduced significantly from previous years to one where overall non-recurring and ongoing production costs are substantially lower.

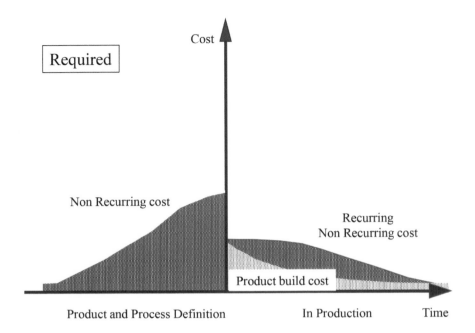

A new product and process definition process would ensure that the product was engineered and designed in the Least Waste Way, that Standard Work for production would be in place when production started, resulting in Least Waste Way cycle times and manufacturing costs. Leaving the product, its design and specifications, well positioned for recurring cost improvement over the next 20 plus years of program life.

This would require:

- The application of Toyota Production System principles integrated into a new Lean Product Development process.
- Prudent common material and process selection.
- Common engineering standards and methods.
- Careful management of new technologies.
  o   Incremental, distinctive and breakthrough categories
- Well defined common hardware definitions, standards and preferences. (hardware, latches, fasteners, etc.)

- Consideration for cost-effective manufacturing and special processes, such as chemical, thermal, and specialty coatings.
- Input from experienced shop floor employees to ensure, via their decades of experience, that least waste way manufacturing and assembly processes, methods and techniques are utilized.

As indicated in earlier chapters and on the "Three Track Chart," we learned that care must be taken to first establish and nourish a positive culture with appropriate continuous improvement and organizational strategies and tactics.

What follows is the record of the transition of Engineering and Research and Development departments into the new culture and the development of new tools and techniques to support business goals.

Well into the 1990s the Rohr Engineering and Research and Development cultures could be described as "somewhat isolationist" and remote from operations and not always receptive to input or change:

- Helping only when requested.
- Outlining technical barriers to suggested process changes and revisions.
- Providing indifferent support for the Three Circles
  o Input and support for continuous improvement in operations was not evident.

As the business recovered, credibility with key customers through well-sustained quality, cost and delivery performance, the real possibility of new business emerged. With strong Goodrich support, investment was made to pursue new program opportunities.

With the award of two relatively small in scope and volume programs, in the late 1990s, engineering was pulled into developing a Lean Product Development process and utilizing a modified Toyota Production System. This subsequently required Research and Development to integrate with engineering on the development of a new materials system.

The cultural journey and steps we took to this ultimately unique yet effective organizational structure, are outlined in the following sections.

Continuous Improvement Strategy and the Lean Product Development process

We consciously outlined and then detailed new engineering processes based upon Toyota Production System principles. It was essential to build upon lessons learned within operations, and continuous improvement learned there combined with engineering practices matured over the years.

Consequently, a selected progressive leadership team integrated Lean Principles and established engineering principles, germane to the existing product and process definition process, into the framework for a Lean Product Development process.

Much of this new process framework and supporting information came from our consultant and selections from numerous books and papers on product development within Toyota. Some of these reference sources are noted in the Appendix.

Once again, learning, developing and applying on projects as we went proved to be invaluable and we were fortunate that the process went through several iterations where we gained understanding, experience, traction and process maturity.

The next chart summarizes the framework noted above, outlining first the intent of the new Lean Product Development process followed by deployed actions to achieve that intent.

Lean Product
Development   *Actions to achieve*
Intent

Lean Product Development Intent	Actions to achieve
Toyota Production System Deployment	**Positive Pro-active Culture** • Extensive communication, training and engagement in Operations Three Circle activities to drive behaviors and culture
Linkage and Flow of activities	**Broad Cross Functional Participation in product and process development** • Organization structure and collocation to drive engagement and participation
Management via Visual Controls	**Chief Engineer Organization** • Positioning of overarching technical governance, through the Value Stream structure
Standard Work and Standard Processes	**Traning and Development** • In Continuous Improvement, technical skills and subsequently Lean Product Development
Common materials and processes	**Voice of the Customer process** • Development of a process to understand customers needs beyond specifications and other documents
Reduced Days To Process	**Uniform and balanced Product Development Process Flow** • Development and maturation of specific, visual, Lean Product Development processes
Reduced design iterations	**Apply Rigorous Standardization** • Development of part and process Standards and of an Engineering Standard Operating Manual
Non-recurring cost reduction	**Engineering & Operations Least Waste Way processes** • Development of effective Lean Product Development, Design For Manufacturing and Assembly and 3P Processes
Production Direct Labor cost reduction	
Least Waste Way @Unit #1	

As experienced in the past within operations, leadership engagement at the outset was mixed, "that's the way we do it" was heard more frequently than had been heard in operations.

Over time new leaders emerged and fully engaged in the new way of doing business while others either retired, removed themselves or were assigned to other areas.

Again, constancy of purpose was vital, as new processes were introduced, became recognized as the new standards and produced superior results.

First Generation Lean Product Development

The somewhat basic and preliminary framework of the new Lean Product Development process was first deployed on the nacelle and pylon for the C5 Galaxy, a military aircraft.

Aerostructures had the contract to redesign, manufacture and replace both of these components on this aircraft.

The nacelle to be used was a commercial nacelle already being produced and had minimal engineering activities to test out any new engineering development ideas or concepts.

The pylons were an entirely new design but were nearing design completion. We were, however, able to deploy and test several of the new Lean Product Development processes and tools as the program transitioned into production.

The linkage and flow of information and data feedback from operations to engineering improved and subsequent engineering changes were effectively implemented. Assembly Flow II events and the development of Standard Work in operations ensured pylon assembly costs met the required goals. Lessons learned regarding the standardization of engineering analysis methods were captured, reviewed, and integrated as appropriate into further updates of the Lean Product Development process.

The C5 pylon also provided an opportunity for a whole new cadre of employees, engineers, in particular, to go to the manufacturing workplace, do time observations and develop Standard Work, for the assembly of the product, on a new program from the ground up.

A first-time occurrence and eye-opening experience for many engineers and technical employees.

Although the bulk of engineering activity had completed, ample opportunities were observed that reinforced the belief that a new way of designing, certifying and tooling a new program was needed and could be accomplished. This indicated to those engaged in changes to current practices and processes that things, in engineering, were going to be different moving forward.

Even with the limited use of Lean Product Development processes and tools on the C5, it was clear that some old school, "this is not the way we do things" and resistance to change was to be encountered as we moved forward.

The changes to the culture and behaviors in engineering were going to be as challenging as the changes to the product and process definition process itself.

Much reflection and discussion followed the Lean Product Development activities on the C5.

It had been both designed and introduced into production in a traditional manner. Given it was the first significant new program in many years, this may have been predictable.

What was clear was that issues, problems, and opportunities in engineering abounded and that even with limited deployment of an immature Lean Product Development process, we had much confidence that this offered a promising way forward.

What we had identified were specific processes and tools to manage the Lean Product Development process, the next visual are those processes and tools in the sequence of their deployment:

Lean Product Development
Product and Process Definition

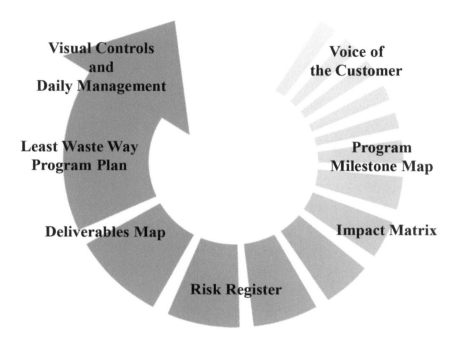

- Voice of the Customer (VOC)
  - A structured process requiring customer engagement, non-leading questions and active listening
    - Exposes Customer "intents, wants and needs," beyond those stated in contracts and specifications.
    - Helps drive mutual understanding
    - Builds relationships
- Program Milestone Map (PMM)
  - High-level plan defining program requirements and sequence:
    - Configuration Development, Detail Design and Optimization, Preliminary Designs Reviews, Customer Design Reviews, Build and Test, Certification, Production and Aftermarket.

- Impact Matrix (IM)
  - Follows VOC/PMM input
  - Identifies program Facts, Assumptions, Issues and Requirements (FAIRS)
  - Establishes program success criteria
  - Drives impact assessments and priorities
  - Helps identify countermeasures and planning for implementation
- Risk Register (RR)
  - A risk assessment tool
    - Mitigation Planning
    - Contingency Planning
  - Problem-solving reports
  - Continuous review and updates
- Deliverables Map (DM)
  - Follows VOC/PMM/IM Input
  - Defines detailed program deliverables
  - Timeframe
    - Milestones identified
  - Establishes process flow and linkages
    - Dependences identified
  - Defines critical path
- Least Waste Way Program Plan (LWWPP)
  - Turns deliverables into defined tasks and activities
  - Right to left mapping to understand dependencies and aggregate cycle time float
    - Cycle Times are included without waste
  - Enables resource planning
    - Percent Loading
  - Contingency management
- Visual Controls and Daily Management
  - Wall Walks of the PMM, IM, FAIRS, RR, DM and LWWPP
  - Progress reporting
  - Balanced metrics

- o Real Time Problem Resolution
- o Bias for action

It was also clear that the transition of a new product into actual production required the inclusion and use of some additional processes and tools within the Lean Product Development process.

Second Generation Lean Product Development

The first full use and significant development of the Lean Product Development processes and tools came when the CF34 nacelle - inlet, fan cowls, exhaust and engine build-up contract was awarded to Aerostructures. The thrust reverser and tailcone were awarded to other suppliers. This engine/nacelle is primarily used on a number of Bombardier and Embraer airplanes.

Concurrent with this award, Aerostructures was completing the process that resulted in the Value Stream structure. This structure and the realignment of responsibilities and employees dovetailed into the deployment of continuous improvement into the product development process.

The desire for participation on the new CF34 program/Value Stream was high, and we had the opportunity to select motivated and engaged employees to increase chances of success within the new Lean Product Development processes.

The leader selected for the CF34 program was someone who had previously engaged in change and the deployment of continuous improvement processes and tools across a wide range of functions in Aerostructures with much success. The team was made up of some other individuals in leadership roles who had also been actively engaged in change and continuous improvement in operations and then a full complement of design and stress engineers.

Being a new program also provided the opportunity to hire some new engineering talent, integrating them directly into the new process. The bulk of the new hires were recent college graduates or individuals relatively new to aerospace engineering. They had little traditional "aerospace engineering baggage" and proved to be more amenable to the new processes being introduced. The entire team was also collocated.

With expectations set, leadership leading by example, use and development of the Lean Product Development tools advanced significantly. This was well supported by Policy Deployment reviews to monitor progress and additional specifically detailed "new program" engineering reviews.

The lessons learned and the processes and tools identified in the first generation deployment of Lean Product Development, on the C5, were used, confirmed and built upon.

The CF34 part family was subsequently designed, tooled, certified and phased into production using the new Lean Product Development processes. These processes and tools were explicitly for the management of the design process itself.

The need for an additional set of processes and tools, identified previously for the transition of a new product into production, was also confirmed with the tools subsequently introduced as part of the process.

Some of these processes and tools for the transition into production were not original, but many were new to Aerostructures, and almost all had to be modified and developed for our use.

Lean Product Development
Production Transition

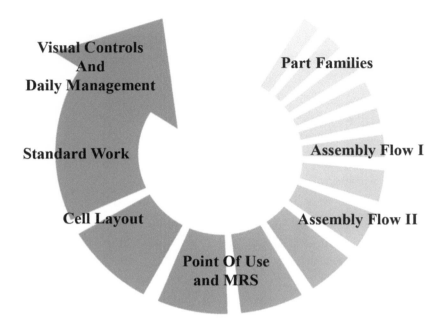

- Part Families
  - o Identification of like parts and process steps to minimize variation in:
    - ▪ Manufacturing processes
    - ▪ Materials
  - o Placement of work options both internally and externally
  - o Supplier negotiation leverage
- Assembly Flow I
  - o Primary fishbone product flow, sub-assemblies into final assembly
  - o Broad process steps
    - ▪ Identification of equipment and major tools used
    - ▪ Enables the identification of some issues, problems, and opportunities before production starts

- Assembly Flow II
  - Detailed fishbone product flow of each sub-assembly and final
  - Identifying for each process step:
    - Hand tooling
    - Chemicals, solvents, and adhesives
    - Consumables
    - Shop aids
    - EH&S issues
  - All of which are inputs to cell layout and Standard Work, Least Waste Way
- Point of Use and Material Replenishment Systems
  - Ensuring that everything is within easy reach from the work location, with minimal movement required to access needed items
  - EH&S considerations
  - Materials Replenishment System, a system that identifies and replenishes the stocks of parts and items used in production without interrupting production activities
  - All inputs to cell layout and Standard Work, Least Waste Way
- Cell Layout
  - Configured to minimize the seven kinds of waste
  - Right-sized for production activities
  - Accommodates all required tooling and consumables
  - Right-sized for incoming materials
  - Initial SWIP calculations
  - Strong EH&S focus
- Standard Work
  - Definition and documentation of the Least Waste Way
  - A basis for further cost reductions – close the gap activity
  - Identification of staffing needs - percent load
  - Identification of safety and quality requirements
  - A training aid

- Visual Controls and Daily Management
  - Work area walks
  - Progress Reporting
  - Balanced Metrics
  - Real Time Problem Resolution
  - Bias for Action

The Lean Product Development toolbox was expanding.

Once into production, feedback from the production employees on the shop floor was "that the CF34 went together, noticeably much better than anything else we have seen before," with significantly fewer Quality issues. Formal Quality data and reports supported this claim.

The actual direct labor hours booked to the program components as production ramped up were also significantly lower than any "learning curve" calculation would suggest.

With the CF34 success, Goodrich took an active interest in the Aerostructures Lean Product Development process, and it was renamed the Goodrich Lean Product Development process and became a central component of Goodrich marketing campaigns competing for multiple contracts on the new Boeing 787 aircraft. Goodrich began to develop and deploy this Lean Product Development process in earnest across the company with focal points assigned from Aerostructures to ensure continuity.

Of interest to Aerostructures were the General Electric and Rolls Royce engine versions for the 787 aircraft, both of which needed new nacelles. One aircraft but potentially two new nacelle programs.

Aerostructures capabilities, much-improved relationships with Boeing and competitive commercial contract terms, resulted in the contracts for both engine nacelles being awarded in 2004.

Third Generation Lean Product Development

The 787 provided the third opportunity for further Lean Product Development.

Responsibility for the 787 was given to two leaders. One of whom was the leader of the 717 program who had had his continuous improvement epiphany in Foley earlier and had become a staunch advocate of Lean Product Development and its continued use and development.

The other was the former leader of the CF34 program who was ready to build on the second generation Lean Product Development processes and tools.

Given the cost challenges on the 787 program, application of the Lean Product Development processes and tools was going to be necessary to achieve non-recurring and recurring costs.

A number of both leader's staff had many years of experience with continuous improvement in operations. This worked to our advantage, creating a strong culture supporting change.

With change, culture and continuous improvement in mind, the Lean Product Development process had evolved over two distinct phases in engineering. These phases had engaged many employees from various engineering disciplines over the years but not all of them.

When staffing the 787, emphasis was placed on recruiting engineers who had the benefit of being on the C5 and the CF34. In addition, some highly technical employees, who had limited new product and process development experience were also added. Like the CF34, both of the 787 nacelle teams were collocated and reported to the Value Stream leadership.

Very early in the 787's development a number of the employees, without the C5 or CF34 experience, faced with changes to behaviors and processes, chose to seek other opportunities.

A number of them had skill sets and expertise that were not easy to replace, but we were going to continue to develop and use the Lean Product Development process, to enable achievement of both product performance and cost requirements on the 787 program. This required everyone involved in that quest to be fully committed and engaged.

This new aircraft required new and state of the art non-metallic material systems, methods of analysis and innovative designs to reduce weight, increase aircraft efficiency and reduce noise levels.

The then in place composite material systems at Aerostructures were somewhat dated and only marginally capable of meeting new requirements. A new materials system was to be developed and certified.

New material Testing and Certification

The 787 aircraft itself required significant weight reduction to enable required aircraft fuel efficiencies and this, in turn, would drive the use of lighter composite materials across a number of structural components of the aircraft, including nacelle components.

To address this issue, the decision was made to:

- Leverage a single standardized new advanced composite material system across all new programs
- Develop common material testing, design allowables (engineering limits) and design and analysis techniques to be leveraged across multiple new programs

This had the potential to reduce both material costs and the cost of complying with potentially multiple diverse customer requirements.

The concept of a single new material system to support multiple customers and new programs was revolutionary for the business.

This idea was generated within the Airworthiness Organization and is a solid illustration of the strength of the new positive culture and engaged employees.

Leaders of the Research and Development and Airworthiness organizations then assumed responsibilities for new material testing and certification with the FAA, using an existing Supplemental Type Certificate.

This massive effort required around forty thousand material test coupon samples. Testing and analysis was carried out in concurrence with the design and analysis of the 787 and subsequently the A350 nacelles.

Drawing from operations experience the Research and Development value stream set up dedicated material development and testing teams to manage the production of the test coupon samples to the required rates.

- Testing and certification teams were established and collocated in Riverside.
- Meaningful driver measures were developed and put in place.
- Standardized development and testing processes were developed.
- Takt times, cycle times, Standard Work and SWIP, with percent loading of staffing requirements, were identified and developed.
- The linkage and flow of design and analysis processes were defined and improved through robust countermeasures.
- Visual controls were established to show daily progress
- 5S was deployed in the work area and to the associated electronic data files.
- Continuous improvement training was provided.
- Real Time Problem Resolution was implemented.

Since their inception, the Research and Development Value Stream had been included in the weekly Policy Deployment business reviews with uniform scorecards and metrics, so this effort and progress towards it was visible via appropriate metrics in their Policy Deployment package.

Success was achieved with the FAA qualification of the new materials system, all driven by a well-organized, lean tool driven approach.

Both 787 nacelles and the incorporated new composite material system were fully developed using the Lean Product Development process.

The new Lean Product Development process had matured to the point where it was working very well.

At the date of writing the 787 nacelles are approaching two million hours of in-flight service performing well within specifications.

Other Lean Product Development Opportunities

As often happens, a new aircraft launch from one airframer is usually countered by a new "like" launch aircraft from the other airframer. In this instance Airbus, who offered a new A350 aircraft also requiring innovative materials and designs.

Unlike the 787, the A350 had only a single engine option, the Rolls Royce Trent XWB, and consequently, only one nacelle variant.

Airbus had their own variation of a "Voice of the Customer" process that was known as the "Plateau phase" where potential suppliers worked with Airbus to identify, define and evaluate requirements, options and supplier capabilities. In addition to demonstrating the ability to meet technical and performance criteria for the nacelle.

This necessitated months of on-site at Airbus representation by Aerostructures personnel.

Airbus knew full well that a Lean Product Development process was being used on their competitor's 787 nacelles currently in product and process definition at Aerostructures. The progress being made with Lean Product Development was a factor that weighed in Aerostructures favor, and in 2006 the A350 nacelle, less the inlet, was awarded.

The company had gone from no new programs of any substance to two planes requiring three nacelles, with the opportunity to bid and win other future aircraft replacement programs.

We now had the opportunity to again, further develop and mature the Lean Product Development processes and tools.

A lesson learned from the 787 program. It was advertised that it would be staffed by a rigorous selection process that engaged only the "best of the best engineering and operations personnel." Not a good move, as this implied that those not selected for that program were "second best" which caused a level of division over time as the A350 and other programs were awarded and staffed.

A case could be made that the 787 did in fact have many of the "best of the best" individuals, who on occasion struggled to work together as a team.

Alternatively, a case could also be made that the A350 had individuals who demonstrated teamwork beyond that seen on the 787.

The objective, of course, was to place qualified, skilled and engaged individuals on all new programs utilizing the new engineering processes. To support this, some movement of resources, across new programs, was made as the needs and opportunities of different programs became clear and skill sets became available.

While meaningful 787 program design and Lean Product Development progress had been made, the A350 had considerably increased the workload on engineering.

Moreover, given the years of minimal product development activity, the resultant downsizing of engineering had resulted in minimum staffing in key nacelle design and analysis specialties, in some cases down to the last one or two people who had in-depth knowledge and experience within several complex technical disciplines.

This shortage of engineering talent, combined with the demands of multiple large development programs, put the Lean Product Development process under stress.

As further new nacelle programs were won in the late 2000s, requirements and competition for aerospace engineers, with often scarce highly technical disciplines, became common. This was an Aerospace industry-wide issue, given the number of new aircraft and engines in development.

From an Aerostructures perspective, this applied stress and pressure not only on the overall workload but also on the development of the Lean Product Development process. In reality, a considerable portion of the large commercial aerospace industry's new nacelle design workload was being managed by Aerostructures.

Regardless, the third generation of Lean Product Development continued and was completed and documented. Previously developed training modules were updated and additional training undertaken.

All driven from humble beginnings in Riverside and the relentless leadership application of a the Positive Employee Philosophy and culture change.

As company ownership changed to Goodrich in 1997 and then to United Technologies Corporation in 2012, both companies provided much needed financial stability and support for the continued development of the Lean Product Development process and the significant changes in Engineering and Research and Development to support their managed evolution.

Building on the three-plus phases of Lean Product Development application and learning

While the use of the Lean Product Development process was now extensive, customer demands, such as those for total nacelle weight, cost, and certification metrics were a recurring challenge.

With the Lean Product Development process there had been progress made towards uniform engineering standards and methods. However, challenges remained.

Component design options, fundamental technical decisions regarding the use of composites versus metallic materials and the methods of analysis all began to noticeably diverge across different program teams. These were becoming driven by personal experience and preference rather than the uniform application of data and methods.

The certification workload was tremendous for each new program. In addition, bond panel manufacturing methods, utilizing traditional manual layup or multimillion dollar automatic machines, were in discussions and dispute.

With minimal exception, "engineers are highly educated and love to engineer." Unless effective guidelines and standards are in place, every new program presents an opportunity to "start again" and re-engineer product designs and introduce new manufacturing methods.

Even though there were, and are, more than sufficient and appropriate "products, engineering callouts, designs and manufacturing methods and data," available that meet many requirements.

The maturation of the Lean Product Development process had been across multiple programs. The process and the Value Stream organizational structure had become the standard.

What was also in place to support the organizational structure was a small, but not insignificant, central Engineering and Quality organization that included:

- Chief Engineers Office
- Central Engineering governance group
- Specialty Analysis - Acoustic, thermal, dynamics
- Quality and Technical Compliance
- Research and Development

As noted earlier, during the late 2000s significant additional new or derivative programs were awarded. These new programs, now eleven in total, had projected total development costs of several billion dollars.

The need for uniform engineering standards and methods, and the total development costs being faced drove a modified Lean Product Development structure, leadership, and organizational approach.

That was the next evolutionary but necessary step relating to the Lean Product Development process.

Component Value Streams

The then president of Aerostructures, Marc Duvall, had made the same observations and provided strong support and leadership in the development of what would become a centrally controlled Component Value Stream organization structure.

In this structure, co-located Component Value Stream teams were charged with resources and responsibilities for completing the development of each new program in partnership with other programs utilizing standard design, analysis and certification principles, and process Standard Work. All with the required personnel and training to be successful.

The key to success in the Component Value Stream structure was that it enabled a uniform, standardized focus on *specific nacelle components* across all programs. Rather than a program focus across all nacelle components.

This allowed component engineering teams to gain high levels of expertise and productivity in each of the various component team disciplines enabled by intensive continuous improvement and technical training.

Over a period of seven months, cross-functional teams developed a formal *component-centric*, integrated "Engineering and Lean Product Development process." Including redefined engineering principles, part, process and analysis standardization and effective process application methods within a coordinated framework.

This carefully managed process was driven with broad participation and support from senior leadership, outlined in the following process:

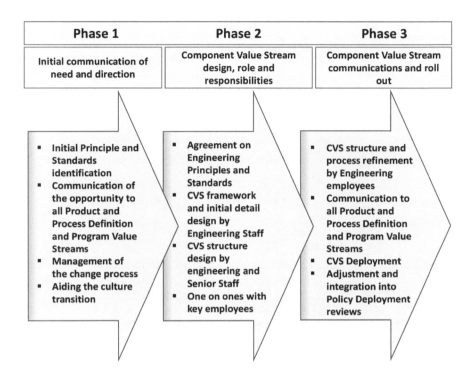

Phase 1	Phase 2	Phase 3
Initial communication of need and direction	Component Value Stream design, role and responsibilities	Component Value Stream communications and roll out

Phase 1
- Initial Principle and Standards identification
- Communication of the opportunity to all Product and Process Definition and Program Value Streams
- Management of the change process
- Aiding the culture transition

Phase 2
- Agreement on Engineering Principles and Standards
- CVS framework and initial detail design by Engineering Staff
- CVS structure design by engineering and Senior Staff
- One on ones with key employees

Phase 3
- CVS structure and process refinement by Engineering employees
- Communication to all Product and Process Definition and Program Value Streams
- CVS Deployment
- Adjustment and integration into Policy Deployment reviews

This revised product development framework, Component Value Streams, launched in 2010, required significant changes in leadership and organization and it is a credit to the now mature culture that these significant changes were implemented smoothly in structured and measured fashion utilizing the steps outlined.

The basic structure of the Component Value Streams is shown on the following diagram:

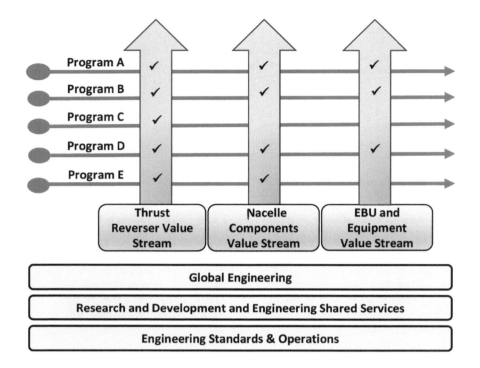

Nacelle Components above, being Inlets and Fan Cowls.

Engineering Principles and Strategies

In the new organization, the goal was to drive and further mature the Lean Product Development process, through constancy of purpose, emphasizing standardization and balanced engineering and program Value Stream continuous improvement activities. This was developed as part of the now standard strategic planning process and benefited from excellent input from engineering leadership who were heavily engaged in engineering's transformation.

Elements of the strategy were:

- Engineering principles and application
- Program management
- Managed technology applications

- Technical compliance
- Quality compliance
- Least Waste Way cost, for non-recurring engineering and recurring production

We differentiated between Lean Product Design and Lean Product Development as follows:

- Lean Product Design - the design, analysis and development standards.
- Lean Product Development - the process by which the product design, analysis and development is accomplished.

There are generally multiple ways to approach manufacturing and engineering problems. However, with each, it is important that once viable standard methods and processes, often referred to as Standard Work, have been established that they are followed closely. As more is learned through use, these standards are modified accordingly.

Engineering principles are foundational to engineering Standard Work and provide the firm foundation that processes can be built upon.

Key to this approach was a standardized design and analysis re-use strategy leveraged across multiple programs using:

- Single Source of Data
  - Common design and analysis tools
- Common Material Systems
  - Metallic and non-metallic
- "Draw Thin"
  - Easier to add weight back than to take weight out
- Design for the normal; accommodate the abnormal
  - Adding weight and complexity for potentially rare, if ever, failure events should be challenged
  - Drive to understand how the structure can be modified to withstand events likely to happen only once in a lifetime

- Common hardware selections
  o Uniform standards for fasteners
- Data and component design re-use
- Standard analysis methods
  o Consistency with defined methods
- Standardized bonding, testing, and chemical processes
- Uniform drafting practice and part numbering system

All while maintaining a line of sight on product and process improvements within the engineering process and the production processes called the Least Waste Way as we know it today. Over time this approach evolved and was documented in an Engineering Standard Operating Manual (ESOM)

Expansion into Global Engineering

As the aerospace business both expanded and ramped up, the availability of experienced nacelle engineers within California and across the US, as noted, had become quite limited.

Established overseas Research and Development activities at Goodrich locations had been successful, and following an Aerostructures strategic directive, Global Engineering design and analysis centers were established at company facilities in Bangalore India, Singapore, and Mexicali Mexico, under the following parameters:

- All employees were full time, not contract.
- Training the new employees in the Three Circles, Lean Product Development processes and tools and standard engineering processes and systems was mandatory.

The intent and value of this model was to ensure close linkage and alignment across locations regarding business strategy, the engineering organization function and its use of the lean tools and processes for product development and process improvement.

The company emphasized the uniform application of the Three Circles and common metrics throughout the business. It is interesting to note that these global teams, from diverse backgrounds, successfully implemented and thrived within a Three Circle culture. The Global nature of extended linkage, flow and co-location limitations were minimized via virtual (electronic) co-location systems and in-country work schedules that fostered round the clock activities leveraging time zone differences.

Following significant and extensive technical training, these global engineering professionals would prove to be vital to the success of the business.

This new organization was designed and implemented across a 12 month period with team members from multiple engineering disciplines and levels being led out of Singapore with strong organizational support from Chula Vista.

Component and Program Value Streams, Global and Central Engineering

As Engineering Principles and Strategies were being developed the Component and Program Value Streams along with global and central engineering functions were in their "final" evolutionary structure.

The following visual attempts to show how product development activities on a program, are supported by the Engineering/Component Value Stream organizational structure to produce a compliant product, meeting customer performance, weight, schedule, and quality requirements. Moreover, ensuring the entire multiyear, multi-million dollar project comes in at or beats, the contracted cost.

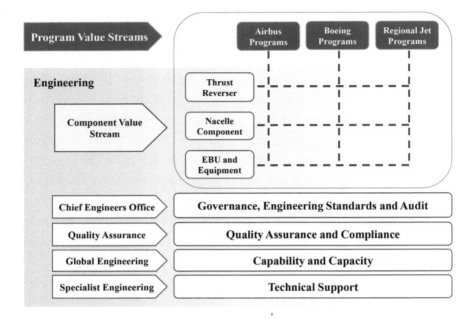

The new Component Value Stream structure had engineering employees assigned by component and by program, collocated with the program leadership and staff. This also required supporting organizations to be appropriately placed, staffed and engaged to ensure functional governance, compliance with all requirements and new process adherence. The structure shown fostered coordinated and leveraged design of components, strong technical input and validation, quality assurance, and disciplined process reuse.

At the same time, progressive career development was enabled as it allowed clearly defined design and analysis and leadership progression steps.

Defined roles and responsibilities were updated or developed for Component and Program Value Streams.

Both are outlined here:

Program Value Streams	• Overall program management • Customer commercial interface • Program finances • Change management • Program integration • Program scheduling • Transition to production
Component Value Streams	• Specific component design expertise • Engineering execution • Customer specification requirements interface • Employee development • Engineering continuous improvement
Chief Engineers Office	• Functional governance • Specific component design expertise • Engineering execution • Meeting customer specification requirements
Quality Assurance	• Engineering quality standard compliance • Product and process compliance • Government authority compliance
Global Engineering	• Specific engineering task capability and capacity • Flexibility
Specialist Engineering	• As required specialist / technical support

Research and Development remained integral to the Lean Product Development process and to the Component Value Stream structure and process. It also remained a separate Value Stream focused on its primary mission – Research and Development.

A Reflection

Over 10 years the Lean Product Development process was outlined, subsequently developed and matured. On the way, numerous challenges were encountered and dealt with.

Integration of the revised Lean product design and Lean Product Development processes and tools within the Component Value Stream Engineering process is shown on the next illustration.

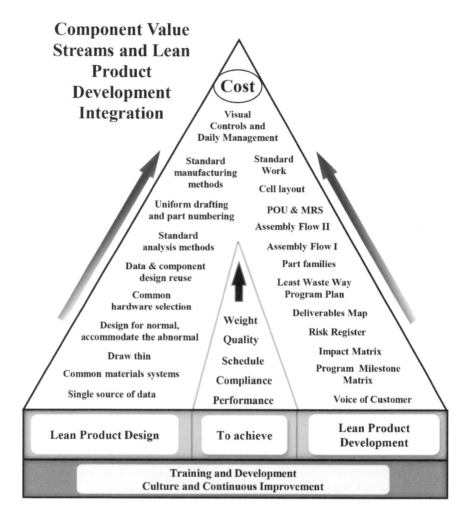

Over the years, some functional aspects of the Lean Product Development process and of the standardized engineering methods and practices were, of course, questioned - "will it work like that."

Some genuine understanding questions were asked of the process - "I have not used this tool before and need help."

Unfortunately, some pushback statements were also made - "it won't work like that."

All were all addressed appropriately as we maneuvered through the years.

We were not going to go back to how we used to do it. We were determined to address and resolve the issues as we faced them and to keep moving forward to a process that would deliver the needed results.

We were fortunate to have significant programs spread over the ten year period enabling us to develop and refine a Lean Product Development process. The significant steps taken in the development of the Lean Product Development process are shown on the following diagram:

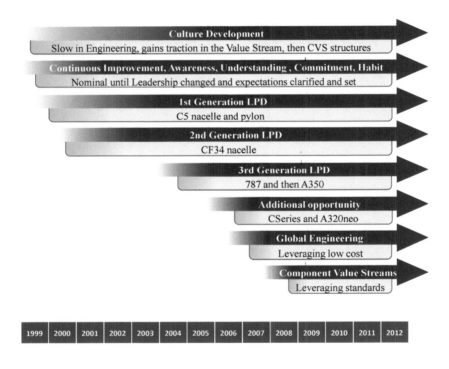

Results to date continue to show significant and ongoing reductions in both non-recurring and recurring new program development costs from conception through complex certification requirements.

While results are orders of magnitude improved, as with other areas of the business, the potential to continue to improve is almost unlimited.

Through 2006, and prior to the aforementioned CVS transformation, we were progressing well:

What we learned along the way – a Summary

- We had an engineering process that was the result of evolution rather than managed development.
- Lean tools can work as well in product development as in operations.
  - However, we did have to appropriately align and use them with engineering processes
- Within a positive culture, team members were willing to propose, try and own new methods and processes
  - A single new material system, qualified within an existing Supplemental Type Certificate is an innovative example.
- Engineering, Research and Development as in all organizations had employees reluctant to change to new methods and processes.

- o Some eventually "came to the party" and performed well; others removed themselves; new leaders emerged; progress accelerated.
- Engineers new to the company had little idea of the past "journey" and perhaps did not always value the environment they were working in.
  - o While they usually adapted well to the new culture, the multi-year steps of the change journey that preceded their employment was a frame of reference they did not have the benefit of experiencing.
- Design engineers are educated to engineer and design and given the opportunity will do just that.
  - o This can be at cost if an acceptable design is already available.
- Small incremental improvements were far more evident than major leaps forward once process and cultural guidelines were in place.
- The 5S of electronic data yielded significantly more opportunity in product development processes than in Operations. (More on this subject in Chapter 6)
- Focusing on linkage and flow, visual controls in support processes yielded similar high results as in operations.
- While event participation was high, new standard processes and methods were more difficult than anticipated to implement within an engineering environment.
- Global engineering highlighted how different diverse cultures approached and solved problems.
  - o Value was attained by leveraging the strength of each.
  - o Global teams fully embraced and enhanced culture and processes.
- Engineering does not stop after design, tooling, and certification are complete. The product still has to enter into production at the required labor hours and cost.
- As Lean Product Development was maturing its application and further development was invaluable.

Things you may wish to consider – a Summary

- Are our continuous improvement expectations of engineering the same as they are in operations?
  - If not why not?
  - Do we have metrics to track engineering continuous improvement progress?
- Do we have an explicit visual representation of the process flows in Engineering, Research and Development, Product Development?
- Do we understand how our engineering costs are driven and measured?
- Are development activities focused and classified - Incremental, Distinct or Breakthrough, and aligned with strategies?
- Are our engineering leaders focused on the customers' requirements, beyond those documented?
  - What do they use to understand the requirements and their progress towards achieving them?
- How often do our engineering employees participate in shop floor activities on the products and processes which they are responsible for?

Chapter 6

A *maturing Operating System and the introduction of a formal Macro Planning process. Real Time Problem Resolution, the opportunity raises its head again. Right-sizing the Chula Vista campus. A regular stream of visitors interested in "culture, change, and continuous improvement." An updated Continuous Improvement model and a looming second crisis.*

A Maturing Business, Firing on all Cylinders

The progress Aerostructures had made with not only the Lean Product Development processes internally, but also in the marketing use of these processes with customers through their pre-contract award phases contributed significantly to the 2004 award of the Boeing 787 nacelle for both General Electric and Rolls Royce engine versions. Moreover, the subsequent award of the Airbus A350 nacelle contract in 2006.

Given the staggering costs of developing, tooling and certifying a new nacelle system it is easy to understand our interest in applying continuous improvement to this endeavor. As previously noted, the success and the potential of Lean Product Development processes appealed to many in the Aerospace community as parallels could be made with developing, tooling and certifying other aircraft components.

Operating System

Internally all components of the operating system had continued to evolve and mature. The Strategic Planning process, the entire Policy Deployment process, the Enterprise Excellence Assessment and the continuous improvement processes were being used continually and effectively and were now part of the Aerostructures DNA. The operating system had evolved as had the understanding of it with all leadership and many employees across the business.

The Operating System:

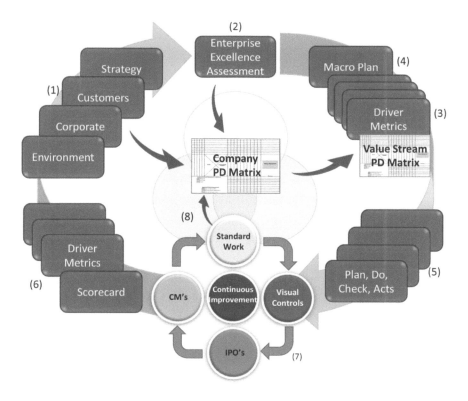

A summary of how this worked:

(1) External influencers along with the Strategic Plan were understood, focused upon and included as inputs to the annual Policy Deployment process and matrix.

(2) The Enterprise Excellence Assessment had matured significantly, and an Improvement Target tying back to Enterprise Excellence progress was established each year for all Value Streams.

(3) All Value Streams had in place their own annual Policy Deployment matrix and increasingly meaningful driver and result measures.

(4) Significant additions had been made to the operating system including the development of a Macro Planning process. More on Macro Planning later in this chapter.

(5) The Plan, Do, Check, Act process was active in all Value Streams, and constant coaching ensured everyone used the process as required, albeit some better than others.

(6) There was a documented Policy Deployment Review process, outlined in Chapter 3. All Improvement Targets required visual driver measures metrics that had a plan line through to achievement, with subsequent weekly/monthly actual status shown alongside the plan line throughout the year. With enough clarity that minimal explanation was needed.

Visual controls across the business, all facilities, all information boards, and all posted metrics, used simple color-coded symbols that could be readily seen. Including every Improvement Target in the Policy Deployment packages. Color coding "status," again outlined in Chapter 3.

Significant steps being taken to achieve each Improvement Target pulled directly from the detailed Plan, Do, Check, Act documents, were also shown in summary at the bottom of each metric page.

The weekly Senior Staff Policy Deployment Review process had become quite efficient. All Senior Staff were in full attendance every week with minimal exception. The reviews were of approximately six Value Streams each week. Over the course of six weeks, all Value Streams had been reviewed and the schedule repeated. Some new program and high "bottom line" impact Value Streams were on a more frequent cycle than some with lesser business impact. Each Value Stream review ran to a specific cycle time. Times for the reviews varied by Value Stream per the criteria just noted.

(7) One benefit of timely, meaningful, visual and actionable metrics, was that opportunities or needs for continuous improvement and lean countermeasures became crystal clear. Where focus was needed to improve performance and reduce cost was no longer elusive or opinion based.

(8) When a kaizen event was to be held, the "Standard Work for an Event" package included a specific step to link the Objectives of every event to the Goals of the business. Each kaizen event team was required to complete this step as required event pre-work, which enabled them to understand the linkage of the event Objectives to the Goals of the business.

In the early days of continuous improvement and kaizen events, we had been concerned about creating a situation that we labeled as "Kaizen Olympics." That is, running events because "running events is a good thing," but without a good understanding of business impact or any event prioritization.

On many occasions, all that was needed to change and improve a situation or opportunity was an immediate "just do it" action rather than a kaizen event. Appropriate "just do it" actions were encouraged.

The operating system now developed and mature, ran against the background of the "Three Circles," which were routinely reinforced as a point of reference.

The Values and the Positive Employee Philosophy contributed to the risk-free environment where there was an expectation and the encouragement to raise and discuss issues and problems that may be hurting performance. When particular issues and problems were raised, leadership considered them opportunities for improvement, and following review and discussion required firm countermeasures to be established.

One Aerostructures president remarked when reflecting on the Policy Deployment process "I know more about this business than another business unit president knows about theirs." This was undoubtedly as a result of the maturity of the Policy Deployment process, the structure, focus and simplicity of the process and the clarity of both driver and results metrics that had also matured and stabilized over the years.

The frequency of reviews and the risk-free review process itself provided visibility of plans and status to plans. Activities driven by a focus on driver measures delivered exceptional business results.

One side benefit of the Policy Deployment Review process was that it provided an opportunity and forum for leadership development when members of a Value Streams leadership, other than the leader themselves, were given the opportunity to present the Policy Deployment package. This was quite a common occurrence and contributed effectively as a small, but essential, leadership development element.

By 2004 Standard Work had become the primary focus, central to waste identification and removal and cost reduction. Once Standard Work had been established frequent "close the gap" events were run to identify any waste that had crept back into processes or any other waste not previously observed. These "close the gap" events were often referred to as "peeling the onion," once one layer of waste is removed another one can invariably be seen. Programs that have been in production for many years are still holding "close the gap" events and revealing opportunity. With basic continuous improvement tools in place, good Standard Work and sustained close the gap events, direct labor hour savings in the range of 50% to 90% plus were common, on both mature and the soon to be seen new programs. To be expected, percentages diminished over time but were never seen to end.

Standard Work, the associated Visual Controls and the collocation of support personnel resurfaced the issue of "Real Time Problem Resolution." The process as outlined previously was that when a shop floor employee ran into a problem and could not follow Standard Work for any reason, they would turn the in place visual control, usually an Andon light, to "red status." Value Stream support personnel were trained to respond to red lights or signals immediately, and make every attempt to resolve the problem "real time." Our discipline to this process was not always as good as it should have been but over time progress was apparent.

Our consultant went to great pains to explain and assure us again, that problems can indeed be solved real time when the "evidence" relating to the problem could be located or seen, discussed and countermeasures identified on the issue, real time.

As we established process discipline, this proved to be the case and we re-energized the teams and the process, through another round of training and expectation setting.

Things improved, although not always in real time. On occasion, a problem would be resolved sufficiently to enable shop floor personnel to resume activity with "root cause" analysis to follow.

The Enterprise Excellence document continued to be frequently revised and updated and worked exceptionally well in driving culture, change and the continuous improvement process. The feature that required leadership's continuous engagement and other requirements that had to be accomplished each year had been expanded and now included:

- Two Value Stream personnel other than the Value Stream leader have presented the Policy Deployment package during the current year.
- The Value Stream Leader has participated in four kaizen events and led two of those events in the current year.

- 50% of the Value Stream staff have participated in two kaizen events in the current year.
- The in-place Standard Work is less than six months old, excluding Takt Time change updates.

This Enterprise Excellence Assessment feature and the visibility through the Policy Deployment review process ensured that all Value Streams were automatically recalibrated every year to maintain a focus on leaders and employees engagement in the continuous improvement process. Maintaining and supporting the constancy of purpose essential for continued progress.

Macro Planning

As mentioned previously, Macro Planning was a process introduced in the early 2000s when two distinct opportunities noted below became visible:

1) The need to have a visual process to plan, schedule and manage significant activities in what was a dynamic and demanding environment.
2) Recognition that not everything fit conveniently into a 12 month Policy Deployment "Improvement Target window." Some Value Streams had issues and opportunities in front of them that required discussion and planning for beyond the current year. For example, pending a production program startup or close out that could require actions over several years.

To provide themselves with this visibility it was seen that some Value Streams had taken the initiative and had developed a visual process to help with these two points. Value Streams were indeed identifying issues they saw beyond the current year that needed consideration and a placeholder on this visual for these issues.

The focus for the Value Streams using this process was the full year, but particular attention was given to the near future, as a sub-element of the Macro Plan which became known as the "three-month rolling plan." The Value Streams doing this were linking and coordinating this visual and their Plan, Do, Check, Acts effectively, and the entire process was working quite well.

From this a Macro Planning process was formally developed, once again utilizing a matrix type process that had the following features: on the X-axis was a weekly calendar extending out a minimum of a year by the week and on occasion a second and third year, by month. The Y-axis usually had the annual Improvement Targets and other issues deemed to be of importance to the Value Stream. These significant activities, in support of specific Improvement Targets and other important issues were noted on a "stickie" at the matrix intersection of the Improvement Target and other important issues with the planned week. A simple process for the "stickies" was developed.

The Macro Plan and use of "stickies":

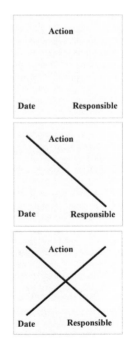

Actions are entered with the date for the action to commence placed in the bottom left-hand corner. The name of the person responsible entered in the bottom right-hand corner. Different color "stickies" can be used to denote types of activities or for other categorizing needs. A colored dot, usually red, is entered if the date is changed from the original. The original date is always saved.

A single diagonal line indicates that action has begun.

Once the action is complete, it is crossed out.

The Macro Plan once developed by each Value Streams leadership team was reviewed weekly by the team, with a focus on the plans, the scheduling of required resources and the associated planning on the upcoming three months activities, the three-month rolling plan.

Adjustments were made to the schedule as appropriate, and additional items added to the Macro Plan as the year unfolded and opportunities arose.

An example of a Macro Plan below:

Month	January				February				March					April				Ma'	
Week	1	2	3	4	5	6	7	8	9	10	11	12	13	14	15	16	17	18	19
Improvement Target 1																			
Improvement Target 2																			
Improvement Target 3																			
Improvement Target 4																			
Improvement Target 5																			
Improvement Target 6																			
Improvement Target 7																			
Important Issue 1																			
Important Issue 2																			
Important Issue 3																			
Important Issue 4																			
Important Issue 5																			

In this example, a marker, moved weekly, indicates the end of week five and that all actions to date have been completed, on schedule, except one relating to Improvement Target 3 that has outstanding items to close out. Some prework has been started for the activity on Improvement Target 7 which is scheduled for week 6. An action relating to Improvement Target 5 has been moved out from the original date.

Standard Work was of course developed for Macro Planning development and the weekly Macro Plan Reviews by the Value Stream leadership.

The Standard Work for the weekly Macro Plan review process, once the visual was in place, included these key elements:

- Review past issues/activities that are still open
  - o Identify plans and resources required for closure
- Review current week activities
  - o Identify items requiring special attention
- Review Events and activities planned over next 2 to 3 weeks
  - o Ensure kaizen event pre-work and team membership
- Review/discuss activities that are scheduled, or that need to be added to, the next three-month window
  - o Identify any pre-work, resource, information requirements.
  - o Identify any items requiring rescheduling
- Identify any new issues/activities for further review

Attention to a process such as Macro Planning, and many other processes we introduced, required discipline to be successful.

Through many of the processes we introduced, we were changing years of behavioral conditioning from reactive to proactive. For some this was a welcome and relatively comfortable change to make, for others it required the conscious reconditioning of behaviors.

The business was indeed firing on all cylinders and leaders were leading.

Outstanding performance progress was being made possible through:

- The engagement of leadership and all employees in continuous improvement activities.
- The effectiveness of the Value Stream structure and the progress with Standard Work and waste removal in manufacturing and support Value Streams.
- The operating system that was in place, providing real time issue, problem and opportunity visibility, enabling course corrections and tactical adjustments to be made.

- The introduction and use of a Macro Planning process
- The Enterprise Excellence Assessment tool as a practical and focused guide and measurement of real continuous improvement progress.
- The in-place Gainsharing incentive scheme that encouraged and helped sustain employee engagement.
- The constant communications that reiterated and reinforced where we were going and how we were going to get there – a constancy of purpose.
- The winning of significant business that had boosted the already high morale.
- The positive environment and culture that was being developed and sustained.

All of these things reinforced the understanding, belief, and buy-in that employees had regarding the "Three Tracks" that we were traversing, now modified to include Standard Work, Real Time Problem Resolution and additional items encountered on the journey.

The organization and culture was changing to one where leaders led and employees readily engaged in process improvement activities in the business. The lean journey and our understanding and proficiency of how to use and leverage the Toyota Production System processes and tools was continually increasing.

Functioning in a state reflective of Enterprise Excellence, was nearer.

By 2004 the Aerostructures metrics were progressing well:

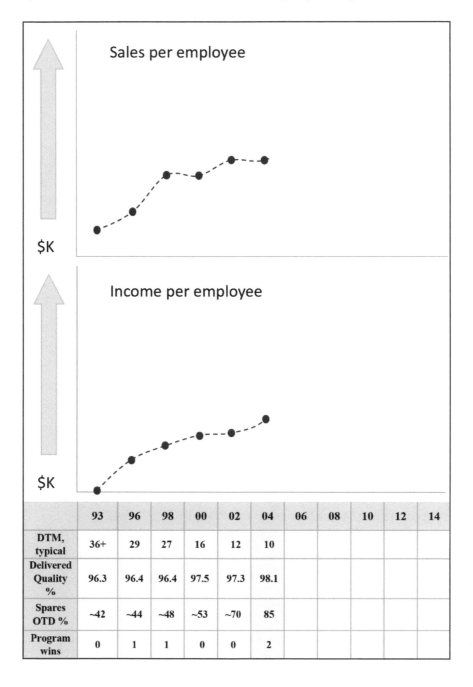

	93	96	98	00	02	04	06	08	10	12	14
DTM, typical	36+	29	27	16	12	10					
Delivered Quality %	96.3	96.4	96.4	97.5	97.3	98.1					
Spares OTD %	~42	~44	~48	~53	~70	85					
Program wins	0	1	1	0	0	2					

The direct labor as a percentage of the total cost was now down to 8% as follows and again with no offloading, the "apples to apples" comparison maintained:

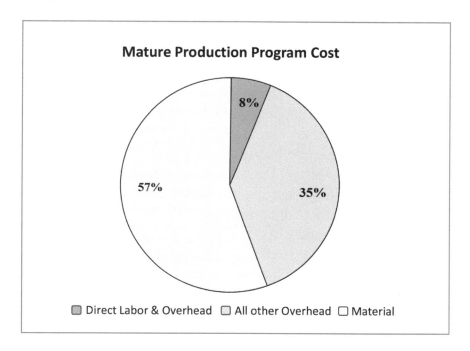

Good progress was being made in Support Value Streams, although we were still experiencing employees in those organizations who were resistant/reluctant to change and who required additional support, education, and encouragement.

Those Support Value Stream employees who grasped the Toyota Production System processes and tools and deployed them effectively were recognized and supplied with the required support and leverage.

What helped with those resistant/reluctant to engage was the inclusion of revenue generating Value Stream employees, usually shop floor personnel, in Support Value Stream continuous improvement activities. In addition, Support Value Stream employees were encouraged to participate in revenue generating Value Stream continuous improvement activities on the shop floor.

This "cross-pollination" between revenue generating and support value streams enhanced learning and understanding of how all areas contributed to the business and their joint identification and elimination of waste proved to be an epiphany for many in Support Value Streams.

The focus on continuous improvement training and education continued through 2004 by which time we had run around 78 Continuous Improvement boot camps, and approximately 2600 employees, customers, suppliers, and other Goodrich business unit employees had participated in this training.

At this time the Chula Vista facility had made considerable headway with linkage and flow, right-sizing equipment and where feasible, placing equipment in-line. Some innovative point of use processes had been developed and also put in line.

One significant development was the design, manufacture, and placement of right-sized, in line "degreasing equipment." The background to this effort was that a large "central, one-stop part degrease" piece of equipment had been purchased and installed in the early 1990s. It could degrease hundreds, if not thousands, of parts at a time. However, a downside was that parts had to be transported to this equipment, and scheduled through it. Then loaded into the equipment and processed. Upon process completion, the equipment had to be unloaded.

One problem was, once the parts were degreased and unloaded, they had to be matched back up with their paperwork, as the paperwork could not accompany the parts through the aqueous degrease process. To complicate matters, the parts themselves did not have part number identification on them. Consequently matching parts with the appropriate paperwork, was a time consuming, non-value added process with many opportunities for error.

To further complicate matters most metal parts fabricated in Chula Vista at the time, required degreasing, at least once, some parts multiple times and the process itself became a choke point. From leaving a process step to be degreased, to the first process step after degrease, the elapsed time was in excess of six days on average.

The actual cycle time of the degrease process itself was less than thirty minutes.

A more efficient option was required and was identified in an event in one particular manufacturing area with the degrease issue. It was suggested that an inline degreaser was an option. A somewhat obvious, but up to that point, not anticipated, revelation. A prototype degreaser was designed during the event.

This first right-sized in line degrease equipment, was manufactured in-house, in place and fully EPA compliant within two weeks, proved to be so successful that over the next several months, all locations where degrease was required had right sized degreasers installed, some manufactured in-house, some purchased.

This enabled employees fabricating parts to do the degreasing of those parts, often within the cycle time of their standard process steps. Central aqueous degrease was no longer required. Massive savings in time and labor alone were realized.

Leadership of the manufacturing area then wanted to use the space this large, now obsolete, equipment occupied, to accommodate other manufacturing activities that were being moved from other locations into the facility. This was a somewhat sensitive step as the equipment had been expensive, and was not yet fully depreciated. Once again, leadership took a bold step and decommissioned and removed the central degrease equipment.

One other significant step was to introduce operator self-verification of their work, eliminating transportation to and from many central Quality inspection locations. This was achieved through:

- Training, monitoring and then validation of their process proficiency over a specified period.
- Documentation of their associated process yields reaching and sustaining acceptable criteria and levels.

The right sized in-line degrease equipment combined with operator self-verification, additional right-sizing, linkage and flow and other continuous improvement activities contributed to reductions in material handling equipment, part travel, waiting, days to manufacture, space requirements, management time and of course reduced cost.

It also enabled the next right-sizing of the Chula Vista facility.

By 2004, the space occupied by manufacturing had been reduced from approximately 1.6 million square feet to 1 million square feet. In making these moves, hundreds of forklifts, material handling aids, carts and other transportation devices were removed from the facility.

Aisles that had formerly been full of these material handling aids, carts and other transportation devices, some moving, many waiting to be moved, were now free of traffic.

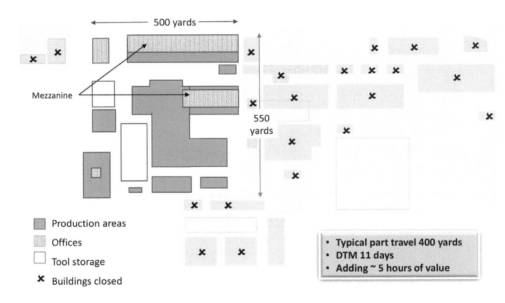

Not to scale

Continuous improvement activities on the shop floor continued to identify and drive waste out of the business. Continuous improvement remained a focus in support functions and real process performance was to be seen across the support Value Streams.

A problem that was seen daily across all Value Streams and locations was finding and accessing files and documents "in the system."

An associated problem was that as a company we were running out of electronic storage capacity and were exploring options to increase capacity. The Information Technology team did indeed take steps to eliminate redundant and obsolete files from server storage locations that alleviated the problem somewhat.

A second countermeasure was an "electronic 5S" process that was developed, following the workplace 5S process, and focused upon "electronic files and data" stored on servers. All Value Streams deployed the electronic 5S process, and massive amounts of additional obsolete, duplicate and unnecessary files were identified and deleted, eliminating server storage space issues and the need for additional servers.

A "Final" Continuous Improvement model

Based on the progress to date, the results seen and the benefits to "all concerned" the Continuous Improvement model had progressed to what became its "final" configuration.

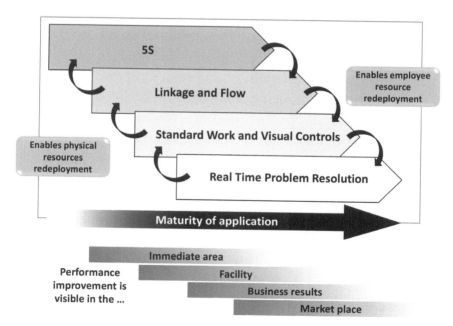

Note the arrows going from right to left. We came to understand that while the journey may be from left to right, as we "peeled the onion" there were multiple issues, problems and opportunities exposed that caused us to go back, and apply the same tools to new levels of waste. We learned that this is part of the process and a potential goldmine of performance improvement and cost reduction. Our consultant often remarked, "the Toyota Production System, the gift that keeps on giving."

Another observation was that we were able to redeploy physical resources early in the transition process as we eliminated waste from processes and right-sized workstations, freed up machines, equipment, and floor space. As the process continued, we created employee capacity. This capacity was filled with the closure of some facilities and the transfer of work to where we could redeploy employee resources. And of course, as the new work we had won entered production it was absorbed into the capacity being created.

Also of note is where the results of the continuous improvement efforts are visible in business results. For example, when our first aggressive continuous improvement efforts were made in the core fabrication area of Riverside, significant positive results were visible in that area's metrics. However, they were not broad or impactful enough to be seen in the overall Riverside facility metrics.

Following about six months of continuous improvement activity in multiple areas of the facility, the Riverside facility metrics began to move in the "right" direction, and after twelve months it was clear that these metrics had improvement momentum. Moreover, given the significantly sustained metrics beyond 12 months at Riverside, improvement was visible in the business metrics of the company.

In subsequent years, well into the 2000s, against a background of sustained performance improvement, we were able to keep financial results on positive trends despite general inflation, increasing material costs and accommodating increasing customer demands for restructured/reduced costs. Continuous improvement and reduced costs were influencing and enabling new customer contracts.

By the end of 2006, with continuous improvement highly active and meaningful, the Aerostructures metrics continued to improve:

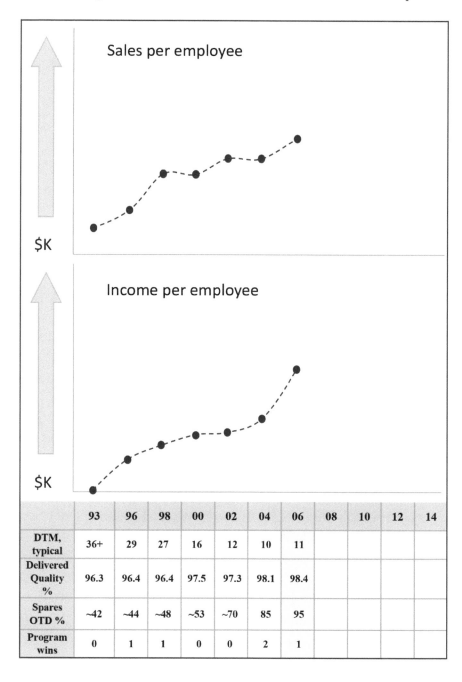

	93	96	98	00	02	04	06	08	10	12	14
DTM, typical	36+	29	27	16	12	10	11				
Delivered Quality %	96.3	96.4	96.4	97.5	97.3	98.1	98.4				
Spares OTD %	~42	~44	~48	~53	~70	85	95				
Program wins	0	1	1	0	0	2	1				

Visitors to Aerostructures

By the end of 2006 the number of visitors, hosted primarily at the Chula Vista and Riverside facilities, totaled around 2100 and the visits followed the same structured and scheduled one day process:

Arrival, welcome and introductions

- By the Aerostructures president if available, a senior leader or two, other continuous improvement zealots and several hourly and support employees.

Show and tell

- An overview of what was now known as the "lean journey," a documented chronicle of the steps taken, issues dealt with, lessons learned and progress made on the "culture, change and continuous improvement path." Outlined were actions taken to drive cultural change and our deployment of the Toyota Production System processes and tools as we understood them and the development of the operating system.

A plant tour of applied Continuous Improvement processes and tools

- Invariably focused on the workplace deployment of these processes and tools, over the years as our understanding of the processes and tools increased so did their implementation, effectiveness, and visibility in the workplace. Visitors were encouraged to have ad-hoc discussions with shop floor and support employees, to understand their thoughts and observations on culture, change, and continuous improvement.

Questions and answers with Aerostructures Leadership

- Nothing off limits, all questions were welcomed.
  - o We learned a lot about our customer's culture and continuous improvement activities from the questions their employees asked.

Question and Answers with shop floor personnel

- Again, nothing off limits. If the plant visit was taking place in Chula Vista or Riverside, they were and still are unionized facilities. Consequently, Union members and support staff made up the Question and Answer panel. Leadership employees were not included in the session, but were available for follow up questions.
- The balance of Aerostructures US facilities are not unionized.

Final Questions and answers with Aerostructures Leadership

- Then departure, with the hope that the visitors carried a positive message and some degree of advocacy, for Aerostructures as a supplier, back to their respective locations.

These visits were a pleasant, momentary diversion and they did contribute to the cultural change. Employees felt good that visitors were coming to look at what they had achieved and were proud to share change, culture and continuous improvement methods and progress, along with many personal anecdotes regarding their experiences with the visitors.

An interesting question that got asked at almost every visit was "if you could boil all this down, what was the one thing that you did to change and make the progress you have made?"

What was being asked, of course, was," what is the shortcut to the end game, what magic wand did you wave?"

The one-day visits had opened eyes to the progress and performance improvement to be seen in the Aerostructures processes and metrics. The program wins, the enthusiasm of the workforce in their role in the ongoing business transformation and all the hard work over many years to achieve these things, were undoubtedly enviable.

The answer to the question was "many, many things over a good few years" and we often gave that answer.

It belatedly dawned on us that a better, more concise answer to the question could be that we had worked relentlessly to change the culture.

On subsequent visits when the "usual question" was asked we replied, "we changed the culture."

It came as a bit of a surprise, although it should not have been, that a follow up question then became "if you could boil all this down, what was the one thing that you did to change the culture?" ...

We were reminded of a quote we came across during our lean journey:

> "The reason most organizations leap to adopt the latest advances ... is to spare themselves the painful commitment to the basics."

> – Allan Cox. Leadership Consultant and Author.

We were constantly reminded of this when many people, visitors, and others, repeatedly asked for the "one thing, the shortcut" to meaningful performance improvement.

Our transformation was days, weeks, months and years of discovery and understanding on the journey to Enterprise Excellence. Developing processes and visuals to help us on the journey, such as the Three Tracks and Three Circles, and once making progress, figuring out what we needed to do next to sustain momentum.

Communicating frequently, extensively and maintaining a constancy of purpose was vital.

We were often reminded that change and culture need constant attention. Moreover, that continuous improvement is not something that's gets completed. It is something you do, continuously.

A journey versus a destination.

We are not aware of any shortcuts, although we did speculate that we could have possibly done things in a shorter time frame.

How much of a reduction could have been achieved is open to debate when considering the leadership and cultural maturity of the organization, the "awareness, understanding, commitment, habit" change process, and how many times this cycle had to be repeated by multiple employees, in multiple locations, and the sheer number of processes, tools, and behaviors that were introduced or changed.

By 2006, progress along the "Change Triangle," now looked like this:

It was on the heels of successful marketing campaigns, new business wins, excellent business results and Gainsharing contributing to a great place to work at, and an excellent culture to work in, that the president through this period reflected on this progress and remarked about a potential new crisis, which he paraphrased as:

A Crisis of Complacency

A relatively simple Operating System delivering consistent, exceptional business results

Gainsharing enabling all employees to enjoy the financial success

High customer satisfaction

Winning significant new commercial programs

A great culture

Wide recognition of the success with Continuous Improvement

… and he added, "with all the new programs we have won, we have considerably upped the ante on continued success."

What we learned on the way – a Summary

- The operating system proved to be invaluable.
  - o Linking Strategy, Policy Deployment, the Enterprise Excellence Assessment, Macro Planning, and Continuous Improvement, all with meaningful metrics.
  - o Frequent reviews by senior leadership are part of the process that sustains the operating system.
  - o The operating system had become part of Aerostructures DNA.

- Kaizen events should be viewed through a "qualitative lens."
  - It's not the number of events held but the quality of the event in terms of waste removal and performance improvement.
- Most problems can indeed be resolved real time if there is discipline to a Real Time Problem Resolution process. Years of not being collocated with the product they support, prioritizing something else other than addressing problems in real time, appeared to have created a resilient culture in our case.
- Macro Planning can be a simple visual to help in the planning and scheduling of significant improvement activities.
- The "show and tell" visits we hosted, most of which were by customers, helped change the view of Aerostructures from negative to positive.
- There is no silver bullet or shortcut to cultural change and sustainable performance improvement

Things you may want to consider – a Summary

- Do we have an integrated, effective operating system or do we have uncoordinated activities and a "bunch of charts?"
- Can we see our continuous improvement plans or are they in someone's mind or on a computer somewhere?
- Are our continuous improvement activities delivering performance improvement?
  - How do we know?
- Are our continuous improvement events structured processes with defined scope and boundaries?
  - Do we utilize the right participants?
- How do we train employees in continuous improvement?
  - Who trains them and are they proficient in their delivery of the Continuous Improvement training?
  - Is it effective?

- o How do we measure that?
- Do we view continuous improvement as something we have done, need to do or are doing?
  - o Is continuous improvement a component of our mission?

Chapter 7

*E*stimating new business opportunities and not winning any. Changing the source of estimating data and improving the estimating process. Securing multiple new program contracts. Growing the global supply chain and our own global operations. The differences and challenges to "change, culture and continuous improvement deployment" in these global locations and the support that was required. Becoming part of a large corporation and the challenges experienced. Interest in continuous improvement from a local municipal entity. Achieving Enterprise Excellence levels. And a third crisis.

Growing Pains

Prior to winning the 787, parametric estimating was Aerostructures primary method for quoting new business. This system utilized historical labor hour and material data sources based on previous similar components and assemblies. This outdated methodology was a likely contributor to the situation where Aerostructures was unable to win any significant new business from the early 1980s, up to 2004.

The reasons parametric estimating had outlived its usefulness were twofold.

1. The data and performance metrics being used were dated and relative to old designs, technologies, and manufacturing processes. In addition, they did not align with "today's marketplace" where competition was, and still is, intense.

2. By now, overall Aerostructures business performance and efficiency had improved dramatically. Labor hours generated on programs, old and new, were radically below traditional learning curve performance predictions. Production cycle times and performance to schedule were significantly improved, and support organizations had made marked progress on their efficiency. Overhead costs were being managed effectively and were also reduced from previous years.

These consistent productivity improvements, resulting in reduced direct labor hours and overall costs, were evaluated to be part of a predictable long-term business-wide reduction trend. These types of results would be required to compete for and then win the important and challenging Boeing 787 nacelle competition.

As a result, Aerostructures presented an extremely aggressive 787 nacelle quote package that contained projected direct labor hour reductions considerably below any results to date. However and as a result of recent experience, we had high confidence that the labor hours being quoted were, in fact, achievable given the current and sustained positive trends.

The 787 labor rates quoted were similarly competitive. The labor rates used in the quote process were below Aerostructures facility labor rates in place at that time. These labor rates were used with the understanding that if the program contract was awarded, work placement would require identification and establishment of some new production sources where the labor rates were supportive of business requirements and competitive for the geographical locations chosen.

Raw material costs were at a projected market price. Equipment costs remained a challenge. The improved overhead rates contributed to the overall aggressiveness of the quote package. Some sourcing option costs, yet to be clearly defined, were also included in the quote package.

As noted earlier, the 787 Nacelle program was awarded to Aerostructures. Subsequently, a comparison was made between the quote package submitted and one completed via traditional parametric estimating. As a result, it was determined that had labor and overhead costs been parametrically estimated, they would have been over 40% higher than the actual labor and overhead costs utilized in the quote.

It was clear that parametric data and traditional learning curves had little relevance to current performance trends and market requirements.

This was to lead to further dramatic changes in the Aerostructures business.

As noted in Chapter 5, the Lean Product Development process was in place on the 787 and was both developing and maturing as it was used to fulfill the need for lower product and process development costs.

Operations Global Expansion

Another significant challenge was to determine the manufacturing locations of the product to support the quoted program cost. Current fabrication sources were external, managed by the supply chain, with the balance of fabrication being in the Chula Vista facility. The assembly of existing products was primarily accomplished in US or European Aerostructures locations.

During the quote development period, it became apparent that drastic measures were needed to achieve Boeings aggressive price targets. One option considered was to develop an Aerostructures facility in Mexico for 787 work. Following a further detailed review, a campaign was launched to find a suitable site for the fabrication and assembly of parts in Mexico.

Location options and financial incentives were subsequently evaluated. Proximity to the Chula Vista facility, the availability of technical and engineering resources, local incentives, competitive labor rates and the availability of suitable shop floor employees were critical evaluation criteria that resulted in the selection of a Mexicali site.

This required a new manufacturing facility to be built and 787 work, and work from other programs at Chula Vista and at suppliers, to be placed there to support the necessary, aggressive, financial assumptions modeled in the business plan.

Product development work was to be retained in existing US facilities and the overall outlook for Aerostructures was better than it had been for many years.

This planned move to Mexicali also kept the work internal to Aerostructures rather than locating to some external perceived low-cost country supplier, with any cost/productivity improvements contributing towards Aerostructures bottom line, rather than a suppliers.

To be successful Mexicali would have to be brought up to the same continuous improvement capabilities and performance being achieved in the existing US Aerostructures facilities. Construction of the Mexicali facility started in 2007.

While the lower business costs and labor rates in Mexicali potentially resolved several aggressive part fabrication and assembly cost issues, the overall Riverside composite bonding load remained as both significant cost and capacity issues. Composite bond manufacturing options were developed to address both issues. One option that was promoted by Goodrich was to use an available site they had in Tianjin China. Established with the intention of developing a manufacturing facility and foothold to leverage the aerospace market there.

Goodrich encouraged Aerostructures to develop and use this facility as a location for low technology, simple bond panel work. This encouragement was heeded.

Culture within cultures

Concerns were raised, regarding the deployment of the Three Circles in Mexicali and Tianjin. Would they be implemented with the same rigor and success at these locations as was being enjoyed in the other Aerostructures sites?

Most if not every country has its own environment and culture that manifests itself in many ways. What was clear was that while both Mexicali and Tianjin were traditionally hierarchical "top-down control" environments, the degrees of "top-down control" varied by the environment a person happened to be in.

At a macro level, that environment could be - the home environment, a social environment, the street environment or a work environment. Within each setting, this will again vary at the micro, level dependent on where the person is at the time. For example, in a work environment, an employee could be at their actual workplace, in a meeting or in the cafeteria.

In prior years we had chosen to fully deploy the Three Circles in our Scotland, Singapore and Dubai Maintenance Repair and Overall facilities. With the belief that it was the right thing to do and that while we were not going to change and develop a culture outside of the work environment, we were confident that we were capable of success within the work environment.

At all of these locations, the Three Circles and integration of their requirements along with the corresponding positive culture was in place and evident.

We were prepared to work and develop the Three Circle Culture at both Mexicali and Tianjin, to an understanding, competency and comfort zone with all employees, given the known benefits of the environment it would create.

Mexicali had noticeable upside, it sits on the border of the US, and it is a short commute to and from Chula Vista. The general manager was to be a US transplant, as was the operations manager who spoke fluent Spanish. Some Mexicali residents recruited into leadership positions were educated in the US and were bilingually proficient.

Consequently, from the outset, the environment in Mexicali was well positioned to make a successful cultural transition. However, we did recognize that additional communication, nurturing, training and support would be required to be fully on a par with our other overseas facilities at this stage in their development.

Tianjin did not have the location benefits we experienced in Mexicali. However accepting the "macro versus micro" view of cultures and environments, the Three Circle Culture was deployed there and is developing and well supported to this day.

When visiting an Aerostructures facility in the US or around the world, it is easy to see that they are all part of the same organization and one can see with clarity and consistency that the same Three Circles are deployed.

It is also clear where the local environment has had some impact on the facility work environment. This is generally apparent in the progress the employees and the facility are making regarding cultural change, evaluated within the change process of "awareness, understanding, commitment, and habit." It is different depending on location, but all Aerostructures facilities are moving in the same positive direction.

More business wins

Good progress continued with the design, certification, tooling and production preparation for the 787 General Electric and Rolls Royce nacelles, all effectively supported by Lean Product Development processes. The A350 made similar progress through design, certification, and tooling, having the advantage of running in the wake of the 787.

Commercial aircraft development was buoyant during the 2000s with several companies actively working on new aircraft, many of them planning to utilize the "in development" Pratt & Whitney Geared Turbo Fan engine.

Against the background of a much-improved reputation in the industry combined with lower costs, and the alignment of Aerostructures with Pratt & Whitney in the UTC portfolio, Aerostructures was awarded the GTF nacelle contract for the Bombardier CSeries and the Mitsubishi Regional Jet.

The maturation of the operating system and the deployment of continuous improvement processes and tools continued to drive performance while significant multi-million dollar investments in new programs were being made.

By 2008 the Aerostructures metrics were:

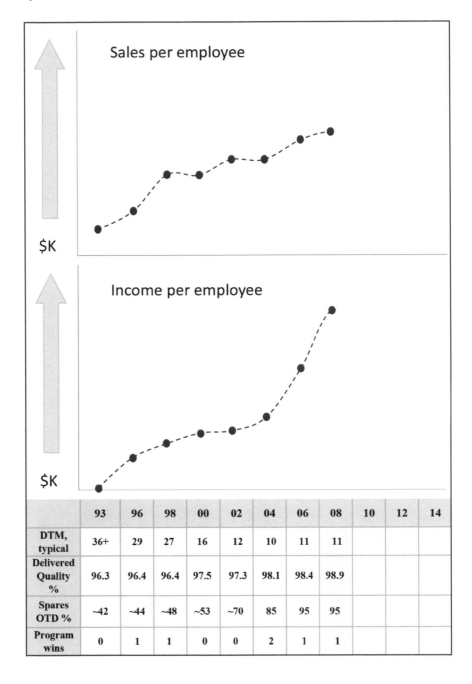

	93	96	98	00	02	04	06	08	10	12	14
DTM, typical	36+	29	27	16	12	10	11	11			
Delivered Quality %	96.3	96.4	96.4	97.5	97.3	98.1	98.4	98.9			
Spares OTD %	~42	~44	~48	~53	~70	85	95	95			
Program wins	0	1	1	0	0	2	1	1			

The "Performance Sweet Spot" 2004 – 2008

At this point in the narrative, it is appropriate to summarize business results driven by the changes in the business represented by the detail on the Three Tracks and the Three Circles.

Their gradual understanding and deployment had produced remarkable results during a "sweet spot" period from 2004 – 2008, as compared to 1993.

During this period:

- *Almost twice as much product was being produced*
- *In half the space*
- *For several years in less than one-third of the time*
- *With one-third of the resources*
- *Consistently on schedule*
- *With best in class quality*
- *Sales per employee had grown by a factor of 4.5*
- *Moreover, an estimated $60 - 70B in new OE and Aftermarket business had been won*

Quite an achievement given the perilous situation the company had previously been in.

Supply Chain Global Expansion

Work placement at competitive costs was becoming increasingly challenging. Several suppliers had been identified for major nacelle sub-assemblies and components, primarily machined parts and some large composite assemblies.

With the exception of two suppliers who were based in Europe, all of the others were in Asia.

It was anticipated that the European suppliers and two of the Asian suppliers would require only minimal technical or business support as they were industry experienced suppliers, already supplying hardware to Aerostructures. Albeit one of the experienced Asian suppliers was bringing a new South East Asian facility online during this period.

A third Asian supplier was taking on a considerable increase in its workload and needed to build another large building to accommodate that growth. We realized we would have to provide significant on-site technical and operations resources over an extended period to ensure their success. A fourth Asian supplier, while a large business, was a novice with regard to high tech, high volume parts and was struggling with new products from other aerospace companies in addition to its existing business.

The "Crisis of Complacency" referenced earlier, continued to be a concern. Whenever an opportunity presented itself, increased emphasis was provided on the importance of The Three Circles and continuous improvement activities across the company, while vigorously reinforcing the Values and Positive Employee Philosophy. Communications highlighted progress being made, and Gainsharing payout supported this position.

The need to sustain a focus on the new programs, and the continued deployment and development of the Lean Product Development process driving Least Waste Way design and manufacturing processes, was clear. Production facilities were tooled and positioned with pro forma Standard Work and ready to produce at labor hour and cost levels that were significantly below "traditional" new program "learning curve" levels.

There was also the need to continue to drive change and continuous improvement at all Aerostructures locations with existing production and support activities driving waste out of our processes, creating capacity and providing business returns to help finance these new programs.

One noteworthy achievement during this period was at the Aerostructures Toulouse facility where engine build-up (EBU) was and still is, accomplished to produce an integrated propulsion unit for a number of Airbus aircraft.

This involves painting the nacelle components in the livery of the airline to which the propulsion unit is destined and then mating the nacelle components with the engine in the engine build-up process.

The EBU process is complex, requiring electrical, fuel, fire suppression, hydraulics, pneumatics and oil systems to be routed, and installed within and across the two components – the nacelle and engine. Traditionally the EBU had been completed with the engine hanging on a static I beam with all EBU requirements accomplished in situ. Although Toulouse had made advances with continuous improvement, there was still a local leadership position of "this is the way we have always done it, why change?"

Those on both sides of the Atlantic with a greater belief in continuous improvement and "keener eyes," envisaged significant improvement opportunities, should a moving line concept be developed and introduced for the A320 EBU process.

This took on an extra challenge as what was proposed was a high volume mixed model moving line. The A320 had a choice of engines, and that choice was with the buyer of the airplane. The moving line would have to accommodate a mix of both engine types in an irregular cadence. This introduced a significant challenge in ensuring that the right parts were in the right place at the right time as the line moved to the Takt Time. Not a simple replenishment process to develop. Toulouse rose to the challenge and working with moving line designers and suppliers with automobile assembly experience, configured a moving EBU line capable of accommodating two engine types. The Toulouse team did an outstanding job of designing a kitting and part supply process that did indeed ensure the "right parts were in the right place at the right time." The moving line came online in 2010, and prior Standard Work was quickly updated. The line ran supporting customer requirements, shown on a large Takt Time counter that was visible by the teams working on the moving line. Introduction of the moving line went exceptionally well with a minimum of startup problems.

- In the six years before the installation of the moving line, direct labor hours had been reduced:
  - ~ 15% on Program A
  - ~ 22% on Program B
- There were ten stationary "I beam" workstations, occupying 13,350 square feet.

- Six years after the moving line introduction direct labor hours had been reduced a further:
  - ~ 21% on Program A
  - ~ 29% on Program B.
- Six workstations on the moving line occupied 5,400 square feet.

Quite amazing reductions given that this EBU activity had been in place since the late 1980s and the production rates were higher than they had ever been. Close the gap events have run, and additional waste removed, on the EBU line ever since.

As with any site, acceptance of continuous improvement had its nuances in the Toulouse facility. However, enabling employees to see and understand customer requirements, the competitive marketplace challenges and the results achieved by continuous improvement, resulted in robust "change engagement" by the entire Toulouse team.

At an Aerostructures level, the direct labor as a percentage of program cost was now at 7%, and again, with no offloading, this remained an "apples to apples" comparison.

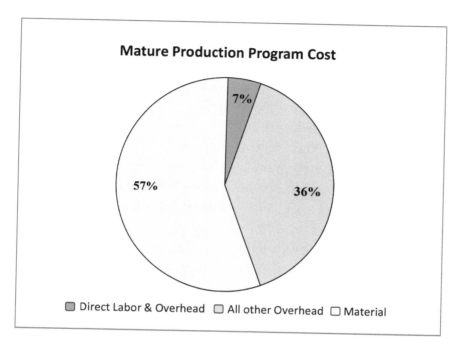

It was, however, the last time we were able to do this baseline analysis as products from both new and mature programs were being sourced and resourced into the external supply chain.

Meanwhile, Mexicali produced its first fabricated parts in October of 2010. Product quality and facility performance started out positively and continued to improve, and the Rolls Royce 787 thrust reverser assembly work was then transferred, to Mexicali, per the plan in early 2012.

This transfer took place following two years of maturing the Mexicali fabrication production processes and preparatory work for the thrust reverser assembly. It is of interest to note that while the Rolls Royce 787 thrust reverser assembly process was stabilized in Chula Vista, a new innovative multi-station assembly line was designed and developed by the new Mexicali team with continuous improvement support from several other Aerostructures facilities.

The thrust reverser assembly line choices were either a moving line similar to the one implemented in Toulouse, or a pulse line, where movement of components through the assembly stations is not continuous but instead indexed to a Takt Time cadence. Given the extensive and challenging operator access requirements during the thrust reverser assembly operation and also with "creativity before capital" in mind, a pulse line was facilitized and introduced.

The pulse line quickly paid dividends regarding both quality and cost. Customer schedule requirements were supported effectively, with the usual, new program high anxiety moments. These high anxiety moments caused nervousness with the customer, and they vetoed the planned move of the General Electric thrust reverser assembly to Mexicali.

Many of the employees on the GE thrust reverser line in Chula Vista, were contract labor. A contractors priorities in life may not always align with whom they work for. This appeared to be the case when it came to our drive for implementing continuous improvement, the development of Standard Work, the identification and removal of waste and the reduction in direct labor hours – cost. Contractors usually seek high hourly labor rates, regular overtime and some security or longevity of assignment. This was not a good match for our needs at the time.

Until the customer's nervousness was eliminated, continuous improvement and GE thrust reverser cost were going to remain a challenge.

Then in early 2013, 787 supply chain part supply and quality issues from other suppliers to Boeing overshadowed the now diminishing issues the customer had with the GE thrust reverser assembly in Chula Vista. In mid-2013 the GE thrust reverser assembly moved to Mexicali onto its own ready and waiting pulse line. Once again quality and cost improvements were quickly seen through the development of Standard Work, close the gap activities and waste elimination all created within the Three Circles environment.

Airbus had previously announced a significant upgrade of the A320. It included new engines and new nacelles, and the plane was renamed the A320neo. Through the late 2000s the A320neo opportunity was pursued, and although we were the incumbent, we knew that Airbus was reflecting on all the commercial nacelle business we had won from 2004 through 2008 and was considering alternatives to keep other nacelle providers as viable, reliable suppliers. That and the not unusual political consideration for work placement among companies in the Airbus European supply chain became factors in their sourcing decisions.

In 2010 Aerostructures was awarded the nacelle contract for the Pratt & Whitney Geared Turbo Fan engine on the A320neo aircraft. As with the A320, the A320neo had two engine choices, the Pratt & Whitney GTF or the CFM International LEAP. The GE LEAP engine nacelle was awarded to Nexcelle, a GE/Safran joint venture.

In support of Aerostructures new nacelle business, outsourcing of assemblies and components to low-cost countries continued during the late 2000 period. Finding capable, qualified and low-cost suppliers proved challenging. Most if not all airframers and suppliers to them were scouring the globe for the same supply capability, capacity, and low cost.

Along with the growing global supply chain footprint, Aerostructures business continued to expand its own global footprint – production facilities in Mexicali and Tianjin, engineering facilities in Singapore, Bangalore and Mexicali, Maintenance, Repair & Overhaul facilities in Brazil, Turkey, and Tianjin.

All of these locations were started with the "Three Circles" to the fore. Expectations relating to and deployment of the Positive Employee Philosophy and continuous improvement were communicated, training provided and support maintained. This, of course, put increased strain on the resources providing that training and support.

In addition, from 2008 to 2010 eleven new low-cost major component suppliers were either in the process of a production ramp-up or were already in full production, along with multiple new smaller suppliers doing the same.

One concern shared by Aerostructures leadership was the perceived level of support required by some of these new low-cost country suppliers as they worked to introduce new products, pass first articles, ramp-up production and achieve production, and quality stability.

It was apparent that many suppliers needed a lot of unanticipated, unplanned, and unbudgeted support.

Unbudgeted support, quality issues, schedule impacts, transportation, contractual support and costs, international trade issues and a multitude of other issues brought the "high price of low cost" clearly into view around 2010.

There are tangible, and readily calculable costs associated with suppliers of highly engineered products, that often increase as a global supply footprint expands. These costs can pale in comparison to the intangible costs.

One significant intangible cost is associated with the extended linkage and flow, and fragmented communications contributing to delayed real time problem identification and resolution which in turn can be alarmingly challenging and expensive.

Receiving a delivery and finding a part with a problem can be devastating to both schedule and cost if there are more parts in shipment, more in transit and yet more still being produced, all with the same problem. Identifying a root cause that occurred potentially thousands of miles away and weeks, or months ago becomes challenging.

A "Total Landed Cost model" was developed and did indeed provide a clearer picture of the "full cost" of a product in addition to the price on the invoice. This model was not fully developed or used as schedule demands took precedence and attention.

Time has assured us that invoice cost and total landed cost are different, with total landed cost always being higher. And that if parts and products are sourced and managed effectively in a proficient low-cost location, it is often a more financially viable alternative to in-house manufacture. Prudence is recommended in these decisions.

Performance trends showed some mixed results.

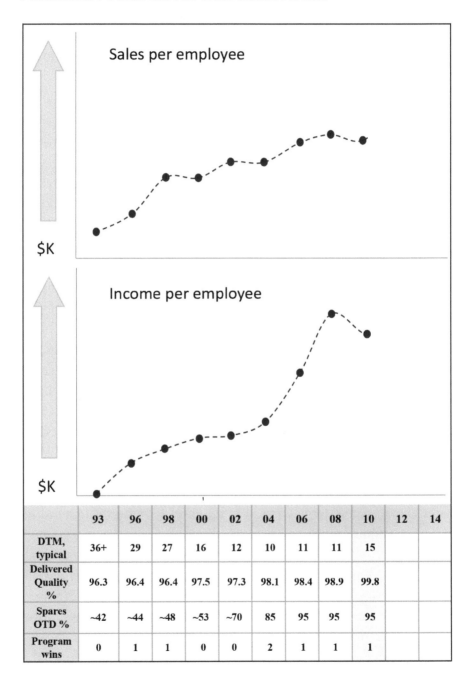

	93	96	98	00	02	04	06	08	10	12	14
DTM, typical	36+	29	27	16	12	10	11	11	15		
Delivered Quality %	96.3	96.4	96.4	97.5	97.3	98.1	98.4	98.9	99.8		
Spares OTD %	~42	~44	~48	~53	~70	85	95	95	95		
Program wins	0	1	1	0	0	2	1	1	1		

One metric with a distinctly negative trend is the Days To Manufacture metric. This was driven by the transfer of primarily, fabrication work, and shortly after that assembly work, from Chula Vista to Mexicali which required planned buffer stock to facilitate the production transfer and protect customer schedules.

Growing pains outlined

By the close of 2010, growth problems driven by the success of the business were categorized as follows:

- Following intense continuous improvements efforts over the years, mature, stable "in-production programs" were delivering quality products on schedule while meeting business financial needs. Airframer customer relationships were generally positive, and aftermarket airline support well understood and maintained.
  - o The business was now transitioning from these programs with over 20 years of history (many with outdated technologies supplemented by extremely competent and motivated employees) to new nacelle products and technologies emerging from multiyear Lean Product Development activities entering into full production. And the Aftermarket business was increasing rapidly.
- New processes, new manufacturing techniques, and new material systems were now required to achieve demanding customer requirements including:
  - o Automated processes, new materials and new systems, all required for reduced weight, increased sound attenuation, deicing capability, high reverse thrust performance, maximum aerodynamic performance and of course reduced cost.
- Nacelle hardware was fundamentally changing from the 1970s – 1980s technology where metal bonded components

were common, to advanced composite systems for reduced weight and generally increased performance. Although composite bonded components had been around for many years, their application was limited. By the 2000s, materials and supporting technologies had advanced enabling the use of composite bonded assemblies on a vast array of components. Reference many of the significant sections of airplanes today now being composite.

o Composite materials are procured in a pre-cured state requiring freezer storage until production use. When removed from cold storage, useful material life is limited to around only ten to thirty days during which production operations must be completed.

o Composite materials and many composite components require special material handling.

o In addition, composite bonded panels once fully cured tend to distort more than corresponding metal bond panels in the "free" or unrestrained state. The predictability of that movement can be challenging, consequently "quality and or assembly issues" can emerge.

• Aerostructures, although having deep experience with all nacelle components, did not have a full nacelle system in production. In production were components of nacelles.

o The challenge was the management, coordination, and integration of entire nacelle components and systems through design, tooling, manufacturing, and certification. This brought much more load and activity in the engineering phase and new challenges in the manufacturing and supply chain processes.

• Historically the component manufacturing supply chain had consisted of 70% "make in-house, and 30% buy from suppliers." As a consequence, support functions had adapted over the years to support this supply distribution and all it required to function.

- o This was now changing rapidly to 30% make, and 70% buy. This was a seismic shift, and the Supply Chain and other support Value Streams struggled to adapt at the same pace as the make-buy distribution was changing.
- In line with this "make-buy" change, the supply chain had traditionally been US-centric with many of the suppliers being on the West coast, with a concentration of them in the Los Angeles basin.
  - o As noted previously, this was also changing rapidly to a global supply network, another seismic shift that required an entirely different type and different level of support we had yet to understand fully. The Aerospace industry as a whole was searching the globe for capable, qualified, low-cost providers. Competition for capability, capacity and cost was fierce.

In 2012 Aerostructures workload increased yet again with the award of the nacelle contract for the Embraer KC390 and E2 aircraft both utilizing the new Pratt and Whitney Geared Turbo Fan engine.

Then things really changed. UTC acquired Goodrich in July 2012.

The ex-Hamilton Sundstrand businesses, already part of UTC, were merged with Goodrich business units and became United Technologies Aerospace Systems (UTAS). This brought three different cultures together, a different management structure with remote central functions and increased reporting requirements to those central functions. One other significant difference was the approach to culture and continuous improvement.

The now Goodrich Operating System developed at Aerostructures was continuous improvement centric. The Enterprise Excellence Assessment document and process, a vital component of the operating system, had been purposely and thoughtfully hard-wired to drive improving business results and had been delivering excellent business results and returns, at Aerostructures, for many years.

The UTC continuous improvement approach and process, ACE – Achieving Competitive Excellence, was hard-wired to achieving levels of ACE requirements, expressed as Bronze, Silver or Gold.

While UTC business performance was generally good, we did have concerns regarding implementation of their ACE process within Aerostructures. With that in mind, we ensured that relevant sections of ACE were reinforced with critical cultural and operating system elements germane to our business. These elements included specific and strong emphasis on - leadership engagement, communications, Policy Deployment and Standard Work.

In practice, this was an integration of continuous improvement philosophies, and we recognized that ACE did provide some improved processes and tools relating to "in process and delivered Quality." A broad portfolio of tools that could be used to drive quality issues and problems to "root cause effectively."

Interest in the Aerostructures culture resulted in some UTC executives attending the one-week Positive Employee Philosophy clinics, and Aerostructures continued to operate via adherence to the "Three Circles" under new ownership.

UTC provided deep engineering leadership and resources and were supportive of the new nacelle development programs underway and the Aerostructures Lean Product Development process.

As time passes, the ACE and Enterprise Excellence Assessment processes continue to transition and align with increased benefits across both businesses. The UTC - Goodrich cultures are merging, and approaches to leadership and management also continue to align. As happened when Goodrich acquired of Rohr.

One thing in life is constant, and that is change! We were pleased to move on with our new owners and their requirements and maintained a crisp focus on our business, our customers and what had made us successful to date.

Attrition and skill loss

Another issue that came into play in the mid to late 2000s was both attrition and hiring. Attrition had been at exceptionally low single digit for many years, and Aerostructures was recognized as a great place to work.

Hiring had also been minimal for many years except for critical skill set replacement. However, with the influx of new business combined with some long service employee attrition, over 3000 new employees were hired across the company during the 2004-2012 period.

Of the 3000 new employees, 40% of them were replacements, the balance, new hires. These new employees who generally integrated and aligned with the culture and the business processes had no concept of the struggles of the lean journey of the previous years that created the culture and developed the business processes.

This may seem trivial or irrelevant, but those employees with the experience and knowledge of the time and effort that went into moving from a crisis of survival to one of unmatched business success were irreplaceable when it came to sustaining that lean journey.

They consistently demonstrated the required behaviors, maintained a focus on and were first in line to drive continuous improvement. Their knowledge of, and proficiency within the operating system and use of the Toyota Production System processes and tools was high.

After 20 years, the behaviors and activities of the Three Circles were "what these employees exhibited, habitually."

Compounding the attrition problem and the challenge of the influx of new employees, was the unanticipated loss of a measure of "functional expertise" within the Value Stream structure.

The Value Streams, as outlined previously, had been staffed, in 2000, with the required functional skill sets to achieve their goals and Improvement Targets. This staffing consisted predominantly of employees from manufacturing engineering, master scheduling, production control, sustaining engineering, finance and supply chain, and on new programs, design engineers, stress engineers, tool designers and contracts administrators.

As attrition began to take its course and the business growth demanded replacement employees with the required functional skill set it was apparent that the development pipeline of these skill sets, which had previously been accomplished by central functions, had in some instances, virtually disappeared.

This functional skill set development had been previously accomplished during the residency of an employee, in a function, through both formal employee training and development. This was supplemented by informal learning and development as a result of being collocated within that function and working within a team of employees with the same functional skills.

This began to cause much concern and discussion. In 2012 plans were implemented to reintroduce small central functions to ensure specific skill set standards were maintained, communicated and understood. This ensured that the appropriate training and development was in place to develop employees with specific functional skill sets to maintain a future supply. Additionally, functional governance, which had been lacking, was reestablished.

Beyond Aerostructures and Aerospace

As noted in earlier chapters, Aerostructures is headquartered in Chula Vista, California, which now has a population of around 240,000 people.

In the late 2000s, the city was having some severe budget shortfalls and had unfortunately experienced some significant labor force reductions.

At the time Cheryl Cox was Mayor, she and Jim Sandoval the City Manager, Scott Tulloch the Assistant City Manager and a number of other Council members had become familiar with the continuous improvement activities, the changes and the progress being made at Aerostructures Chula Vista and other Aerostructures locations.

The Council and City officials were anxious to learn about how to apply lean processes and tools on the services and activities of the City, eliminate waste, improve performance and reduce costs.

In 2008, the Mayor's office set up a meeting with all the City Department leaders and Aerostructures leadership to better understand what Aerostructures was doing relative to performance improvement. Representing the City were the Mayor, the City Manager, the Assistant City Manager, the Police Chief, the Fire Chief, the head of Parks and Recreation, the City Controller and a number of council members.

The Mayor and the Council, like many other Municipal Mayors and Councils, were faced with demanding customers, the citizens of Chula Vista, who wanted more and better services and they were faced with limited revenues - city taxes and fees, and resources - city employees, to accomplish and satisfy all of their customers' demands.

An in-depth review of the lean journey at Aerostructures was provided with a primary focus on the Toyota Production System processes and tools, the Three Tracks and the Three Circles.

There were discussions regarding the benefits of each and their appropriateness and application in support of the services and processes performed by the City on behalf of its residents.

There was general agreement across the City Council, and department leaders that they should adopt a lean approach to waste elimination and performance improvement, and Aerostructures offered to help in any way it could.

That help came about through City employees participating in Aerostructures kaizen events in Chula Vista, participation in the one-week "Continuous Improvement boot camps," the Aerostructures Human Resources Value Stream providing Positive Employee

Philosophy overviews and frequent consultations between City employees and Aerostructures continuous improvement resources.

The City identified an employee to be the Continuous Improvement Manager, identified focal points in each City department and went on to make significant progress, improving many of the City's processes and consequently services to the citizens of Chula Vista, for which they received favorable press reviews and visibility beyond Southern California.

In 2012 the City of Chula Vista was recognized by the "International City/County Association" for its continuous improvement application and progress.

2012 had been another memorable year, Aerostructures metrics for the year:

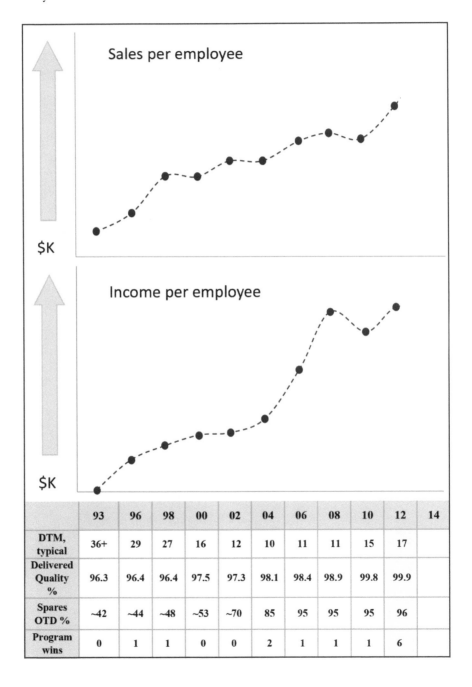

	93	96	98	00	02	04	06	08	10	12	14
DTM, typical	36+	29	27	16	12	10	11	11	15	17	
Delivered Quality %	96.3	96.4	96.4	97.5	97.3	98.1	98.4	98.9	99.8	99.9	
Spares OTD %	~42	~44	~48	~53	~70	85	95	95	95	96	
Program wins	0	1	1	0	0	2	1	1	1	6	

The growth in days to manufacture continued as additional buffer stock was put in place to enable and manage work transfers to not only Mexicali, but to other external to Aerostructures suppliers.

Enterprise Excellence

It is worth pausing to reflect again on progress made on the "Cultural Change, Continuous Improvement Journey," the lean journey, we had been on.

From the 1994 period and the plight we found ourselves in, through 2004 where significant progress was made in creating a culture capable of change. The business identified and removed waste, improved performance and reduced cost with increased efficiency and effectiveness. Evidenced by now positive operating margins on programs that were decades old and had been non-profitable, or at single-digit margins before 1994.

As mentioned, the "sweet spot" in performance came in the years 2004 – 2008 when days to manufacture were at their lowest, on-time delivery to airframers was, with few exceptions at 100%, delivered quality was increasing year over year and was close to 99%, on-time delivery to airline request date for spare parts was at ~95%, and significant new business had been won.

It must be noted that during this period, planned growth in the Aerostructures Aftermarket accelerated, driven by the increase in both total and aging aircraft in airline fleets. This contributed significantly to the margin improvement.

Were we operating at an Enterprise Excellence level?

As reflected on the "Change Triangle" we had not comprehensively put in place or mastered all of the enabling steps identified on that visual. However, we were winning business, delivering significant operating margin and income, had created a culture that drove performance improvement and an environment that employees enjoyed working in.

And the business success that was getting much external recognition.

Through the years 2008 – 2012 these excellent trends continued, schedule, quality and cost metrics continued to improve, albeit as the previously mentioned days to manufacture was deliberately increased. Gainsharing was a contributing factor in achieving this performance, with employees seeing and benefiting from their engagement and contributions. Moreover, additional programs had been won.

Progress by 2012:

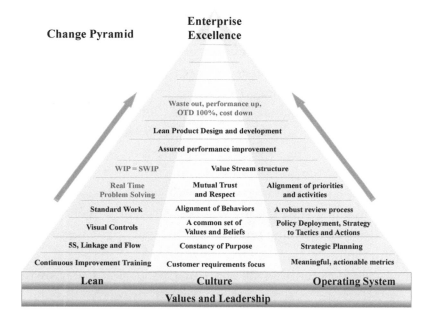

The steps where we believed we had ongoing opportunities:

- Although much time and effort had been put into Real Time Problem Resolution and SWIP, they remained constant challenges. While we were making progress with both elements, significant opportunities remained. They both require almost perfect stability of processes and production schedules, linked with discipline to the management of SWIP and real time problem resolution. We could not yet declare victory on these two items.

- Some performance metrics took a wrong turn as we spread our global footprint and that of the supply chain and although on time delivery was sustained at above 99.5%, the occasional delivery miss occurred, fortunately, few and far between.
- We were driving waste out, and driving performance improvement up. We were also far from any level of waste reduction where we thought we could relax and there were still lots of waste/non-value added activities that required removal.
- With regard to "choosing customers," this is a bold statement. In reality, the customers were choosing us rather than the other way around, and we needed to maintain a firm focus on their requirements and our ability to meet those requirements to positively influence their contract award decisions.

We also believed that after 20 years of focus on cultural change and meaningful continuous improvement, the programs won, the business metrics being consistently achieved and the work environment created, we were operating close to the "Enterprise Excellence zone."

The challenge was to sustain the culture that was driving meaningful change. Some key employees were retiring or moving on, and a significant number of new employees were entering a business that had a unique, uncommon culture.

Moreover, as previously discussed the growing pains being experienced were demanding much of leadership's attention.

As we moved through 2012 a third crisis was seen:

A Crisis of Distraction

New owners

Challenges integrating business cultures

Central management functions and demands

Additional layers of management

Significantly increased reporting requirements

Different approaches to Continuous Improvement

A significant number of new employees

As mentioned, noticeable employee attrition started in the late 2000s and continued into the early 2010s, particularly those employees with around 20 - 30 years of service. These employees all benefitted from experience gained driving change and continuous improvement deployment across the business. Their exit from the business weakened the overall team strength and depth of change and continuous improvement knowledge, experience and capability.

Moving into the mid-2010s, some senior Goodrich leadership who had been instrumental in change moved on, and some significant, experienced and supportive "change agents" had followed that leadership. The Aerostructures global footprint was significantly bigger and more complex. The pool of employees with the visceral proficiency and experience of change and continuous improvement" principles, processes and tools, from the days of a Crisis of Survival, was diminishing rapidly.

Another decision acted upon in this timeframe was to eliminate Gainsharing as this incentive methodology did not align with UTC's incentive structure.

What we learned on the way – a Summary

- How we estimated costs of new product opportunities was way past its sell-by date.
- The transformation of the business from legacy programs with a domestic-centric supply chain to new programs with a global supply chain was counterintuitive to "linkage and flow."
- Invoice cost was not the price we were paying.
  - o The need to identify and understand Total Landed Cost emerged.
- The linkage and flow of products is challenging, the linkage and flow of data and information is both a minefield and an area of great opportunity
- We were experiencing growing pains with a number of issues
- Some major suppliers need significant support, much more than anticipated.
- The City of Chula Vista demonstrated that they could deploy continuous improvement tools to good effect in their "business environment."
- Enterprise Excellence is not a place or destination. It is the creation of a culture and environment that achieves and sustains operating levels and business metrics that are the envy of the competition and continually wins the lion's share of the market.
- The merging of different cultures presents both opportunities and challenges.
- The merging of different continuous improvement approaches and requirements again presents both opportunities and challenges.

Things you may want to consider – a Summary

- Do we have a robust competitive cost estimating capability?
- If we can improve performance to the point of winning much new business, can we handle it?
- Do we have a robust functional skill set development pipeline?
- Do we know how much time and cost do we incur supporting our suppliers?
- Do we understand our total landed costs of supplier parts?
- Are we agile enough and prepared for future technology, materials, process, manufacturing or business techniques?
- If we need an influx of technical resources where are they going to come from?
- Do we have a robust employee development process to ensure the continuity of our culture?
- Should we choose to offload work, what do we anticipate the response from the workforce will be and are we prepared to deal with that?
- Are we winning the "Lion's share" of business opportunities?
  - If not do we know why?

Chapter 8

The importance of culture and leadership. Leading and managing with principles, rather than rules as the basis for decisions. Employees and their often underappreciated talents and value. Indicators of meaningful, positive cultural and behavioral change.

Culture and Leadership

We believe that the importance of Culture and Leadership cannot be overestimated. There are multiple books on both subjects written by distinguished people who study, understand and can relay the intricacies of each much better than we can. According to one 2015 study, over 50,000 books on Leadership alone have been published in English in the last century.

However, to understand progress within the business that began as "Rohr," it may be of value to relate our experiences in building a robust and successful business with a leadership culture that still endures to this day through two business ownership changes.

All companies have a culture. This culture will either contribute to and enhance business results or degrade from them. For employees to function efficiently and succeed personally and contribute to the business mission, it is essential that they understand and buy into the culture they are working in. This requires understanding and committing to that culture and its requirements, while habitually demonstrating appropriate cultural behaviors.

We believe that the culture we established over time was a pivotal contributor to overall company success.

Essential and critical items of that culture are listed below:

- Customers are placed first in priority.
- A constancy of purpose, where we are going, how we are going to get there, the processes and tools we are going to use and the required behaviors are clearly communicated.
- Shared beliefs, values, norms, and practices are established, communicated frequently and continually demonstrated.
- Positive Employee Philosophy Principles to create the work environment are the norm.
- Business processes and practices are clearly defined within the operating system.
- The use of Toyota Production System processes and tools is non-negotiable.
- Behaviors not acceptable are exposed and dealt with.

While many elements contribute to Culture and Leadership, the underpinnings of the Positive Employee Philosophy process referenced in earlier chapters and above, were essential for success. For example, without "Effective Two-Way Communications" and "Mutual Trust and Respect" cultural gains would have been improbable if not impossible.

Fundamental to our understanding of the changes in the business, we did learn that "culture trumps leadership and business strategy every time." Without a robust supporting culture, the best-laid plans can become of minimal value and gains can become temporary at best.

A quote seen quite often:

"A leader is a person you will follow to a place you wouldn't go by yourself."

Joel Barker. "Futurist."

For a leader to accomplish this, we believe there are a minimum of five required characteristics:

- They must have a clear, vision and can consistently articulate that vision.
- They must lead the quest to that vision from the front.
- They must define clear roles and responsibilities, set expectations and then hold themselves and others accountable for results.
- They must be able to exercise influence.
- They must praise and encourage effort, and success. They must also praise efforts that result in less than desired results. In both cases ensuring those applying themselves continue to do so willingly and with fervor.

Even with the above elements in place, there is no guarantee that effective leadership can be practiced without defined methods, systems and processes.

This is where the "Three Circles" – the Values, the Positive Employee Philosophy, and the Operating System, came together and leveraged talent from across the business to produce extraordinary business results over decades.

As the business environment at Aerostructures changed and evolved, it became apparent that providing effective leadership was demanding, even when operating with appropriate values, norms, and practices within a supportive culture.

Rather than a traditional rule-based system as a backstop, leaders were now required to:

- Make positive assumptions about people; ensuring Adult to Adult behaviors.
- Identify and eliminate negatives; working within principles rather than relying on "thou shalt, thou shalt not" rules. This meant that circumstances had to be considered to "do the right thing," which was not always the "same thing."
- Rely on communicating and listening skills.
- Implement practices designed to be fair, but not always equal.

We learned that even the most talented leaders could achieve little if our culture did not allow them to influence employees toward a common goal. Nothing exists in a vacuum; effective leadership cannot function or survive in the wrong culture.

Effective leadership is always combined with competent core management and decision making skills, demonstrating the essential ability to close on obligations and commitments.

As we began to change the business at various levels and at different sites, it became apparent that while fundamental leadership requirements and values were consistent, the skill level and personality of the leaders needed to be considered when assignments were made. This enabled needs and opportunities within the business to be addressed or leveraged.

For example, the general manager at Riverside who led significant business structure changes was well matched to achieve to the first generation of changes, which were heavily "culture-centric." After two years he was moved to a facility that needed this same culture-centric focus. The replacement general manager who had been at Riverside during the cultural change was well suited to institutionalize the new ways of doing business via the acceleration of the Toyota Production System processes and tools.

After about one year, this leader, in turn, became the "culture change agent" at the San Marcos Texas business, and was replaced with a strong cultural leader from within the Riverside team. The replacement at Riverside was a leader who had been fully engaged through the transformation to date and had the benefit of understanding this change, being an active part of it and had a cadre of leaders around him with the quickly developing skills to continue the quest.

The leadership development process was reinforced by these key leader positional changes that brought the right skill sets, at the right time, to the facilities needing them while continually developing talent and skills in the leadership ranks.

Early in the change process we did recognize and understand that a critical leadership responsibility was to establish a constructive, risk-free work environment where employee morale could flourish even when under adverse business conditions. This led to involved and engaged teams at many levels who "kept climbing the mountain of achievement" despite occasional setbacks.

As we progressed, we saw that Culture and Leadership are intrinsically woven together, and it's the many, small, simple, easy to do things that change the culture. However, you have to be honest, unrelenting, and consistently reinforce the right behaviors through demonstrated actions, words and management skills. That is the art of getting things done, completed or closed appropriately within the "Three Circles."

On occasion, we did encounter leaders who demonstrated a strong commitment to the Values and the Positive Employee Philosophy. However, they lacked supporting management, organizational, and continuous improvement skills which hampered their ability to close on commitments.

What we can relay, is how we came to understand and apply focus on the cultural elements in our business, managing the change from ineffective culture and leadership practices to ones that enabled dramatic business improvements.

Some things outlined throughout this book seem very basic, and the reader may ask "why is this basic stuff even in here?"

The answer may lie in the quote, included earlier in this book that resonated with many of us at Aerostructures, which is worth repeating:

"The reason most organizations leap to adopt the latest advances ... is to spare themselves the painful commitment to the basics."

– Allan Cox. Leadership Consultant and Author.

All too often, the latest software, the latest whizz-bang machine, the most recent business fad, some high-priced consultants or another round of management reorganizations are seen as answers to business problems and the achievement of a competitive advantage. These moves usually come at high premiums, potentially long lead times and too often only offer a temporary advantage if any at all, until the competition gets or does "the same thing."

Through unyielding attention to leadership, culture, and application of the Toyota Principles, processes and tools we were able to reinforce our "competitive advantage goal" constantly. Previously stated, as "doing what we did, at better performance and cost, than our competition."

Leadership and Culture entering the Crisis of Survival

In the early 1990s a traditional, somewhat "Theory X" culture was in place at Rohr. This culture exhibited traditional workplace values and autocratic assumptions that assumed team members:

- Disliked work and would avoid it if possible
- Avoided accountability
- Lacked responsibility and drive
- Must be coerced, controlled and directed to apply themselves

- Were not capable of thinking through work method improvements
- Needed specific direction to function

This functionally driven "Theory X" culture essentially drove the business to be somewhat dysfunctional as exhibited by uncoordinated activities, unaligned priorities and the general malaise of the organization described in earlier chapters.

This was further evidenced by an "office versus shop floor" separation whereby shop floor support was inadequate in an "us versus them" environment. Marginal product and process quality and delivery levels continued, and we frequently heard the refrain from engineers and other support employees that "if only they, shop floor employees, would follow the process, use the system, do what we tell them to do, then all would be well."

However, when these engineers and support personnel were challenged to go to the shop floor and oversee work or help with a process or system issue, they usually found that many manufacturing and support processes and systems were, to say the least, lacking in functional capability or their availability.

We realized that positive cultural and leadership changes were vital to success.

This required change can be illustrated by the example below of a problem with a scheduled delivery to a customer:

One leader's input:

- "Somebody dropped the ball. I want everyone in this weekend, set up both shifts, spread support employees out on second shift as well as first. I want conference calls mornings and afternoons on both Saturday and Sunday. I want a detailed report of the weekend in a conference call on Monday, 5:30 am. I am not going to miss a shipment."
  o This yields one response

A different approach:

- "We have a customer delivery scheduled for Monday that we must make and we have some issues that we need to resolve to ensure delivery. I appreciate everyone's focus so far to make that happen, but we have a little way to go yet. Please get the team together, include me too, and let's figure out what we need to do to make sure we support the customer's requirement and let's see if we identify what went awry and fix the problem at root cause."
  o This yields an alternate more meaningful response.

It was obvious that the appropriate culture must be in place whereby a question or request and the subsequent response and actions yield the best outcome for all concerned. We could not throw a switch and say "the culture on Monday next will be one of everyone doing the right things, harmony and bliss." Aerostructures worked on leadership and culture constantly.

Changing Leadership and Culture

As the culture changed, we recognized that we could not inflict change on employees. It was vital to develop engaged employees, part of the principles outlined in the Positive Employment Philosophy while acknowledging that involvement and engagement are two entirely different things.

A myriad of simple things contributed to positive cultural change - we had changed and relaxed the dress code and the separate cafeteria for management had been mothballed, both in the late 1980s. Reserved parking was long gone. Moving into the mid-1990s office doors, which were few, were rarely closed, if at all. Leaders and support employees were collocated with the people, product, and processes they supported. Rules had been replaced with Principles. With expectations set, understood and acknowledged, leaders began to lead. Employees were seen and treated as assets capable of significant contribution, they were actively listened to and activities were coordinated rather than directed.

We needed employees to feel safe implementing change, and we encouraged and enabled managed risk taking and decision making at the working level. This was accomplished while communicating the consequences and responsibilities of risk taking and decision making within established boundaries, principles and processes.

Any one of these actions alone means little, but they all, and many others, contributed to cultural change. Leadership's behaviors and the environment that reflects those behaviors drove the balance of the cultural change we experienced over the years.

By consistently demonstrating the required behaviors through their actions leadership confirmed that traditional autocratic behaviors were being replaced by behaviors that reflected an environment and culture where team members would readily:

- Come to work to contribute
- Engage in the process to make that contribution.
- Want to do the right thing
- Exercise self-direction toward objectives to which they are committed
- Engage in continuous improvement
- Exercise their capabilities and potential
- Provide input and make decisions

Formal broad communications plans were implemented and sustained as outlined earlier, supported by "Leadership walking about," being seen in the workplace every day and listening as much, if not more than, talking.

Leadership was required to be engaged and informed regarding the ongoing business changes and processes:

- Being transparent and consistent in all their communications of "where we were going and how we were going to get there."

Getting everyone to understand that:

- The customer and their needs were the most important things for all employees
- We were all coming to work for many of the same reasons; to pay rent/mortgages, buy groceries, raise children and send them to college.
- The competition was the enemy (quite a challenge in such an interwoven business as Aerospace)
- Moreover, by "doing what we do better than the competition" would keep the customer coming to us, providing increased reward and job security. Given the fact that this security was not the case when company employment went from 13,300 to a little over 4,000 (3,300 to 380 in Riverside alone) this was quite well accepted.

We listened to employees, acted upon their input, and if the response was to be "no" we discussed the rationale for the answer with the employee. We talked and engaged with employees about something other than work – their wellbeing, their families, sports and other items. We were after all, all employees coming to work each day for the same reasons.

Cultural change at Aerostructures created much outside interest. One amusing anecdote to share was during a visit we made to a large customer where "Cultural change" was an agenda item. The customer's representatives, all of them in dress shirts and ties, described in detail and ardor the focus they had on the issue, the support of their leadership, the cultural changes they had made, and how this was to be seen in their work environment. As this conversation unfolded, through the window could be seen a fleet of somewhat expensive automobiles, all in quite obvious reserved parking spots. They were being washed, one by one, by an elderly gentleman in a long trench coat, carrying a bucket and sponge, while light drizzle fell.

It was reminiscent of a scene from "Downton Abbey." The vision did not seem to support the cultural change being so passionately described.

Indicators of Positive Cultural Change

As we deployed the Values, the Positive Employee Philosophy and the Operating System, we saw significant cultural changes in broad areas of the business. Some of the changes we noted were:

- **Communications**
  - The more we communicated the direction of the business, increased levels of communications and information were requested by employees.
  - Input and feedback from employees was provided freely and routinely.
- **Positive future**
  - We got feedback of increased optimism about the future of the business.
  - Union leadership began to state that "perhaps this time they, leadership may have got it right and we have a chance of survival."
- **Senior staff visible engagement**
  - The visibility of senior staff participation in the workplace and in continuous improvement events had a significant positive effect on culture and results.
  - Seeing the presidents of Rohr and then Goodrich, in the workplace documenting reality and applying countermeasures was always impactful.
  - "Leadership walking around" provided visibility, support, and opportunity for informal discussions.

- **Visual Controls**
  - With basic visual controls in place indicating performance to driver measures, team members were able to see and understand how they were contributing to the business.
  - There began a sense of urgency to get issues and problems resolved to ensure success.
  - Many employees expressed appreciation of being able to stop producing charts and data that they knew were of no consequence.
- **Process Engagement**
  - Increased numbers of employees, from Finance, Engineering, and Manufacturing et al, came forward requesting training and engagement in the changes being made and the continuous improvement being deployed.
  - From these employees, new leaders emerged who engaged in the changes being made.
- **Continuous improvement activities**
  - Improvement activities were being undertaken independently of formal kaizen events.
  - A waiting list of employees wanting to participate in formal kaizen events was required and maintained.
  - A waiting list of employees wanting to participate in the "Continuous Improvement boot camps" was also required and maintained.
- **Engagement**
  - Many employees who had been "standing on the sidelines," under previous management saw the opportunity to engage in change as issues causing their previous hesitation were melting away.
  - Employees encouraged to contribute, take risks, participate in continuous improvement activities did so with increasing effect.
  - Many employees who had leadership potential but had not previously wanted to embark on that path now did so eagerly.

- **Union employee engagement**
  - Company and Union relationships were excellent.
  - The contract negotiations that took place in the era discussed throughout this book took on a positive business focused tone. Both parties represented their "constituents," but the focus of both changed to one of recognizing the competitive nature of the business environment we were in. Resulting in contract language that balanced union employee representation, compensation and welfare with the flexibility to generate returns for the business, and its employees, as a whole.
  - A "rider" documented and inserted into the contract in the late 1990s stated, "In a kaizen event, production classifications are waived except for situations where technical skill sets are required." Enabling the kaizen event teams to do much real time "hands-on" change.
  - Union grievances reduced from around 50 per month in the early 1990s to one to two per month in the mid-2000s to early 2010s.
  - The chief Union official at Riverside was elected to office on a documented "Lean Ticket" in the mid-1990s.
  - The "second in command" Union official at Chula Vista was a regular participant in the "questions and answers" sessions when we had visitors on site reviewing the continuous improvement and cultural change progress.
  - Union members were leading continuous improvement activities and "kicking off" events with positive comments.
  - Time observations being done by union members, on union members. That was momentous!
- **Attrition**
  - The overall attrition rate that had been running in the teens through the 1980s into the 1990s dropped to slightly less than 2% and stayed there for many years. As noted it did pick back up and went back to double figures in the early 2010s.

- **Customers**
  - o Customers became aware of positive changes as business performance to commitments improved.
  - o Although performance was still far from required levels, the drive to remove work and place it with alternative suppliers, essentially stopped.
  - o Following 2400 customer, supplier, and other visitors, from the late 1990s through the mid to late 2000s, external recognition of continuous improvement and cultural change progress was high.
- **External Recognition**
  - o A number of newspapers and magazines had recognized and reported positively on changes to the business, the performance improvements, and the financial results being achieved.

And the "gift that keeps on giving" – keeps on giving:

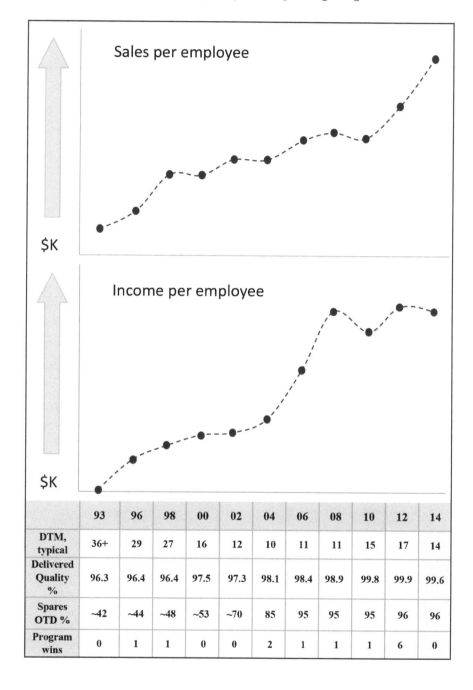

	93	96	98	00	02	04	06	08	10	12	14
DTM, typical	36+	29	27	16	12	10	11	11	15	17	14
Delivered Quality %	96.3	96.4	96.4	97.5	97.3	98.1	98.4	98.9	99.8	99.9	99.6
Spares OTD %	~42	~44	~48	~53	~70	85	95	95	95	96	96
Program wins	0	1	1	0	0	2	1	1	1	6	0

As the "Sales per employee" positive trend continued "Income per employee" results became mixed. This was the result of new programs entering into production, where Standard Work - close the gap activities had yet to be vigorously deployed to identify and remove waste and cost. Income per employee is estimated to have ramped back up significantly, as these activities have been effectively utilized in recent years.

It is also of note that once launched, these new programs demonstrated much lower waste and cost than on previous development programs. The traditional learning curve was, once again, shown to be obsolete.

Days to manufacture can be seen beginning to reduce, as the buffer stocks for work transfers were being eliminated.

Delivered quality took a downtick as suppliers ramped up, deliveries to the customer increased and quality issues were found by the customer.

What we learned on the way – a Summary

- Leadership defines Culture and Culture defines Leadership
- Culture change happens over time, provided leadership defines the culture and reflects that culture in every spoken word, action, and behavior.
- If someone in leadership is unable to support, after training, expectation setting and coaching; then removing them from their position is necessary.
- The cultural change enabled (unleashed) thousands of small ongoing process and flow changes that fundamentally changed the business.

Things you may want to consider – a Summary

- Do we have a constancy of purpose?
- Do we have a communicated and understood vision?
  - o Does everyone know where we are going and how we are going to get there?

- Are Values established, communicated and clear?
- How do we communicate with our employees, from formal business communications all the way to daily interaction and everything in between?
  - Is leadership visible, in the workplace, every day?
  - Who is communicating what to who?
  - How is that communication accomplished?
  - At what frequency?
- What do our leadership communications, actions, and behaviors inspire and yield in the workplace?
- Do we lead or do we manage?
  - What do our daily actions and behaviors look like?
  - What do our employees think we do?
- What is our working environment reflective of?
  - When considering this question am I thinking of the environment I work in, or the workplaces our employees are in?
- Do we measure or gage our culture across the company?
  - How do we do that?
  - At what frequency?
- Where are employees located in terms of whom they interact with and support on a daily basis?
- How would a knowledgeable visitor describe our:
  - Leadership style?
  - Work environment?
- How would a knowledgeable observer describe our culture and our continuous improvement activities?
- What are the indicators of our culture?

Chapter 9

*E*very day was and is a learning opportunity. At times when we stopped moving forward, we had to look in the mirror and accept that what we were doing was not working. We often needed to "course correct" and relearn many things to continue to make progress. Over 20 plus years we learned a lot from our experiences and mistakes, with a number of them outlined below. Reflection is a beneficial process.

Lessons Learned, what we underestimated, missed or got wrong

Looking back it's relatively easy to note areas and events where our assumptions, actions and sometimes results were less than ideal. This proved to be part of the continual learning process, and much experience and knowledge was gained as a result of getting something wrong.

When mistakes were made we readily agreed that looking for "those guilty" was not a good use of time and this became a thing of the past.

However, we did learn that picking ourselves up from mistakes, understanding the issues and putting countermeasures in place, was much more effective than any other alternative. This fostered continued, engagement and measured risk-taking by employees and enhanced the overall change process and subsequent results.

Some of the more pertinent items are noted below:

Leadership

On occasion, we waited too long to make a change with leaders who were not committed to the path we were on. Approximately 75% of the senior leadership team in Riverside were replaced over the first eighteen months of change activity. Chula Vista operations experienced the same scale of leadership changes over a similar but later period. However the rate of change was much slower in several operations sites and support organizations and in retrospect, we waited too long to take action. A leader who is "not on board" can be a significant overt and covert, impediment to change.

Value stream mid-point (Where and what do you improve first?)

The first significant changes toward the required culture, continuous improvement deployment, and a viable operating system were implemented in our Riverside bonding facility. Bonding operations are early to mid-point in the value stream of the production build and had we started in an assembly site, at the higher end of the value chain, earlier bottom-line results could have quite possibly been attained. In the 1990s the Foley assembly site was well positioned for improvement with Values deployed and the Positive Employee Philosophy in place and may well have been the first to drive major improvements had we been given that option. It was, however, Riverside that was faced with closure and where decisive actions were needed.

Cultural enablers and the operating system

While the Values, Positive Employee Philosophy, and supporting leadership were positioned and essential to establishing a viable culture, it was the operating system that brought everything together enabling significant improvements in business results. These increases in results were far greater than we had anticipated early in the journey. Just as leadership cannot exist in a vacuum without a supporting culture, then the culture needs a viable operating system to be successful. Although company Values and the Positive Employee Philosophy were in place in the 1980s, it was the final "Third Circle, the operating system" that closed the loop in the late 1990s and enabled major cultural and business performance gains.

Linkage and Flow

As our lean journey was starting, the final touches to a "Centers of Excellence Strategy" for nacelle production were being made. A "Centers of Excellence Strategy" may have its advantages in some circumstances. However, these advantages were not apparent on our lean journey, and much waste was removed as we addressed linkage and flow opportunities, re-collocated work and closed facilities.

The Centers of Excellence Strategy had extended employment expectations to the employees at some locations that we were, unfortunately, unable to keep.

In the facilities that remained, the initial continuous improvement activities were focused on aligning product flows within a cellular manufacturing environment with plans for right-sizing, point of use and visual controls.

The productivity gains from basic linkage and flow activities were so significant that they propelled excellent performance and business results through the first five years of change and continuous improvement. These pleasantly surprising results were supplemented by the speed at which non-conforming products and processes were exposed and dealt with. The time from "detect to correct" went from months to days, then to hours and finally some to Real Time Problem Resolution.

While this was all positive, it did take much time and effort to undo decisions of the past.

The concept of linkage and flow invariably leads to vertical integration opportunities in single rather than multiple locations, with major production activities all on one shift supported by the appropriate, collocated production support.

This minimizes inventory levels and costs, and reduces overhead costs, while enabling dramatically reduced cycle times and improved business performance, driven by real time communications, real time problem resolution, and ongoing waste elimination and cost reduction activities.

While the location of a business may be important, we have found that the criteria mentioned above drive success rather than the particular location of the business.

What we were able to accomplish in the first 10 years of change and performance improvement was clearly driven by linkage and flow, moving substantially in the direction of vertical integration while delivering outstanding business performance.

The most recent 15 years at Aerostructures, has seen increased global outsourcing, essentially a strategy counter to linkage and flow, driven by time and circumstance. While Sales per employee have understandably, continued to increase, Income per employee has become a little blurred and conceivably challenged.

We believe that wherever possible the premise of doing as much as possible "in one location, on one shift" enables maximum business performance.

Then gradually insourcing appropriate outsourced work, filling the capacity that will be created. At which point you have the opportunity to identify and remove waste, thereby reducing the cost, of the insourced work.

Performance improvement through incremental gains

The real learning was that waste comes in layers and improving a process or product by removing waste exposes the next level of incremental improvement opportunity. This was earlier labeled as "peeling layers of the onion," and we were slow to realize and react to this phenomenon and remove waste that was in reality, right in front of us. We learned that multiple incremental gains repeatedly made, were far more fruitful than focusing resources on proposed "breakthrough, step function gains" that are often slow, expensive to implement and very often deliver less than promised. That is not to say we closed the door on "breakthrough step function gains," we just became prudent in our investment of them.

The high price of low cost

As mentioned earlier, this issue did come into view as we expanded the supply chain in search of lower costs. Subsequently, we did develop a "Total Landed Cost model" that provided additional information on the actual costs. There were, and still are, many incurred costs that are not included on a supplier invoice. In addition are the "quality, engineering, supply chain and other" resource costs, required to manage and support low-cost sources that are, more often than not, understated.

Once core and non-core manufacturing capabilities and products have been determined for a business (a measure of vertical integration), the supply chain supports the procurement of materials for the work to be done in-house.

As continuous improvement identifies and drives waste out of internal processes and capacity is created, the opportunity to add back some non-core manufacturing into the mix, increasing vertical integration increases. As does the opportunity to remove waste and cost from those products and processes once insourced. See "A fourth crisis looms" in the Summary.

Supply Chain

As noted above, manufacturers will invariably utilize a supply chain, and we did not initially recognize significant "low hanging" waste reduction opportunities available at a number of our suppliers.

For example, a supplier provided a kit of multiple parts for an "Engine Build-Up" process with each unidentified individual part wrapped in protective material and placed randomly in a pallet sized box about 30 inches deep.

Once received the parts were unwrapped, laid out for identification and then put into kits aligned with their assigned sub-assembly locations. This process took around two hours, occurred multiple times per week and had been in place for many years.

As a process improvement, the supplier, who jointly identified this opportunity, was requested to separate and pack the parts in the sub-kits, on robust rotable foam shadow boards complete with part identification, to enable direct delivery to the appropriate sub-assembly station.

A significant savings in time and cost for both parties that the supplier was frustratingly slow to incorporate. Perseverance paid off and the countermeasure requested was eventually put in place.

One does wonder what took so long. Could it be that the way things were packaged was "the way they had always done it?"

Multiple other supplier transportation methods, packaging, kitting, delivery frequencies and delivery location opportunities were subsequently identified and leveraged.

We were slow in identifying the wealth of opportunity in the interfaces with suppliers.

We severely underestimated the amount of support suppliers both established and new, would need across the globally expanding supply chain and its increased workload.

WIP - SWIP

While we leveraged linkage and flow and Standard Work that resulted in reduced product cost, we did not focus on inventory for many years. We had to understand the consequences of the difference between "Work In Progress" – WIP, or "Standard Work In Progress" – SWIP. As outlined previously, SWIP is reflective of the least amount of inventory that should be in place to satisfy customer demand. SWIP is calculable, dependent on the Takt Times and cycle times of the required processes.

As we progressed into the 2000s, we began to understand, calculate and manage to SWIP levels and freed up vast amounts of capital. Given the number of facilities and suppliers now across the globe, we are left to wonder how much inventory is in these manufacturing locations, in-transit, in multiple buffer stocks and hardware in holding areas, awaiting problem resolution from afar.

Continuous improvement in support organizations

As previously outlined, we had some great success in support organizations, and we had some "heel dragging." In retrospect, we should have done more to educate employees in these organizations and helped them understand and identify available improvement opportunities and how to deploy continuous improvement tools to leverage them.

And quite possibly have made some additional leadership changes earlier.

When we last looked at overhead costs, they were approaching 40% of total production program cost. That is a wealth of opportunity.

Functional erosion and skills development

When we deployed functional expertise – putting employees with specific functional skills into the Value Streams, the staffing of some functional organizations was, of course, reduced significantly. These organizations established standards, provided governance, maintained processes and developed proficiency within key disciplines.

Over time, through retirements and other personnel movement, some of these functions, as noted earlier, effectively disappeared – notably Manufacturing Engineering, Master Scheduling, Production Control and ERP support. We belatedly realized that without central or core organizations we would eventually run out of employees with the specific functional skill sets.

In the late 2000s, these organizations were back in place to provide standards, governance and training.

Career progression

Following on from the previous issue, those who enjoyed and wanted a career in a specific function, their career progression paths became blurred, or even non-existent, as many functional positions disappeared.

One interesting positive aspect of this was observed. Support personnel collocated into the Value Stream structure were exposed on a daily basis to the inner workings of other skill sets assigned there. This resulted in many of them gravitating to, and excelling in the skill sets of functions that were not in their interests when embarking on their initial educational or career paths. This subsequently resulted in a number of these individuals rapidly increasing their capabilities and value, with many of them progressing in their careers and becoming leaders within the Value Stream structure in a number of roles.

Engineering

The deployment of Toyota Production System principle's, processes and tools and the development of the Lean Product Development process in engineering and research and development was a significant "learn as you go process."

General resistance to new materials, designs, processes, and methods was high early in the deployment and development of Lean Product Development. However, following the consolidation of engineering into the Component Value Stream structure, combined with the associated changes in leadership and clearly defined accountability, buy-in became higher, and subsequent process and product innovations followed.

In retrospect we allowed the highly technical content of the product to obscure and delay changes required regarding employees and processes who were obstacles to the culture.

For example, having once again been surprised that a nacelle, once actually weighed, was found to be well over calculated design and contract weight requirements, the entire weight management process was mapped in detail. This process mapping revealed that nacelle design engineers were alternately utilizing uncoordinated weight management systems. The product Weights Engineers, as they went through their process, were not qualified for, or even authorized, to access and use the processes used by the design and stress engineers.

With the mandate for a "single source of data," and a single weight management process, valid component weights became available to all with clear, consistent methods to calculate them.

It was surprising that this type of action took so long and was typical until the new Component Value Stream structure and leadership were in place to drive Lean Product Development and the discipline and culture required to support it.

Culture change speed and site differences

During the change process, it became apparent that Riverside employees were quite resilient and ready for change. Possibly driven by decades of surviving the questionable tactics and directions of previous leadership. Recognition of the reality of the "burning platform" enabled change to establish and flourish relatively quickly. While the Chula Vista site did implement positive change, it was at a slower rate than at Riverside, even when supported by former Riverside leaders inserted into leadership positions in Chula Vista. Also, some of the newer sites did not have a survival type of history or belief that there was a "burning platform." As a consequence most were slow to change and some, as noted previously, were eventually closed with work being transferred to other sites "engaged in change" and driving performance improvement. Underestimating the rate of required leadership change contributed to a slower than desired rate of continuous improvement deployment and subsequent results.

Reflection

Reflection was not a strong point or done in any meaningful way at Rohr in the 1980s and early 1990s. Management were paid to make decisions. Not to sit around pondering what may have been. Quite probably a symptom of the environment at the time.

We found that to understand an issue or opportunity in detail, or to make tactical adjustments to strategies and actions being deployed, that reflection, as a deliberate action, increased the quality and impact of countermeasures, or course corrections, that were subsequently made.

That is not to say every issue or every opportunity resulted in reflection. We were judicious in what it was that needed review and understanding through reflection. It was invariably focused on the major changes and plans being deployed to drive change and culture. And often reflection was undertaken by a small group of senior leadership at the leading edge of change. We found it very revealing and beneficial.

Summary

We were fortunate and challenged to have experienced a number of crises over the years. The first one in particular initiated significant cultural changes, the continuous improvement focus and various supportive sub-elements that made up the remarkable lean journey Aerostructures subsequently embarked upon.

This crisis in the early 1990s caused a dramatic reaction and drove a significant step back review of the business including:

- Business leadership and leaders
- The enterprise management processes
- The culture and associated work environment
- Performance improvement methods and processes

Could this have been accomplished without this crisis? Our belief is, it could not. The crisis caused a type of reaction that an opportunity rarely does. A second key element was the Constancy of Purpose. We were indeed focused on, and consistent with, where we were going, how we were going to get there, the processes and tools we were going to use on the way and the behaviors required on the journey. This required leadership with foresight, determination, and stamina to lead from the front.

There was a third crucial element. Since 1994, there have been seven Aerostructures presidents, each of them working with the same core group of Aerostructures senior leadership, who themselves were in place from the mid-1990s through the early-2010s. All actively engaged in the business transition, enabling continuity of progress with their unique capabilities, experience, and ideas. The cohesion, ability, and leadership of these individual leaders to work together as a team was unique. The authors have experienced this esprit de corps, only once, during their broad and long working careers.

> **A Crisis of Survival**
>
> Poor customer schedule support and quality issues
>
> Customer dissatisfaction
>
> Investment community dissatisfaction
>
> Employee unrest
>
> Leadership unable to resolve performance or financial issues
>
> One step away from bankruptcy
>
> Adrift without a plan

Initial opportunities and issues were methodically addressed with the expansion of the company Values and Positive Employee Philosophy integrated with the first implementation of Toyota Production System processes and tools. Over several years this expanded to include deep dive reviews of business elements with opportunities identified and countermeasures implemented. This ultimately resulted in a significant overhaul and positive change across almost every facet of the business.

The second crisis occurring in the late 2000s was one of complacency, driven by a feeling of (false) security as a result of solid overall enterprise performance, multiple significant new program business wins and employee participation in the Gainsharing incentive plan. Another contributor to this "crisis of complacency" was the substantial external recognition received as a result of the cultural changes, continuous improvement progress, and exceptional business returns.

A Crisis of Complacency

A relatively simple Operating System delivering consistent, exceptional business results

Gainsharing enabling all employees to enjoy the financial success

High customer satisfaction

Winning significant new commercial programs

A great culture

Wide recognition of the success with Continuous Improvement

This was a crisis that we were able to effectively define and communicate by providing awareness of longer-term competitive risks with clear plans to ensure positive progress was maintained in all areas.

We cautioned against complacency as a result of the "good times" described above. Leadership strove to lead and maintain a strong continuous improvement focus and the supporting behaviors and activities. We were dealing with this crisis when the book "How the Mighty Fall" by Jim Collins was published. This book was widely read and became a source of information and inspiration for leadership.

For us a timely and very useful publication.

A third crisis, still unfolding, is one of distraction, as the integration of Aerostructures into the United Technologies Corporation business structure continues.

A Crisis of Distraction

New owners

Challenges integrating business cultures

Central management functions and demands

Additional layers of management

Significantly increased reporting requirements

Different approaches to continuous improvement

A significant number of new employees

Looking back, to when Goodrich acquired Rohr, many of the elements noted above were present and indeed had we written this manuscript at the time many of the concerns would have been the same.

We have learned over time that the strong culture at Aerostructures will generally sustain with new ownership, and now strongly influenced by UTC, will continue to grow positively. This growth is a result of the sharing of multiple benefits brought by both entities and leadership's relentless constancy of purpose.

This now hybrid Rohr-Goodrich-UTC Aerostructures culture, leadership and operating system continues to evolve and improve as evidenced by continuing business results.

This business performance has overcome offsetting influences such as an influx of new employees and the loss of employees who contributed so much to the positive change in the business over 20 plus years.

The differences in the approach to continuous improvement between the two companies continues to be strongly influenced by the Aerostructures operating system. ACE remains strong in "quality fundamentals," and has now integrated critical aspects of Aerostructures continuous improvement approach. Aerostructures Lean Product Development process has benefitted from UTC's strong engineering heritage and systems, and it's Technical Fellowship organization.

So, while the visceral grasp of what it takes to "do what you do better than the competition" may be of concern as key employees in the original business change move on, the processes and tools are in place and available to continue to do just that.

As with any business, the crucial requirement is leadership engaging, leading from the front and having a constancy of purpose.

Over the course of writing this book, Rockwell Collins merged with UTC Aerospace Systems, the joint company being now named Collins Aerospace Systems.

It remains to be seen how the cultures will mesh and what form or name the continuous improvement process will take under Collins Aerospace Systems. However, it is anticipated that the strengths of both companies' cultures and continuous improvement processes will be integrated to leverage the expertise of the combined businesses.

Progress on the Change Pyramid

We believe we got many things right and quite a few things wrong through the years.

When we got things wrong, we brushed ourselves off, learned from the moment, did not assign blame, made the necessary adjustments, applied countermeasures and moved on.

We did not fully achieve all items on the enablers of Enterprise Excellence, seen on the next illustration, but the stage was set for continued progress and success.

Key takeaways

- "Constancy of purpose" was crucial. We drove the same Goals, the same philosophies, the same behaviors and the same performance improvement tools throughout the years. Leadership were consistent and fully supportive in their actions and when on occasion when that was not the case, they were found other things to do.

- The Three Circles developed and deployed consistently proved to be invaluable. The Values are indeed binary, and along with the Positive Employee Philosophy and the Operating System, this trifecta guided us to outstanding performance and financial results. It brought industry-wide recognition and beyond. It has provided recognition, reward, and stability to the business and its employees.

- The Three Circle approach works globally with the "right" leadership in place, albeit at different deployment speeds.
- Unflinching and constant engagement and behaviors by leadership reflecting the Three Circles has to be maintained.
- Employee engagement is critical. People philosophies, operating systems or continuous improvement cannot be inflicted on people.
- Keeping things as simple as possible and sharing as much information as practical helped immensely in securing the engagement of "all" employees.
- A knowledgeable Sensei proved to be invaluable. Not only as a source of facilitation, education, and guidance but also as an "outside stimulant."
- Roles, responsibility and accountability have to be clear, understood and accepted. Metrics to ensure alignment with the roles and responsibilities and to track accountability to goals and targets have to be real time, meaningful and actionable.
- Identifying and removing waste/non-value tasks and activities is the key to long-term performance improvement and reduced cost.
- Performance gains are generally driven by thousands of incremental improvements to eliminate waste combined with a much lower number of breakthrough process or system items.
- Problem-solving is best done "real time" by those closest to the problem and the majority of the incremental improvements noted above were identified and implemented at the operator level.
- Awareness, Understanding, Commitment, Habit - change takes time, courage, attention, and patience.
- Being faced with an "Opportunity to improve" when business results are positive, and life is good is different from that of

being confronted by a burning platform where choices can be binary and are somewhat final.

- We not infrequently came across business leaders from outside Aerostructures who when discussing "change, culture or continuous improvement," would remark "we did that" and then begin to describe their current business improvement initiative. We believe this is nothing more than a "flavor of the day" approach.
- Affecting change, developing a culture or driving continuous improvement are not things "to have completed." They are elements of a consistent journey required to reap and sustain benefits and do what you do better than the competition.
- One should of course, be aware of existing and new problem-solving tools or processes available to business and industry and where appropriate, weave them into the operating system.

Other thoughts

One may ask "how are the principles, processes, tools and the leadership approach described in this book, deployed in Aerospace, across the 1990s and into the 2010s, relative to our situation today?" We would answer:

- Values are required and binary, you either have them, or you don't.
- A strategy is required that is clearly communicated, linked and aligned through an operating system that drives everyday actions. Ensuring effective focus, resource and time management to deliver industry leading results.
- Continuous Improvement – eliminating waste improves performance, reduces cost and creates a competitive advantage.
- Having a culture where mutual trust and respect is well understood and bought into, employees will engage and move

the business forward in an environment that everyone can benefit from.

These principles, processes, tools and the leadership approach has worked every time, everywhere and are timeless. The fortitude to plan, execute and sustain is the challenge. Companies that have persevered and are achieving sustained success have invariably taken a long-term view and have made long-term decisions.

Nothing we did was new or revolutionary. The "Principles for Change" as we have identified and outlined in this book, are all well-known business practices and techniques.

The challenge we had was to:

- Understand them and their sub-elements in detail and how they related to each other.
- Combine their deployment in a structured and measured manner.
- Communicate the challenges and opportunities to all employees
- Engage "all employees in the journey."
- Be consistent, demanding and unrelenting of everyone engaging in change. Particularly leadership.
- Develop meaningful metrics to understand plans and progress, and to assure accountability.

What we were able to achieve through cultural transformation and continuous improvement deployment was a competitive advantage for Aerostructures that separated us from the competition. The business won in the 2000s once into production, supported by continued cultural transformation and continuous improvement can provide stability for many years.

The approach, the steps, the sequence outlined in this book worked for Aerostructures and has been the way that business has been led and managed for over 24 years.

As noted earlier in the Introduction, this is not a "how to," but rather a "what we did" journal. A similar path, with the same or similar steps, may work for you.

To sustain the embedded "Three Circle" culture over the next 20 years, Aerostructures will be challenged in many areas, as they seek to continue their leadership in the aerospace industry.

One of which is to ensure that internal leadership and employee development plans are in place as additional experienced employees move on.

An evolving fourth crisis

A Crisis of "Business Cycles"

The commercial aerospace business "up cycle" is now the longest in history

Key employees, including many Leadership, are being replaced through retirement and attrition

Airframers are determined to increase their aftermarket access and Operating Margins

Airframers have cash and resources to invest in vertical integration

Ongoing change, driven by business cycles, continue to be part of the Aerospace industry. These changes are historically driven by people, customers and the economic climate. Typical areas of change are outlined below:

People:

- As employees move on with their careers and lives, businesses tend to change:
  - Leaderships strategy and focus remain important
  - While product and manufacturing technology advances, business management strategies are invariably reworded, repackaged and recycled.
  - Momentum for continuous improvement and culture gains will either increase or decrease via that strategy and focus
  - Sustaining enterprise excellence requires leadership, effort and dedication

Customers:

- Customers will always reach within their Supply Chains for increased market access and increased margin. Traditionally relating to original equipment and in recent years a significant focus on the associated aftermarket.
  - They continually review opportunities regarding key "make versus buy" decisions
    - This cycle, transferring key product from Supply Chain to in-house manufacture can be seen
    - This phenomena of changing source preferences (often referred to as "the clock speed of an industry") requires significant effort and risk when involving complex product families such as nacelles

Economic Climate:

- Industry wide cyclical downturns are a fact of life within the Aerospace industry. Even with the current extensive order books continuing to drive the current business "up cycle," the industry at some point, responding perhaps to external forces, will begin to retract again.

Moving forward using thoughtful Strategy and effective Policy Deployment, Aerostructures is well positioned to respond to the challenges noted above.

These response options are expected to include:

- Reflecting on the things that made Aerostructures successful for 20 plus years - the deployment of the Culture, Change and Continuous Improvement processes and tools that enabled this success, and sustaining them as an ongoing business priority.
  - o This will require a thoughtful discussion on the business strategy to embrace, deploy and sustain, and leadership's role in that strategy
  - o Done successfully, this will also ensure that margins are retained along with high levels of customer satisfaction
- Carefully increasing the work load by expanding product lines to include full nacelle systems for commuter and general aviation aircraft in addition to existing wide body and narrow body.
- Continuing to invest in proprietary Nacelle technologies resulting in next-generation weight reduction and acoustic performance required by Aircraft operators.
  - o Utilizing their unique UTC relationships to develop extended Engine-Nacelle integration opportunities for wide body, narrow body, commuter, and general aviation aircraft
- Selected vertical integration of identified Aerostructures supply chain to leverage their culture and continuous improvement tools across products and processes currently in the supply base to levels of performance and cost previously unknown. There are undoubtedly significant waste and cost opportunities in the supply base to be leveraged.

All the areas and items noted above will position Aerostructures to weather the "business cycles of aerospace" effectively.

Our experience and confidence in the business and the current leadership is that Aerostructures, leveraged by UTC, and now Collins resources, will use all available options to rise to the challenges outlined.

Time will tell.

Appendix

Key Contributors to the Cultural and Business Transformation

- Bob Rau

  Joining Rohr from Parker, Bob became president in 1993. This was shortly after the company flirtation with bankruptcy and Bob's mission was to either save or sell the business. Bob made some early, almost draconian but necessary, overhead reductions. He soon observed and quickly understood the positive impact on the business of the cultural transformation and continuous improvement activities, initially at Riverside and then beyond. Bob supported these activities effectively as they were deployed across Rohr during his tenure.

- Dave Watson

  President after Bob Rau. Dave bought into and eagerly engaged in the cultural transformation and continuous improvement deployment. Energetically and regularly led continuous improvement activities. Dave was a great communicator and was instrumental in driving the business to the Value Stream structure. Dave subsequently went onto a Goodrich Corporate role.

- Bud Wetzler
Vice President of Operations at the outset of the cultural transformation and continuous improvement activities. Early in the change process, when requested by Riverside Leadership to endorse the initial continuous improvement and business changes Bud replied: "you have a green light."

His courage and commitment enabled the journey to transform the business to begin and to endure. Bud set firm expectations for all facility general managers regarding culture and continuous improvement. Moreover, he removed leaders who were not meeting expectations. Bud became president after Dave Watson and completed the restructuring to Value Streams.

- Curtis Reusser
A senior staff member brought in during the transition to Value Streams. Became president after Bud Wetzler, he also understood, bought into and engaged effectively in the cultural transformation and continuous improvement deployment. During Curtis's tenure as president, the company won their first new major nacelle contract in support of the Boeing 787 aircraft. Curtis actively supported and sponsored global Research and Development and engineering activities which subsequently matured into key areas of technical support as the business expanded.

- Greg Peters
Long-term Rohr leader, initially in engineering roles. Was positioned as the Riverside general manager with the mandate to "fix the business within two years or we close it." Greg led the cultural transformation and continuous improvement

deployment. Initially at Riverside in 1994, then across all Rohr operations locations.

He subsequently became the de facto change and continuous improvement leader for Goodrich and became president of Aerostructures in 2008.

The changes, progress and business returns would not have happened without Greg's unwavering leadership. Greg also has the uncommon ability to motivate employees to do remarkable things, beyond their expectations, time and time again.

- Marc Duvall
  President after Greg Peters. Strongly supported and engaged in the cultural transformation and continuous improvement efforts across the business. Ensured Aerostructures cultural and continuous improvement gains continued post integration with United Technologies Corporation. Was instrumental in the deployment and development of Lean Product Development and the next generation of engineering organizational structure - "Component Value Streams."

- Bryan Broderick
  Vice President of Human Resources through much of the cultural transformation. Sustained the deployment of the Positive Employee Philosophy throughout some "indifferent times." Effectively dealt with some bruised egos and sensitivities during the transformation activities. Negotiated multiple Union contracts with continuous improvement and flexibility in mind that benefitted everyone in the company.

- Dave Castagnola
  A long-term Chula Vista leader who was instrumental in driving cultural change and continuous improvement and the

first Standard Work and Real Time Problem Resolution in Aerostructures on the 717 program. Dave was on the receiving end of the Bob Pentland comment "how good do you want to be?" (Chapter 4). Went onto to co-lead the 787 program, with Jeff Rogers, through design and development of the program and moved the entire Lean Product Development process forward.

A popular, committed, engaged and industrious continuous improvement leader.

- Jeff Rogers
  Another long-term Chula Vista leader. Responsible for the CF34 through design and development, generating the first iteration of the Lean Product Development process on the way. Went onto to co-lead the 787 program, with Dave Castagnola, through design and development, and with Dave, moved the entire Lean Product Development process forward. Another popular, committed, engaged and industrious continuous improvement leader.

- Stephan Dion and Tom Spamer
  Active participants in the development and implementation of all generations of the Lean Product Development process. Subsequently, leaders, change agents and drivers of the second generation of the engineering organizational structure - Component Value Streams. These Value Streams continue to successfully launch multiple new nacelle development programs leveraging a culture and revised nacelle engineering principles combined with innovative supporting engineering standards, processes and driver measures.

- Steve Denty and Alan Binks
  Leaders and drivers of the Global Engineering initiatives that established significant contributing engineering centers in

Singapore, India, and Mexico in the 2009-13 period. These engineering centers were planned, staffed and employees trained utilizing the Lean Product Development process in a "Three Circle" culture across different continents. Both Steve and Alan's vast engineering experience combined with their dedication enabled the early success of these ventures. Also crucial in support of multiple new development programs utilizing Lean Product Development processes and tools.

- JJ Perez
  Ensured deliveries were sustained in support of customer needs at Riverside and in later years at Mexicali while cultural transformation and continuous improvement were being deployed. Consistently and effectively supported change and continuous improvement activities. An outstanding people motivator.

- Rob Gordon
  A leader in Riverside who grasped continuous improvement quickly and was instrumental in the first eye-opening improvements made in the core fabrication cell there. Became general manager and key resource at the Chula Vista plant in 1997, driving continuous improvement and performance improvement throughout the late 1990s and well into the late 2000s.

- Jeff Raley
  Initially in leadership at the Foley Alabama site. Over time Jeff made significant contributions to the Foley business that is now viewed as an UTAS showcase for the Three Circles. Moved into roles in revenue generating Value Streams and became an excellent continuous improvement resource for Aerostructures. His contribution to cost reduction on the 787 and A350 programs and the continuous improvement legacy he instilled on these programs is outstanding.

- Crispin Brown
  Ingersoll consultant who spent much time with the Riverside leadership in 1994 and "introduced us" to Cellular Manufacturing

- Bob Pentland
  Bob was ex "Jake Brake," the first US clients of Shingijutsu, and a student of Nakao. Bob was an excellent teacher, hard driver and unrelenting in his efforts to get all Aerostructures leaders to meet his expectations regarding deployment of the Toyota Production System. Bob was with us for almost 10 years. We would not have made the progress we did without Bob's often vigorous encouragement and guidance.

- Marshall Larsen
  Former Chairman, President and Chief Executive Officer of Goodrich Corporation who supported the change and continuous improvement activities at Aerostructures. Including a hands-off approach to the activity through 1999 that led to the Value Stream structure. Marshall engaged effectively in shop floor and office kaizen events and continuous improvement activities at Aerostructures and across Goodrich.

- James Womack & Daniel Jones
  Two legends that should require no introduction. Dozens upon dozens of Aerostructures employees have studied their books. James Womack graciously visited many of the Aerostructures facilities over the years providing input, insight, and encouragement.

- Colin Cramp and Martin Lodge
  Colin worked at Rohr/Aerostructures from 1994 to 2015, and Martin from 1986 to 2015. Both are grateful that they found themselves on a burning platform and had the opportunity

to work with the leader, Greg Peters, who led the Cultural transformation and Continuous improvement deployment at Aerostructures. And to work with the leadership team, and all of the employees who contributed significantly to the company's transformation that led to the outstanding business results outlined in this book.

Of the 23 people listed, 18 of them were employees of Aerostructures during the cultural and performance transformation and made significant contributions to that transformation.

Of the 18 there are 4 who remain at UTAS, now Collins Aerospace Systems. They are Marc Duvall, who has been with Aerostructures since 2008 and has been president since January of 2010. Stephan Dion, currently Aerostructures Vice President of Engineering. Steve Denty, formally Director of Aerostructures Global Engineering, now Head of UK and Value Stream Engineering at Actuation Systems, a UTAS / Collins company based in the UK, and Jeff Raley, now Executive Director of Operational Excellence for UTAS / Collins.

Acronym's, words and phrases

- 3P
  - Is a structured process used to identify options for product and production process design that result in:
    - The design, being the optimum in quality, schedule, and cost to meet customer requirements.
    - The production process, being the layout and manufacturing processes that will enable the Least Waste Way to be achieved.
- 5S
  - 5S is a method of creating a culture that sustains an organized, clean, safe, and efficient workplace. The 5S's are Sort, Set or Straighten, Shine, Standardize, Sustain.
- Ah Ah of the day
  - Something of significance that was a surprise.
- Airworthiness Organization
  - An Airworthiness Reliability and Safety organization ensures that both aircraft and aircraft components are suitable for flight and meet all rigorous design, construction, certification and maintenance requirements as required by FAA or equivalent International Standards.

- Andon
  - A visual control, often a light, that when used provides a status. The basic status is often:
    - Green – Everything is as it should be
    - Amber – I am running into a problem
    - Red – I have a problem, and I am stopped
    - Blue – I need a Quality check.
- Autoclave
  - A pressure and temperature vessel primarily for "curing metal and composite bond sub-assemblies."
- Bottom feeding
  - Living off scraps after all the significant offerings have been taken.
- CapEx
  - Capital Expenditure. A budget line item that is often for plant, machinery or equipment.
- Catalog Automation
  - Buying plant, machinery or equipment with the belief that this will yield the required quality, performance and cost improvements.
- Cellular Manufacturing
  - Locating everything needed to produce a complete sub or final assembly in one dedicated cell.
- Centers of Excellence
  - Establishing dedicated facilities where technical excellence or manufacturing capabilities, through focus, familiarity and repetition can be developed.
- Chaku Chaku
  - Japanese for "load load," and refers to a manufacturing cell that is usually operated by one employee and produces a "complete part" through multiple steps. Parts are often transferred from one operation step to the next one automatically.

- Countermeasure
  - A deployed action or activity to address, resolve or leverage an issue, problem or opportunity.
- Cycle Time
  - The amount of hands-on labor to complete a task.
- Cycle Time float
  - The amount of time in-between the required and scheduled tasks and activities, on a large project plan, that can be used to manage the overall schedule, by pushing tasks out or pulling them in without detrimentally affecting the deliverables or scheduled completion dates within the project.
- Draw Thin
  - Design to meet the requirements. Add material/weight, only if calculations determine additional strength be needed. Not "just in case."
- Driver Metric
  - A metric that can be managed to help produce the result required. For example, the tracking, managing and improving of *on-time releases* of work orders to the shop floor will contribute to the predictability of *on-time completions.*
- DTM
  - Days To Manufacture. The total elapsed working days a production work order is opened, to the day it closes.
- DTP
  - Days To Process. The total elapsed working days a process is started, to when it completes.
- EBU
  - Engine Build-Up. Mating the nacelle and all utility systems with the engine to produce a propulsion unit.
- EH&S
  - Environmental, Health and Safety. In large organizations often specific functions with specialist staff in these three disciplines.

- EPA
  - Environmental Protection Agency
- ERP
  - Enterprise Resource Planning - the integrated management of primary business processes. Specifically those in the scheduling, material and part procurement, manufacture, and delivery of product. ERP generates data and information used to plan and manage these activities.
- Engineering Standard Operating Manual (ESOM)
  - Contains mandatory Nacelle engineering principles, requirements, methods and standards to ensure current best practices are uniformly implemented across all programs and components. The ESOM is updated as required as improvements in methods and processes are developed and implemented.
- Flow Time
  - Same as DTM.
- Kaikaku
  - A continuous improvement activity where large broad changes are made, such as equipment moved, major product flows changed or systems taken down for a short period that usually requires extensive pre-event planning and post-event follow up.
- Kaizen
  - A continuous improvement activity where incremental improvement changes are made, usually an activity conducted and closed out in a week or less.
- Leadership weeks
  - Weeks in which multiple events are planned and leadership, senior and others participate, usually in "team member" roles.
- Lean
  - It is a term made popular in the last 30 years. It is meant to describe a structured process and method for waste

identification and elimination in any process, business or service.

- o Learning together
    - o A formal process introduced to move the collective understanding and alignment of specific issues, by a group, forward.
- o Least Waste Way as we know it today
    - o Documented Standard Work for a process that has had waste/non-value added activities removed. (we are not aware of any process that is waste free)
- o Macro Plan
    - o Is a process, and large visual, that is normally developed and used by leadership in support of Policy Deployment. It is a reflection of the "high level, big picture" of an organization and the identification and management of what actions need to be accomplished and when.
- o Master Matrix
    - o Is a large matrix used in the Policy Deployment process that is used to link the Improvement Targets to the "important things" to ensure they are all adequately addressed. It is a separate matrix from the Policy Deployment matrix.
- o Material Replenishment System
    - o Is a visual, production line, demand-driven system that indicates parts or supplies are required and are replaced in pre-determined quantities to support customer demand.
- o MRO
    - o Maintenance, Overhaul and Repair, of in-service products.
- o Multi-Skilling
    - o Training employees to a level of proficiency with tasks beyond those they normally do, but usually within their function, to increase their skill set and provide coverage for absences. Sometimes training for "one operation up/ down" in a manufacturing cell.

- Offload
  - Transferring the manufacture of parts from in-house, to a supplier.
- OI and OM
  - Operating Income is the difference between total sales and the cost of producing the product or service, expressed as a dollar figure. Operating Margin is operating income divided by total sales and is expressed as a percentage.
- Onload
  - Bringing the manufacture of parts back in-house, from a supplier.
- OE
  - Original Equipment
- OTD
  - On-Time Delivery
- Positive Climate Index (PCI)
  - A process to solicit input from employees as to "what was working, or being done well" and what was "not working, being done well."
- Pick List
  - A list of parts that have to be picked from stock to make up an order to be manufactured or assembled.
- Plan, Do, Check, Act. (modified at Aerostructures to PDAC)
  - An "execution" process that has been around for many years. One where defined "things" that need to be achieved, usually in support of a Policy Deployment Improvement Target, are identified and documented as **Plan** items. The next level of detail to support each Plan "thing," are identified and documented as **Do** items. **Act** is the detailed activity done, by specifically named employees, to a committed schedule, to achieve the Do items. **Check** is the review done to understand the progress and success of the action.

- Plateau phase
  - An Airbus process used during the preliminary design of a new aircraft. Several potential suppliers often competing on the same work packages are collocated with Airbus teams. Key design deliverables and product performance levels are defined, build and component concepts are developed and evaluated. During this phase, Airbus can review and understand suppliers' capabilities and inputs. Contracts are awarded strongly influenced by the activities, outcomes, and learnings of the Plateau Phase.
- Positive Employee Philosophy
  - A practice that creates an environment that is Principle rather than Rule-based.
  - The creation and sustaining of a culture that recognizes employees as key assets, one where employees understand that they are appreciated and one where they engage freely in the performance improvement of the business.
- POU
  - Point Of Use, the tools, and equipment needed to complete a task are available, within reach and serviceable.
- Principles for Excellence
  - Developed and deployed in the late 1980s. Superseded by company Values in 1995. The Principles for Excellence were:
    - *Service* - providing a level of service that keeps the customer coming back.
    - *Commitment* - dependably meeting requirements and expectations.
    - *Ownership* - taking the initiative with challenges and opportunities.
    - *Teamwork* - working together at all levels to achieve common objectives.
    - *Ethics* - doing "what is right" at all times.

- Result Metric
  - Metrics that in themselves cannot be changed. Actual month-end deliveries, costs or quality metrics. Sales made, employees hired or the "score at the end of a game."
- Right to work
  - A term for laws that make it illegal to require that employees join a union or pay the equivalent of union dues in order to be employed.
- Rotable
  - A part or component usually provided to a customer for use, while their part or component is repaired.
- Sensei
  - A word of Chinese/Japanese origins often used to denote a "teacher."
- SIPOC
  - Supplier, Input, Process, Output, Customer. A process by which the SIPOC steps are documented visually to help understand them and to identify opportunities for process improvement.
- STC
  - A Type Certificate is issued by an aviation authority to signify the airworthiness of an aircraft manufacturing design or "type." A Supplemental Type Certificate can be issued to approve a major modification or repair to an existing Type Certified aircraft.
- Takt Time
  - Takt Time is an expression of customer demand. It is time available divided by customer demand. For example, if there are 2100 minutes in a five day, one shift working week and the customer demand is for 50 units a week, the Takt Time is 42 minutes. That is one unit of customer demand must be produced at a rate reflective of one every 42 minutes.
- Theory X
  - A manner of managing that assumes employees dislike work, must be directed, must have rules enforced upon

them and must be reprimanded or punished if mistakes are made.

- o Tiger teams
  - o An assembled team of usually, cross-functional employees, to address and resolve an issue or problem when normal business activities are unable to do so.
- o Total Landed Cost
  - o The actual cost to a business of a product or service beyond the invoice cost. This could include supplier management, technical and other support provided to a supplier. Including travel costs, additional "first articles," and other quality requirements, transportation, taxes, tariffs and customs duties, receiving, un-packaging and stocking.
- o Toyota Production System
  - o Originated in the company, Toyota, in the early 1950s. It is a management strategy and methodology and a supporting set of processes and tools. It is focused on the elimination of waste/non-value added tasks from all activities and improving value-added activities.
  - o Taiichi Ohno a senior engineer in the company gets much-deserved credit for the development and refinement of the Toyota Production System processes and tools in the 1950s through into the 1970s.
- o Total Productive Maintenance. (TPM)
  - o Checks done by the operators of machinery and equipment on a daily basis to check things such as filters, fluid levels, pressures, and cycles, that when not within established parameters, can be addressed before a serious issue or breakdown occurs.
- o Voice Of the Customer
  - o A process whereby the wants, needs, and requirements of a customer are understood beyond the written documents or specifications. Achieved through face to face interview and discussion with all affected parties at

a customer beyond those who compiled the documents or specifications.

o Wall Walks

    o Stand up meetings where visual plans and metrics are reviewed, at a high frequency, by respective teams and their leadership.

Positive Employee Philosophy Overview

o The Positive Employee Philosophy was developed and constructed to help create an environment where employees are valued, engaged in the performance improvement of the business and are treated and rewarded as valuable contributors.

o The Positive Employee Philosophy Principles Are:
  - Mutual Trust and Respect
  - Effective Two Way Communication
  - Identify and Eliminate Negatives
  - Training and Development
  - Employee Engagement
  - Competitive Wages and Benefits

o A four and a half day offsite "clinic" is a central component of a Positive Employee Philosophy deployment. Traditionally Aerostructures held three to four, occasionally five clinics a year. Class size was 24, with employees in leadership roles as primary attendees

o The class was invariably kicked off by Rohr/Aerostructures President who centered their comments around this quote that captures the consistency of purpose we embraced:

"The very essence of leadership is that you have a vision. It's got to be a vision you articulate clearly and forcefully on every occasion. You can't blow an uncertain trumpet."

Father Theodore Hesburgh - former
President of Notre Dame University.

o The class focused on the Positive Employee Philosophy Principles, their meaning and intent.
o The class content was structured to enable leaders and others to develop the skills and behaviors that develop, support and maintain the Positive Employee Philosophy Principles
  ▪ Constructive feedback
    ▪ Giving and receiving
  ▪ Persuasive presentations
    ▪ Changing a culture and the environment
    ▪ The "Change" process
  ▪ What, Why and How communications
    ▪ Handling objections
  ▪ Accountability
    ▪ Avoiding the Victim Loop. IMPAQ©
    ▪ Setting expectations
    ▪ Moving employees from denial to accountability
  ▪ Diversity
    ▪ Leveraging the strengths of diversity
    ▪ Dealing with problems that may arise
  ▪ Myers Briggs (Personality) Type Indicator© feedback and 360 feedback
    ▪ Recognizing, understanding and dealing with different personality types
  ▪ The People Philosophy and Continuous Improvement
    ▪ Catalysts for each other
  ▪ The Win-Win Process
    ▪ Versus Win/Lose or Lose/Lose

- Treating people as adults is a fundamental behavior to develop and maintain a Positive Employee Philosophy. Rules that were put in place because of the conceivably dysfunctional 5% are eliminated in favor of the 95% who do not need nor should be subject to rules.
- In recent years another quote, originally attributable to Sir Richard Branson and subsequently modified below, that captures the essence of the Positive Employee Philosophy was being used at the closing of recent clinics:

  > *"Train employees so that they have the skills to succeed in other businesses of their choice. Create a work environment that recognizes and rewards their engagement and treats them so that they do not want to leave."*

- Positive Employee Philosophy overviews were given routinely to "all employees" and to new employees during onboarding.

Leadership and Continuous Improvement books that were significant and influential on our journey

Book	Author(s)
5 Pillars of the Visual Workplace	Hirano, Hiroyuki
20 Keys to Workplace Improvement	Kobayashi, Iwao
Becoming Lean	Liker, Jeffrey
Control Your Own Destiny or Somebody Else Will	Tichy, Noel M., and Sherman, Stratford
Developing the Leader within You	Maxwell, John C.
Gemba Kaizen	Imai, Masaaki
Good to Great	Collins, Jim
How the Mighty Fall	Collins, Jim
Inside the Mind of Toyota.	Satoshi, Hito
The Knowing-Doing Gap	Pfeffer, Jeffrey, and Sutton, Robert
Lean Thinking	Womack, James P., Jones, Daniel T.
The Machine that Changed the World	Womack, James P., Jones, Daniel T., and Roos, Daniel
The Leadership Engine	Tichy, Noel M., and Cohen, Eli
The Management Compass	Bechtell, Michele
Toyota Culture	Liker, Jeffery and Hoseus, Michael
Toyota Kata	Rother, Mike
Toyota Production System.	Ohno, Taiichi
The Toyota Product Development System	Morgan, James, and Liker, Jeffery
The Toyota Way	Liker, Jeffrey
Who Moved My Cheese?	Johnson, Spencer

The Authors

C olin E. Cramp hired into Rohr Riverside in 1994, after years of leadership experience at Rolls Royce and then General Electric Aircraft Engines. Over the next 21 years of service held progressive leadership positions supporting significant cultural and operating system changes across the business.

These positions included Director of Engineering and Quality at Riverside, then general manager of this critical site before moving to San Marcos, Texas as general manager of the High-Temperature Bonding site, transforming the organization and production systems.

Over the next 15 years, Colin then held varied executive positions within Rohr, Goodrich, and UTC including V.P. Airbus Programs, V.P. Quality and Technical Compliance and finally five years as V. P. Engineering, R&D, and Chief Engineers Office helping bring eleven new/derivative nacelle programs through design, analysis, manufacture and certification all within the evolving culture and operating systems.

Retiring in March of 2015, Colin continues to be actively committed to the support of Culture, Change and Continuous Improvement within the industry.

Martin R. Lodge hired into Rohr Riverside as an Industrial Engineering Supervisor in May 1986. Transitioning to Plant Controller, reporting to the general manager by 1989.

The company replaced the Riverside general manager in 1994. Martin immediately aligned with the new leadership and actively engaged in identifying and developing a way forward that focused on change, culture and continuous improvement.

Engagement in planning and affecting change, and much "learning by doing" followed through to 1997 when he, along with one other Riverside leader, were transferred to Chula Vista where they both assumed the roles of Operations Managers.

By 2000 the role had transitioned to company Director of Continuous Improvement. In the mid-2000's he became V.P. of Operations, adding Supply Chain in 2010. He was actively engaged in the deployment of change, culture and continuous improvement at Rohr, and then Goodrich, through the entire period detailed in this book. Retiring as V.P. of Quality, Manufacturing Engineering, Tooling and SAP Support in March of 2015.

In retirement, Martin continues to consult in various businesses and industries.